L.A. FOLLIES

Design and Other Diversions in a Fractured Metropolis

SAM HALL KAPLAN

CITYSCAPE PRESS

Distributed by
SOUTHERN
CALIFORNIA
BOOKS

ALSO BY SAM HALL KAPLAN

L.A. LOST & FOUND: An Architectural History of Los Angeles
THE DREAM DEFERRED: People, Politics and Planning in Suburbia
THE NEW YORK CITY HANDBOOK, with Gilbert Tauber

Published by Cityscape Press,
823 20th St. Santa Monica, Ca. 90403

Designed by Dana Levy

Produced by Perpetua Press

Printed in the United States of America

Distributed by Southern California Books,
522 S. Sepulveda Blvd., Suite 111, Los Angeles, CA 90049

Library of Congress Card Catalogue Number: 88-93072
ISBN: 0-9622007-0-0

First Printing

Cover photo by Dana Levy

Contents

INTRODUCTON: Design and Other Diversions   10

I. WHY L.A. LOOKS THE WAY IT DOES   13
   The Misshaping of Hathaway Hill   15
   Best High-Rise Knows Its Place   18
   Mini Malls: Scenario for Horror Film   20
   A Lesson For Pershing Square   22
   Skyline Signs Spell "Tacky"   25
   Skidding Along Skid Row   27
   Planning Process Raises Questions   28
   Public Risks and Private Profits   29
   Housing: The Good, Bad, and Ugly   33
   Suburban Dreams   35
   The Future of L.A. Is Now   38

II. WHOSE CITY IS IT, ANYWAY?   41
    Hamilton Goes, 15 Fiefdoms Stay   46
    Neighborhoods Strive For Common Link   47
    Citizens Wants a Hand in Zoning   48
    The Battle Over Prop U   50
    Hope for Local Planning Boards   52
    Mayor's Speech 5 Years Too Late   55
    Little Tokyo Wary of Big Plans   56
    Back To The Nitty Gritty   58
    Hope For a Livable City   61

III. STRIP MINING THE URBAN LODE   65
     Westwood Village Woe   67
     Renovating Houses, and Rent Control   70
     Land Use Abuse Continue   72
     Schools Fail To Justify Home Grab   74
     Museum Ventures Into Real World   76
     Hooray, We Hope, For Hollywood   79
     Better Design For Better Housing   81

IV. ARCHITECTURE, FOR BETTER OR WORSE   84
    Designs For Future Schlock   86
    A Contest for Self-Congratulations   88
    Seeing Light in the Dark of Garages   90
    Post Mortem on Post-Modernism?   91
    Dull Skyline in for a Change   93
    Fox Plaza: Nice Style, Poor Design   95
    A Plus and Minus for Civic Center   97
    A Heaping Portion of Fish Shticks   99
    Architecture as Sculptural Objects   103
    A World Class Housing Need   105
    Competitions: Risk and Rivalry   107
    In The Spirit of Disney   109

V. OF STREETS, TREES AND TRAFFIC   112
    Downtown Debacle   115
    Pedestrians Wait For The Bus   117
    Threats to Library Open Space   119
    Improvements Up His Alleys   121
    Woodsman, Spare That Billboard   123
    A Wider View of Westside Traffic   125
    A Hope (Street) For Walkers   127
    Wrong Way Signs Spare Neighborhood   129
    Taking Narrow View of Sidewalks   131
    Design Debate On Sunset Strip   133
    Cars, Neighbors and Convenience   135

VI. PRESERVING THE PAST   138
    Landmarks in Need of Help   140
    Recycling The Throwaway City   142
    Playing Politics With a Landmark   144
    Pasadena's Threatened Heritage   147
    Struggling West Adams Shows Its Stuff   149
    Craftsman Period: a Time of Glory   150
    Renewed Buoyance About Piers   153
    Historic Houses Need Getty Help   155
    Waiting for the Getty To Step Forward   157
    Preservation: the People's Choice   159

VII. SPECIAL PLACES   161
    On The Plaza   162
    Halcyon Days   164
    Around the Venice Circle   166
    Long Beach Comes of Age   168
    Tail o'the Pup on a Roll   169

L.A. Under The Palms 170
The Heights of Hollywood 172
The City as a Movie Studio 174
An Eye for L.A. Images 175
Covering The Waterfront 177
Schindler's Spirit Survives 178
L.A.'s Mean Streets 179
MacArthur Park Alive 183
Courting a Neighborly Style 185
Semi-Secret Places 186
Rodia's Watts Towers 187
Celebrating Spaces 188

VIII. SPECIAL PEOPLE 191
Julius Shulman, Photographer 191
Lautner Still Ahead of His Time 192
When Lefcoe Missed The Ham, He Quit 195
Cliff May's Quintessential Houses 197
Charles Lee's Glory Days 199
Designing Women 200
Remembrance for UCLA's Harvey 202
An Architect With the Wright Stuff 204
Ain's Contributions Remembered 206
Quincy Jones' Architectural Legacy 208
A Missionary Among Architects 209

IX. PERSONAL PREJUDICES 211
A Public Park As a Private Preserve 213
Fighting Traffic Terrorism Abroad 215
View of Santa Monica and Beyond 217
Viewing Downtown in A Wheelchair 219
A Design That's Worth The Wait 221
Rumbles on the Livable City Turf 222
Aid for Creative, Not Con, Artists 225
Public Art Can Make a Difference 227
Modest Proposal for a Better L.A. 229
Welcome to a Sadder City 230

ACKNOWLEDGMENTS 233

INDEX 234

To My Children, Alison,
  Michael, Josef and Kyle

DESIGN
AND OTHER
DIVERSIONS

THERE ARE TIMES WHEN THE SUN IS BRILLIANT, THE TEMPERATURE JUST right, the ocean sparkling, the mountains in view, the hillsides in bloom, the smell of Jasmine in the air, the traffic light, the storefronts diverting, the parks and beaches inviting, and the architecture appropriate, evocative and fanciful, that Los Angeles appears to fulfill its promise of a comfortable, livable city blessed with a benign climate and a beguiling landscape. Then there are times when the sky turns a pernicious hue of smog, the sun blisters, traffic gridlocks, trash cans overflow, cars moon sidewalks, pollution closes beaches, maxed out mini-malls seem everywhere, and most of the architecture elbowing their way into view is flimsy, banal, and gauche, combining with the frayed ecology to grind into grit the promise of the good life.

That Los Angeles can offer such contradictory visions, depending on times and moods, for me makes it a constantly challenging phenomena to write about. (And when I refer to Los Angeles I am generally referring not to the city itself, but to a multi-centered grid spread across an expanding region consisting of nearly 100 municipalities and authorities; a fractured metropolis. However, with 3 million of the region's 13 million residents, the City of Los Angeles dominates, and, is a prime focus of concern.) Few metropolitan areas in our increasing complex urban society offer such a potential as Los Angeles for an attractive, accessible life style; a potential that is being prompted in part by a rising tide of interest, immigration and investment, flavored with a healthy tradition of a capacity to change. Poised as it is on Pacific Rim at the beginning of what has been labeled the Pacific Century, Los Angeles is one of the fastest growing regions in the western world, a burgeoning center of commerce and culture.

However, in growing over the last 150 years from a cowtown, to a boomtown, to a post-industrial conglomeration, the region has all but been consumed by spectacular, speculative and, generally, slovenly growth. Sadly from my perspective few areas as Los Angeles seem so disdainful of their ecological and architectural heritage, and so incapable of capitalizing on it to generate a more humane environment. Yet in fragmented community enclaves, neighborhood groups, preservationist societies, professional associations, and even in isolated alcoves of government itself, I also see and sense an increasing awareness and appreciation of this frail heritage, and a heartening awakening to the urgency of saving it as a foundation for shaping a better city.

With that long view very much in mind, and with a love of an adopted son of Los Angeles who revels in its once and future cityscapes, I have tried for ten years to somehow entertain, educate, and energize readers' through my columns, commentaries and articles in "The Los Angeles Times" concerning architecture, planning, and preservation. It has been my hope to aid readers to be more sensitive to the role design plays in their lives, while spotlighting who is affecting that design; and how it perhaps can be better fashioned and shaped to make Los Angeles a more livable, aesthetically pleasing city.

As for the effect, design criticism is quite unlike, say, theater or film criticism, where a stinging review just might turn out the lights of a play, or bury a movie. No one has yet demolished a project I have panned. But I can say with pride some significant landmark buildings threatened with demolition that I have called attention to and praised have been saved, some street widening projects I have questioned have been canceled, preserving a few trees offering shade and grace to sidewalks and making various communities a little more hospitable for pedestrians; and institutions like the Getty Trust that I have prompted to become more involved in the built environment have redirected resources to aid specific projects. We do savor our little victories.

And I would be less than discreet not to say that I have taken a certain Old Testament pleasure in calling attention to those who I feel have used their position or profession, be it in the name of progress, power or parochialism, to compromise the city fabric. More importantly, I like to think that my comments concerning what I do and do not like in some way influences the future designs by the myriad cast of characters involved in the built environment; that immodestly my insights are incorporated, consciously or subconsciously, into some form of structure or cityscape to better serve its users, and society, or more simply into actions to preserve a sense of place, and community.

Of course, in journalism, the story is paramount. You live from article to article, which as a colleague once noted is somewhat like leaping from rock to rock in a raging river. You are constantly involved in a story, bearing in mind the old journalistic adage that you are as good as your last printed article. It's all very exciting, and existential. In this respect, most of what I have written for "The Times" over the last ten years has been very much in response to the specific projects, issues, campaigns and experiences of the moment. Meanwhile, Los Angeles keeps changing; new promises are made and new policies are instituted, usually in response to political pressure, to improve situations, only to backslide when the pressure eases; new buildings are built, some better and, unfortunately some worse; imaginative plans are drafted, only to be filed away; and those of us concerned with the drift of design continue like surfers to paddle our boards against the tide, hoping to catch a new wave and ride it gloriously back to the beach, however briefly.

Still, I like to think that my writings of the moment gathered here expressing my hopes and fears, and prejudices and preoccupations, have a certain relevancy, and perhaps can be of value, if only to offer a perspective to what seems to me to be a continuing battle to better shape the growth of Los Angeles. To make them a little more coherent, I have grouped the writings under various chapters focused on different themes, and within each chapter after an essay or two setting the tone put them generally in a chronological order to lend the effort some continuity. Except for a few corrections and deletions, they are untouched. Where some issues were unresolved at the time the columns were written I have added a brief update. And because they were written for the moment, there also are in columns focused on similar issues over a period of time a certain amount of repetition of facts and opinions. When writing for a daily newspaper we must assume that every day the world is reborn. The columns were not written with the idea that they would end up in collected form, to be read in bits and pieces, or as a continuum. As a result, there really is no beginning, middle or end to such a collection. Given the subject, I feel this is appropriate. From my view what we have in the shaping, and misshaping, of the region is a continuing melodrama in a series of acts I have labeled the Los Angeles Follies. Pull up a seat and enjoy.

SAM HALL KAPLAN   Dec. 20, 1988

I

WHY L.A. LOOKS THE WAY IT DOES

TRYING TO BE OPTIMISTIC ABOUT THE DRIFT OF PLANNING AND DESIGN IN Los Angeles is difficult. Witnessing the region's frustrating traffic, persistent pollution, haphazard development, faddish architecture, oppressed pedestrians, abused ecosystem and fragmented governments, one might ask, what planning and design?

Still, being a relatively young, albeit fractured metropolis entering what urbanologists would call its second growth, the potential here for an attractive, accessible, livable city persists.

Certainly, one can take heart in the promise of such projects as First Interstate World Center downtown, the Pike in Long Beach, the fine-tuning of the Pasadena Civic Center, the expansion of Otis Art Institute of Parsons School of Design and the Pacific Design Center.

And then there are the neighborhoods that are slowly restoring themselves, such as Melrose Hill, aided by a historic district designation; West Adams and Highland Park, by a dogged house-by-house rehabilitation effort, and Carthay Circle by simply diverting traffic.

There also seems to be an increasing awareness that the emerging urban fabric of Los Angeles somehow must be better woven and detailed; witness the varied planning exercises now under way to mend Broadway downtown, 6th Street in San Pedro, Van Nuys Boulevard in the San Fernando Valley and the Olympic Boulevard corridor in West Los Angeles.

But, unfortunately, these efforts are exceptions, relative oases in a planning and design desert. As an extended tour of our cityscape sadly reveals, rapacious, insensitive developments continue—the increase in overdesigned, obese residential projects, maxed out mini malls, and cookie-cutter commercial complexes.

For specifics, just look at the march of new prison-like apartment blocks on the edges of Mar Vista and Los Feliz; the nouvelle gauche houses being shoe-horned north of Montana Avenue in Santa Monica; the new, glitzy Brentwood Gardens mall on San Vicente Boulevard, and the overscaled office towers sticking up like sore thumbs in Burbank.

Few days go by without some reader or community group contacting me to protest some outrage or other, be it the construction of a rude building, the destruction of a landmark, the mismanagement of traffic, or, as last week, simply the cutting down of two mature ficus trees on Hope Street downtown because the city felt they might interfere with pedestrian traffic.

Though some of the protests, I feel, have been motivated by prejudice and self-interest, most are valid. How else can one explain the design of the Fairway Building on Ventura Boulevard in Studio City, or the apartment houses mooning Hawthorne Avenue in Hollywood with their parking?

And all this despite the flurry over the last few years over moratoriums and slow-growth initiatives, the promise of government to be more sensitive to neighborhood environmental issues, the airing of the problems by seemingly endless seminars and the gestures of concern by a few politicians, professional associations and public agencies.

GROWTH HAS ALWAYS BEEN THE HONEY POT OF LOS ANGELES, AND NOT necessarily a bad one. Growth can create jobs, provide needed housing, stimulate culture, and generally make a more interesting place to live while holding out the hope for a better life for all.

It was this hope, when combined with Southern California's benign climate, unique beaches, topography and vegetation, that spurred the region's phenomenal growth over the last half-century, attracting waves of immigrants and migrants, myself included. California dreamin'.

Putting a damper on the dream has been unmanaged growth, which is what prompted the broad support of the recent slow-growth initiatives. While a few were defeated, all made their mark.

The initiatives were, in effect, a shot across the bow of government, a warning that something was amiss; the goose Los Angeles, which had been laying the golden egg representing a desired quality of life, was ailing.

But two years after the first wave of initiatives, it has become obvious that growth alone no longer is the prime local issue in Southern California.

A hint of this is offered by the initiative being circulated by an organization labeled Pasadena Residents in Defense of Our Environment, calling for more citizen control of the city's growth policies. (If I lived in Pasadena, I'd certainly sign it.)

What, from my perspective, is emerging from the various slow-growth and environmental movements is a much more crucial issue with ramifications beyond just planning and design. It is the issue raised in the question: "Whose city is it anyway, the politicians', the public servants', the professionals' or the people's?"

INCREASINGLY ACROSS SOUTHERN CALIFORNIA, RESIDENTS AT COFFEE klatches and community meetings are expressing their frustration and lack of faith in the ability of local government to manage growth, protect the dwindling quality of life and to foster a more livable city.

Though the words are there, most government agencies just don't seem to be in gear. Persisting is an "us" and "them" mentality that looks at citizen involvement as an annoyance.

As for the self-described professionals, including academics and architects, there have been a lot of talk, seminars, studies, conferences and consultant teams, but no real effect on improving the quality of life here except on those who collect salaries, fees and fame from such endeavors.

With too few exceptions, it has been politics as usual for the politicians. The most egregious example of late was the defeat of the Showa project that had been proposed for Little Tokyo and endorsed after protracted studies by the community and various city agencies. It lost out to a proposal propped up at the last minute by a gaggle of lobbyists.

Meanwhile, the powers and personalities-that-be seem to be too busy toasting memories of the 1984 Olympics, L.A.'s emergence as a world-class city, new cultural institutions and, most of all, each other, to worry about such mundane subjects as planning and design.

That is why L.A. appears at times to be less a city and more a folly.

—Oct. 23, 1988

The Misshaping of Hathaway Hill

O F THE MANY LOST OPPORTUNITIES IN PLANNING THAT HAVE LED TO A misshapen Los Angeles cityscape, the Hathaway Hill development has to be one of the more grievous.

With 45 of its 95 single-family homes already completed, the development stands as a vivid example of what happens when an acquisitive developer runs up against a recalcitrant community in a vacuum created by an unimaginative city government.

The development looks as if it has been lifted intact from an expensive Orange County subdivision and transplanted in error or jest on a prominent hill bordering the Echo Park and Silver Lake communities just three miles from downtown.

It is not that the houses are uninhabitable. They seem very comfortable, as befitting their $244,000 to $450,000 price range and styles labeled the Ashley, Barclay, Covington and Dartmouth. And their sweeping views of the city to the south, the Pacific to the west and the mountains to the north on a clear day are spectacular.

It is just that the 36-acre hilltop site could have been developed with much more sensitivity to the site and at a much higher density to allow for a mix of housing types the city desperately needs.

In addition, if the houses were clustered in the manner of, say, an Italian hill town, enough land could have been easily saved to allow for a public park or some form of welcoming open space. The prospects now are for the site to be fenced and guarded.

Even the current developer, W & B Builders, a joint venture of Watt Industries, recognizes the site's potential. But it notes it inherited the housing package intact when the initial developer, Cresticon, backed out after community protests.

"We feel we have created a quality product based upon the available zoning," said a spokesman for Watt.

Another bad bit of planning is the development's access, which is limited to McCollum Street, a narrow, curving residential lane connecting the hill to Benton Way and Sunset Boulevard in

Echo Park. A more logical alternative would have been to carve a new street on the northeast slope leading to Glendale Boulevard in Silver Lake.

To allow expensive single-family houses so out of character with its surrounding community to be built on such a site so close to a developing downtown trying to bring some cohesion to a sprawling region is an abuse of almost every planning principle and the city's own urban design goals.

With more and more office buildings rising downtown, along with an impressive array of cultural facilities, has come the need for a wide range of housing in easy commuting distance. Unfortunately, because of high land costs, much of the housing recently constructed downtown and planned for the future is too expensive for the average office worker.

For the downtown to become alive as the urban core of the region, it needs more people who work there and live where they can be close to its attractions, not sitting on freeways in traffic jams.

Such a site for such housing could have been Hathaway Hill if the city and, in particular, its city Planning Department, had taken the initiative and shown some imagination when faced with the conflicting interests of developers and neighborhood residents.

As usual in such situations, the initial developer, Cresticon, a subsidiary of Litton Industries, had wanted to bulldoze much of the hill and build as many units as possible while nearby residents, banding together under the flag of the Silver Lake Residents Assn., wanted as little as possible done to the site.

Among the more outrageous proposals made by Cresticon in the late 1960s was a plan for five 15-story apartment buildings with a total of 2,250 units. This was rejected by the city, as were subsequent proposals for six four-story buildings with 900 units; four six-story buildings with 812 units; and two 10-story buildings from 788 down to 700 units.

The insensitive proposals heightened the resolve of the residents to oppose any private development and press for the hill and its crowning Garbutt-Hathaway mansion to be used for a park, a community center, a residence for the mayor, a school, an arboretum or just about anything that left the land undisturbed.

The City Council eventually granted a zone change on a portion of the property that reduced its density to about 550 units with a height limit of three stories. Not incidentally, the zoning was consistent with that of the surrounding community. This prompted a new proposal from the developer in 1975, calling for 530 clustered units stepping up the hill in a design of some potential.

Unfortunately, the plan was a little too ambitious and involved the demolition of the Garbutt-Hathaway mansion, the saving of which had become a rallying point for the opposition. The plan was defeated.

Though it would have taken a supreme effort, the opportunity was there at the time for the city Planning Department to come up with design criterion that would have respected the site and met the public's needs for both open space and a range of housing choices.

OTHER CITIES INDEED HAVE ACTED AS ADVOCATES IN SIMILAR SITUATIONS, calming concerned communities while wrenching from developers more affordable housing, public parks and better designs in return for allowing higher densities, or simply the densities that are allowed. Such an effort would have meant the Planning Department getting involved in a bitter controversy and putting its principles on the line. Not so in Los Angeles, where planning under the direction of department director Calvin Hamilton is, at best, an academic afterthought to political expediency.

A reading of the public documents concerning the development of the site dating back nearly 20 years indicates that the city did not try to present alternatives or arbitrate the conflicting interests despite numerous opportunities to do so. It seemed to have just stood idly by as residents warred with the developer.

Eventually everybody lost. With the residents continuing to pressure the city, the hill a few years later was downzoned to its present density, prompting Cresticon to sell to a joint venture partnership of Watt Industries, a major California developer and builder. It did not contest the zoning and filed plans for 95 units.

"Of course, it would have made more sense from a planning and sales point of view to have more units," said a realtor involved with the current development. "This hill would have been perfect for affordable cluster housing, and have some land left over for a public park. But that is not what the neighborhood or the city wanted, and Watt wasn't going to fight it."

Supporting the downzoning from R2-1 to R-1, the residents association declared in a 1978 newsletter that the action would "preserve the single family character of the community."

It added that "there is a strong possibility that after the streets, sewers, etc. are put in, that lots may not be processed as 'pads' but will remain in their natural state to be graded as individual homes are built. Obviously, when the streets are dedicated, they become open to the public. If this plan is followed, the devclopment should blend in with the community very well."

The association took particular pride in that the approved plan called for "green planted slopes providing open space and corridors for migrating animals." The plan also stated that trees destroyed by the construction would be replaced on a one-for-one basis.

The association concluded in the newsletter that "the Silver Lake Community can be proud of what it has accomplished through organization."

WHAT ACTUALLY HAS HAPPENED IS THAT THE HILL WAS SEVERELY STRIPPED and graded to provide pads for houses that have no relation whatsoever to the character of Silver Lake or Echo Park; of the 634 trees removed, only 379 have been replaced; and traffic on McCollum Street has become a major concern of residents there.

As for the Garbutt-Hathaway mansion, it has been renovated and was recently sold for $1 million. No visitors are allowed there or, for that matter, anywhere on Hathaway Hill, except to look at the model homes.

With about 40 of the 45 homes built already sold, residents have been discussing forming an association, erecting a gate and a guardhouse for security reasons and to preserve the exclusivity of Hathaway Hill.

"When people call and ask me how to get here, I tell them they have to drive through a little hell to get to heaven," said Gary Williams, a salesman for the development. "What we have here is a little piece of Mission Viejo in downtown Los Angeles. It's strange. But that is what the people wanted, isn't it?"

—Oct. 31, 1983

Best High-Rise Knows Its Place

A RECENT RASH OF OFFICE TOWERS APPROACHING SKYSCRAPTER PROPORtions appears to have sprouted at random across the Los Angeles cityscape.

Casting shadows on the image of Los Angeles, they mar the skyline, block views of the surrounding mountains, dominate streets, disrupt traffic, spur destructive speculation and generally are not very neighborly.

They stand in egregious contrast to the towers downtown and even in Century City, where the structures form a critical mass necessary to lend visual drama and a focus to the skyline. Downtown actually is beginning to look like a downtown and Century City something more than a back-lot backdrop.

But where there is no grouping to which to relate, only low-scale communities to look down upon, the lone towers appear like swollen, awkward thumbs—depressing examples of insensitive urban design, poor planning and sluggish city government.

Many of the buildings are in part a result of the failure of the city's Planning Department to anticipate such development, supposedly a major purpose of the department.

Therefore, when the flagrant development began to happen in such areas as Brentwood, West Los Angeles and Sherman Oaks, the department, which has been headed by Calvin Hamilton for 19 years, could not quickly assert itself to stop or better control the growth or persuade the City Council to do so. Once again, planning under Hamilton was as best a reactive process.

There also was no strong support for more forceful planning policies from Mayor Tom Bradley, other than general statements on the need to control growth and protect the character of existing neighborhoods. The mayor has rarely expressed public concern over planning, but instead seems to let the process drift in a sea populated by politicians, bureaucrats, zoning lawyers and building expediters.

Only lately, after a number of office towers have been built bordering residential areas—prompting homeowners to complain vociferously—has the city, led by the local councilperson, begun to slowly roll back zoning and limit heights so they would be consistent with approved community plans. Many of the plans have been in the works for more than a decade.

Actually, the consistency between zoning and community plans was mandated in 1978 by the state Legislature under a law known as AB 283. No one can accuse Los Angeles of acting precipitously in matters that might affect the property values of potential political contributors.

The city's response also has been slowed by a reasonable confusion concerning the role of high-rise buildings in various visions of the future.

During the last few decades, such buildings generally have been viewed here and in other cities as measures of success—size usually being directly proportional to the value of the land and the investment involved.

High-rises also have been a municipal mark of progress, coveted by most elected officials and public servants trying to keep in step with other cities suffering from what could be called an edifice complex. Every city seems at some time or other to want its own variation of an Empire State Building.

THE HIGH-RISE IS CERTAINLY ARCHITECTURE'S MOST DRAMATIC CREATION OF this century, testing new building materials, engineering concepts, the imagination of clients and the talent of designers and their age-old desire to reach for the heavens while dominating the Earth.

And with the more severe, boxy Modern Style now out of favor with office developers looking for something more distinctive to attract attention and tenants, architects have been given even freer rein to exercise their creative urges. The result is that the design of high-rises is flowering.

Even such a late bloomer as Los Angeles is benefiting. Though the city's fledgling collection of high-rises forming a downtown sky-line does not yet have the excitement and power of New York, Chicago or Houston, or the density of San Francisco, it is emerging as a promising focal point to the sprawling region.

Helping the downtown skyline is its increasing volume and such complexes as the stunning Crocker Center, designed by Skidmore Owings & Merrill. From a distance, the center tends to soften the impact of less distinguished architectural efforts in the area, such as the Union Bank Building. What dominates is the sum effect of the structures that in their bulk and diversity begin to read like a city.

But much less successful—indeed, awkward to a point of embarrassment for a city with world-class pretensions this Olympic year—are a number of other structures that recently have been or are being constructed in what had been relatively low- and moderate-rise communities.

These include the Getty Plaza in Universal City, the World Savings Center and the Wilshire Bundy Plaza in Brentwood, the Crocker Center in Sherman Oaks and Westwood Gateway in West Los Angeles.

They stand like giant glass, granite and steel creations, ominous monoliths that dropped out of the sky. And this, despite some of the structures actually being well engineered and designed, at least as a single building in a vacuum.

WHAT DEGRADES THE ARCHITECTURE IS THE SITING AND MASSING OF THE buildings. They are out of context and out of scale, in some instances backing up against single-story, single-family residences.

To be sure, many of the decisions concerning the siting and massing of such developments are not made by the architects, but by the developers and their investors. In such situations, the architects tend to function in effect as exterior designers.

It is the clients who determine how big a building should be, which more often than not is simply calculated upon what the planning and zoning of an area will allow and what more a savvy lawyer can extract.

Whatever it is called—a high-rise, skyscraper or office tower—in the final analysis the structure is an investment stemming from a delicate equation involving finances, taxes, zoning, market studies and politics, sprinkled with a dash of speculation.

That some of the structures might work as part of a critical mass and lend Los Angeles an emerging urban identity while others stand alone scarring the skyline seems to be secondary.

And, of course, long after the clients and architects involved in the design of the buildings have moved on elsewhere, their creations will be a permanent part of the cityscape, affecting lives and lending Los Angeles an image, for better or worse.

April 11, 1984

Mini-Malls: Scenario for Horror Film

THE RECENT EXPLOSIVE GROWTH OF SMALL, CONVENIENCE SHOPPING centers—they seem to be popping up everywhere these days— have generated some pressing urban design concerns.

If the centers were the subject of a movie, the concerns might be advertised as:

"ATTACK OF THE MINI-MALLS!"
"Watch in horror as one is built in your neighborhood!."
"Shudder with fear as it gobbles up the sidewalk!"
"Weep as it turns your shopping street into a pit stop!"

And in smaller type at the bottom of the billboard:

"Call your local council person, the city planning department or the mayor for help and get sympathy but no hint on how the blight might be blocked."

IT SEEMS THE CENTERS ARE A BIG HIT AMONG REAL ESTATE DEVELOPERS, WHO claim they are relatively easy to finance, build and rent. All that is needed is a site at a busy city intersection, such as where a gasoline station once might have been located. There certainly are enough vacant or failing stations dotting the city landscape.

Developers feel that the success of the mini-malls depends in large part on the visibility and accessibility of their parking area, which means putting it in front of the stores. This results in developments slice up sidewalks with curb cuts, destroy the scale and massing of street scapes, hide store fronts behind rows of automobiles and generally discourage pedestrian life.

The process is a variation on strip commercial development of the type that has defaced surburban highways before business began to drift away to shopping centers, then later to the fancier major malls. Van Nuys Boulevard is often cited as an example of such strip commercial (and is used by some planners as a verb, "Van Nuysing," to describe the process.)

Now, the mini-malls are attracting the small-item, quick in-and-out businesses away from the shopping centers and the major malls. The key word in the operation of the mini-malls is convenience.

City planners here say they are aware of the urban design problems caused by mini-malls but contend there is little they can do because most of the properties involved already are zoned for such use.

They add that only if a developer might need some sort of zoning change can such special requirements be imposed that might ease the eyesore, such as requiring walls and plantings. (The walls the city has required have tended to be excellent billboards for gang graffiti.)

Once again the city is in position, at best, of reacting to a situation instead of taking the lead to prevent further damage to the street scape and rectify the damage already inflicted. Or worse, the city will just stand around and sadly watch the malls "Van Nuys" the streets where they locate.

Among the tools urban designers have used in other cities to prevent the "Van Nuys-ing" is limiting setbacks in commercial zones to maintain a consistent facade, which tends to force parking to the rear of stores.

The same effect—forcing parking to the rear—has been accomplished by city agencies simply denying curb cuts for driveways on busy streets and near crowded intersections. This technique also has exacted from developers such amenities as landscaping and sitting areas.

It is not that the city should deny the development of convenience shopping centers—obviously at present they fill a need—but they can better shape them to be more sympathetic to the cityscape. All that is needed is some gumption, imagination and leadership on a practical level.

If the city is not going to assert itself, the mini-malls could become another blight, just as strip commercial development blighted Van Nuys Boulevard, and in time require a redevelopment program with all its costs and trimmings to perhaps restore some design sensibilities to the street scape. Such a program is now under way on Van Nuys Boulevard. But why must the city always wait until the damage is done to act?

Melrose Avenue is another example of urban design problems starting to nibble away at a street's ambiance. The example is particularly grievous for at present Melrose from about Highland Avenue west to Doheny Drive is perhaps the city's most serendipitous shopping street.

First, there is the needless city and county road-widening project that has cut back sidewalks serving strollers to about six feet in width. In the process, trees have been cut down that had lent protection to shoppers against the glare and heat of the midday sun.

This was done to accommodate a consistent four lanes of traffic and two curb lanes for parking. Not accommodated or apparently even considered was the street's potential for a pleasant urban experience.

Still, pedestrians persevere. But with parking meters, telephone polls, fire hydrants and newspaper vending machines making the sidewalk even narrower, strolling is becoming quite difficult. For the handicapped, it is nearly impossible.

Sept. 30, 1984

A Lesson for Pershing Square

THE NOW-CLASSIC PHOTO OF THE 1972 DEMOLITION OF TWO BUILDINGS IN St. Louis is one of the more ubiquitous illustrations used in various planning texts to dramatize the failure of design. Trashed by its tenants, the buildings in a project known as Pruitt-Igoe had become a high-rise slum.

Actually, the buildings by architect Minoru Yamasaki were quite well designed, incorporating the then-latest theories of making high-rises more attractive to families, such as wide, open hallways and express elevators. The effort won several awards for Yamasaki.

Subsequent studies indicated that Pruitt-Igoe's problems had not been caused by design, but dy the landlord, the St. Louis Housing Authority. It had put too many troubled, migrant families together in select buildings while offering them little if any social services.

If the debacle of Pruitt-Igoe had any lessons to teach, it was that while design might have some effect on a particular environment—perhaps making the lives of some occupants more pleasant—it will not solve the more severe of society's ills.

THE LESSON APPARENTLY HAS NOT BEEN LEARNED IN LOS ANGELES, AT LEAST not by those at present hovering over Pershing Square. Once again, a major effort is being mounted—at a major expense totaling $1.6 million—to come up with a design solution to the social problems that haunt the historic downtown park.

It is not as if the forlorn park has not been tampered with enough over the last few decaes. Many of its obvious design problems, such as the ramps to its underground garage that isolate critical edges of the park from the surrounding streetscape, are a result of past "improvements" that were really veiled efforts to drive out itinerant undesirables.

Certainly, the effort last summer during the Olympics by the Pershing Square Management Assn., an offshoot of the Central City Assn., to sanitize the park with a tacky commercial festival and a few plantings—at an estimated cost of $500,000—was a bust, except for the planning consultants involved who picked up healthy fees.

But the real estate interests with investments surrounding the park, who belong to the nonprofit association are persistent. Once again, they seem quite willing to risk yet more funds underwritten by the city's Community Redevelopment Agency to come up with something, anything that hints at an "improvement."

IT IS NOT THAT THE PARK DOES NOT NEED HELP. ITS OPEN SPACE CAN BE MADE more attractive, its edges softened to become more inviting, its plantings cultivated and its facilities repaired and policed, among other things. Pershing Square needs tender loving care, as do its denizens. Though they don't drink with the yuppies and tourists at the bar in the Biltmore, they are citizens too.

But one has to be concerned about the current effort now gaining momentum. Judging from the association's recent remarks before the city's Cultural Affairs Commission and a review of its generous budget being underwritten by the CRA, there seems to be an overemphasis on a costly design process and no real open discussion about its goals.

Indeed, the impression is that the design process will be full of sound and flurry that—when the smoke settles—will benefit only a select public, while not changing the fate of one blade of grass in the park.

There have been so many failures in the past to improve Pershing Square that it would be terribly sad if, because of a lack of goals, this latest effort only produces a thick set of plans to be filed away somewhere and some nice press clippings for those involved to use elsewhere. Given the past failures to revive the park, no one is going to be blamed if the effort fails. The only loser, of course, will be the city.

PERHAPS, THAT IS WHY THE CITY SHOULD JUST LEAVE PERSHING SQUARE alone for awhile—maybe it will rejuvenate itself as the surrounding area slowly improves itself—or at least not be in such a rush to "lend" the park group the $1.6 million.

After all, the group never did pay back the city the $500,000 it said it would when it launched the summer project, despite statements then by its parent Central City Assn. If the area's private interests are so anxious to "improve" the park, perhaps they should come up with funds up front, as they said they would when this process began a few years ago.

May 5, 1985

THE DEADLINE FOR THE PERSHING SQUARE DESIGN COMPETITION IS FAST approaching, with only two weeks left for submissions. The hope is that the effort generates an imaginative concept for which the forlorn public space, and the city, hungers.

To do so, the submissions, unfortunately, will have to overcome a program that reads more like a laundry list than a clear vision of priorities; a result, no doubt, of the obvious conflicts that haunt the space. These include its role as a garage roof, gathering spot for "undesirables" and an unkempt front lawn to expensive real estate.

Beyond the conflicting program, the challenge is whether the design can overcome the isolation of the space and tap into the increasing flow of pedestrian life downtown, particularly to the east.

It will be a challenge, whatever direction the square reaches out to, given the garage ramps that hold the space in a death grip. The ramps literally and figuratively are a hurdle that must be cleared, reduced or relocated so the square can better connect to the city. The development of downtown has reached a point where people and places must count more than cars and convenience.

As for what will be developed on the square itself, we trust that out of the clutter of the program will not come a clutter of structures.

It was Camillo Sittee who pointed out nearly a century ago in his classic treatise, "The Art of Building Cities," that squares should be open and inviting, with the people energizing the space, not objects. What should be cluttered is the surrounding streetscapes defining the square.

Another concern is the competition's jury. While its individual members are quite accomplished, all are either practicing designers or artists. Though valued, their views have to be limited.

Included also should have been a few denizens of the downtown community, in effect the clients. It would have been good planning and good politics.

Still, the hope is that the well-intentioned competition, however flawed, produces a plan worthy of the site, and the city. As its present condition testifies, Pershing Square has suffered enough.

May 18, 1986

NOT PROMISING IS THE HOPE FOR A REJUVENATED PERSHING SQUARE, AT least as promoted by the forlorn park's forlorn management.

With its confidence exceeding its competence, the association continues to scratch for the funding of the ambitious and costly scheme by the ·firm of SITE Projects, of New York, that won the square's widely publicized redesign competition a year and a half ago.

The association's latest ploy is to try to get the city to establish a special assessment district downtown to foot the bill. While some of the property owners and big-buck builders in the area are agreeable in principle to the idea, most feel the SITE design is indulgent and want it abandoned in favor of a more modest and, they feel, appropriate design that would be easier to operate and maintain.

This sentiment also is gaining favor in the city's Community Redevelopment Agency, which, for three years has been nobly indulging the association, and the city's Recreation and Parks Department. Meanwhile, the historic square continues to deteriorate, along with the credibility of those involved. It is time for an accounting.

March 13, 1988

Skyline Signs Spell "Tacky"

THE BATTLE FOR THE LOS ANGELES DOWNTOWN SKYLINE CONTINUES, WITH the forces of good design counter-attacking real estate interests with a report recommending the banning of lettering and logos at or near the rooftops of new buildings.

The much-welcomed report, prepared by the staff of the city Community Redevelopment Agency and circulated among city officials and agencies and other interested groups, will be the subject of a public hearing.

Given the history of anti-sign efforts, the sweeping recommendation will need all the support it can get as it goes up against the always anxious real estate community at the hearing before the agency.

Many brokers feel that the promise of signs on a tower given them that needed "extra" to close a big lease with a major tenant, and so what if the signs look tacky. Their chief concern, they say, is pleasing a tenant, not an arbitrary urban design policy, even if it might improve the value of the building and the image of the surrounding business district.

At last report, late last year, the good-design forces had lost a skirmish to the real estate interests when the city's Community Redevelopment Agency board yielded to the pleas of the developers of the Citicorp and Coast Savings office towers for permission to erect signs on top of their buildings.

The signs planned by Oxford Properties for the mammoth Citicorp tower, now rising at 7th and Figueroa streets, have been described by those who have seen them as "cheap." One would think that this is not exactly the image a major financial corporation coming into Los Angeles would want.

The signs planned by the Reliance Development Group for the Coast Savings tower under construction at 1000 Wilshire Blvd., are said to be relatively discreet, but nonetheless are not needed to identify the building and certainly not needed to further clutter up the downtown skyline.

As IT IS, THE PRESENT SKYLINE IS NOT PARTICULARLY ATTRACTIVE OR DISTINCtive. There aleardy are too many tacky signs, among them, the Convention Center, Thomas Cadillac, the Hilton, Coldwell Banker, Bank of America and Union Bank, and too many tacky, box-topped, boring corporate edifices.

There is the hope in the near future for a more distinctive skyline of generally thinner, more detailed and tapered buildings; a few with engaging roof lines. It is a hope engendered by such recent constructions as the Crocker and Wells Fargo towers and proposals for Library Square.

However, that hope was dampened by the decision of the agency board to overrule a staff recommendation and allow the Citicorp and Coast Federal signs. The board based its decision on the fact there was no firm city policy regarding the downtown skyline to guide developers, and therefore was unfair to developers.

(Isn't it odd that most city boards always seem so concerned about what is fair and unfair to developers, apparently forgetting that it is the broad public they are supposed to represent, not just those of special interests?)

The decision sent the agency staff scurrying to the drawing boards. I was told that this column helped also when it declared that a sign on a building was a symbol of mediocrity, that "if not blocked before it is bolted down, could become infectious and turn the fledgling downtown Los Angeles skyline into a smear of signs, each one trying to be bigger and shinier than the last. Signs get that way if not controlled."

Six months later the staff has produced a refreshingly frank report reviewing the issues and recommending that not only signs, but also logos, be banned from the tops of all new buildings downtown.

"The complete prohibition of skyline signage would establish a consistent aesthetic while retaining the advantages of easy definition and administration," states the report. It continues:

"In cities such as New York, Dallas, Houston and Minneapolis, signs atop tall buildings are virtually absent; the resultant aesthetic places emphasis on building form by eliminating the distraction of signage. This example set by these cities also indicates that a no-signage policy has little negative effect on the leasability of tenant space if the policy is consistent, universally applied and predictable. In fact, from suburban developments to major business centers, enhancement of the overall image of an area has been known to enhance areawide property values and economic desirability."

In short, good urban design policy pays.

THE PROBLEM, OF COURSE, IS WHAT TO DO WITH THE EXISTING SIGNS NOW strewn across the downtown skyline, which, as the report notes, will be more conspicuous than ever under a policy banning all new signs.

"A number of options are available to mitigate this disadvantage over time, including amortized removal and financial assistance, to bring nonconforming conditions in line with the policy," the report states optimistically.

Following the public hearing, the report and its policies will go to the agency board. If the agency adopts the policies, the report recommends that the City Council "be requested to enact a similar ordinance establishing a compatible policy for surrounding areas, such as Temple/Beaudry, to prevent a clash with the image of the core area."

It is the sort of statement that should send a shiver down the spine of billboard interests and right into the pockets of their lobbyists.

July 7, 1985

The report and its recommendations, alas were buried, while the signs were hoisted.

Skidding Along Skid Row

COMING TO LOS ANGELES THIS WEEK TO TAKE A LOOK AT HOW THE CITY might better deal with its Skid Row housing problem is an advisory panel of the Urban Land Institute, a national association made up mostly of well-meaning developers and public officials.

And while the nonprofit institute's record of accomplishments has not been the best when dealing with the problems of inner-city neighborhoods—it fumbled such an effort in the North Lawndale community of Chicago last fall—its involvement in Los Angeles is welcome.

The city certainly needs all the help it can get, for it and its point bureaucracy on the problem, the Community Redevelopment Agency, have been stumbling badly in recent months in their commitment to provide and preserve decent housing to the estimated 8,000 persons who live in the area's single-room occupancy (SRO) hotels.

It is important to note that these are not the homeless—that is another, and in many ways, greater problem for Skid Row, the city and the nation. These are the poor and the increasing number of down-and-out families with children who have been unable to find any other inexpensive housing in the city.

But many may become homeless as the city procrastinates.

To be sure, there is a mayor's committee supposedly studying the problem. But like the mayor himself, the committee, at this point, has yet to come up with a specific plan to develop needed affordable housing, as well as preserving the existing housing.

At present, there are five more months to go on a moratorium on the demolition of SRO hotels, which earlier this year were being picked off by speculators and developers anticipating a shift into the area by the burgeoning toy manufacturing and warehousing industries, and an increase in demand for commercial space.

Fueling speculation has been a proposal within the city Planning Department to rezone the area, bounded by Main, San Pedro, 3rd and 7th streets, to light manufacturing. This, in effect, would kill any thoughts of new housing there, while undermining the city's *stated* policy to preserve the SRO hotels.

"Stated" is emphasized, for there are persistent rumors that pressures on City Hall by Central City East interests are building to "amend" the policy by flat or inaction and "cleanse" the area.

"The moratorium is just a smoke screen," said a caller a few weeks ago. "For a clue to what the city will, or will not do, watch CRA's budget for rehabilitation funds to correct the seismic defects of the SROs and bring them up to code. A minimum $11.5 million is needed to save about 3,000 units. That's housing for maybe 4,000 people."

Last week, the agency approved $5.5 million for the seismic safety loan program, with the possibility that even some of the funds would be diverted to other efforts.

Perhaps the $5.5 million is all that the agency can handle, for its existing rehabilitation program in the area has been moving excruciatingly slow. Gone seems to be a commitment to program, unfortunately, at a time when the city and those suffering on Skid Row need the most help.

How the city can better implement its policy is what the ULI panel will be studying, or should be studying. There is some talk that the CRA wants the panel to consider whether the policy is appropriate.

That seems to be a question that should be debated by elected officials, not by visiting panelists, study committees or, for that matter, by the CRA board.

July 19, 1987

Planning Process Raises Questions

A SPRAWLING, SCRUBBY 257-ACRE SITE ON TOP OF TOPANGA CANYON IS the latest battleground in the heightening war over the shaping and styling of Los Angeles city-and "suburbanscapes."

Involved in this particular battle—in addition to the usual array of concerned local residents and determined developers—is the credibility of the county planning process.

Scheduled to be aired before the county Regional Planning Commission Thursday is a proposal to develop the Topanga site for a hotel and conference complex, an 18-hole golf course, tennis and equestrian facilities, 224 home sites and a convenience shopping center.

Also included in the ambitious plans submitted by architect and developer Christopher Wojciechowski are police and fire stations and a water treatment plant. The cost of the development, called the Montevideo Country Club, has been estimated at about $100 million.

WOJCIECHOWSKI DESCRIBES HIS DREAM DEVELOPMENT, ENCOMPASSING THE headwaters of Topanga Creek, as a public resource, while residents to the north, on the "valley" side, talk of it as "upscaling" the area, and not incidentally, the value of their homes.

But residents to the south see the development as a major threat to their rustic life style and the canyon's fragile ecology, which is ravaged intermittently by floods and fires. They also note that the grading for the proposed project would destroy hundreds of valued oak trees.

And, as in almost every community these days, there is growing concern over traffic. Topanga Canyon Boulevard already is one of the more over burdened and dangerous roadways in the area, due, in part, to the penchant among local residents for souped up pickup trucks, or at least it seemed that way during a recent visit there.

Whatever, there is little question that Topanga Canyon is a unique area, caught in a sort of comfortable, if not funky, 1960s time warp in which the reality of a 1980s real estate packaging, embodied in the Montevideo Country Club, is not particularly welcome.

BUT IN ADDITION TO THE CONFLICT OF STYLES, THERE IS THE QUESTION OF land use. The general interim plan for the site prescribes light agricultural use and about 100 single-family houses.

Though the plan has been adopted, its implementing zoning has not. Still on the books is the old zoning, which, in this case, would allow 529 home sites.

Nevertheless, the intent of the plan has been quite clear for some time. One wonders why the county goes through the trouble and expense, and residents the time and good will, that preparing and approving a plan demands, just to see it so blatantly ignored by developer after developer requesting variances.

The situation seems to have taken its cue from the infamous business practices of the entertainment industry, where producers, having signed a detailed contract, have been known when putting down the pen to comment, "now that it's done, let's negotiate."

NO MATTER HOW WELL DESIGNED, THE PROPOSED MONTEVIDEO COUNTRY Club is so out of scale and of context that it raises questions concerning the good faith of the county's planning process.

It is just this type of situation—the obvious abuse of zoning prescribed by a general plan—that frustrates community groups trying to play a responsible role in the development process, and that sends them over the thin line from conscientiousness to contentiousness.

When communities in the Los Angeles area had elbow room and traffic flowed freely, such developments as Montevideo would probably have been approved without much debate, perhaps even welcomed.

But as the area continues to urbanize and becomes more dense, such developments demand more scrutiny, and the planning process more credibility.

May 23, 1986

A modified scheme eventually was approved.

Public Risks and Private Profits

LOS ANGELES PLAYS HOST THIS WEEK TO THE ANNUAL MEETING OF THE Urban Land Institute, a national organization of private entrepreneurs and public officials dedicated to development. These are the people who, for better or worse, generally shape our cityscapes.

It is the private entrepreneurs who turn realtors loose to assemble sites, who hire architects and tell them what to design; who support politicians through generous campaign contributions, and who pay for the lawyers to finesse needed zoning and environmental approvals.

For them, ULI is a clearing house of sorts for business and political contacts, common concerns and, on occasion, enlightened strategies to various problems plaguing our cities today.

As for the public officials who belong to ULI, they tend to be the ones who embrace developers and let them pick up the tabs for drinks and dinners beyond the pale of their expense accounts.

But all is not play at the conferences. The officials recognize well that their future depends on getting the private sector to build things that generate jobs, pay taxes and pad their bureaucracies, as well as pleasing the politicians who oversee their agencies and who might be indebted to a developer or two, or three.

In addition, today's public official often is tomorrow's private developer, or at least a well-paid consultant to one. This tends to make ULI a big family, and mutual back scratching, along with some back-biting, an informal conference activity more important that the formal program.

But another way, there is a lot of buttering of both sides of the bread at ULI gatherings. It is in these sessions that the private/public partnership, the recent popular catch phrase for development, was once defined for me as projects in which the public secctor takes the risks through granting land write-downs, zoning bonuses and tax abatements and the private sector takes the profits.

To be sure, this does not mean that what comes out of the deals struck at ULI conferences or elsewhere under the banner of private/public partnerships are necessarily bad.

Indeed, there is a recognition in the more responsibile segment of the development community that projects to be successful really must work for the public good as well as for private interests; that doing good can be translated into making good. This is a point that ULI has emphasized in its prestigious awards program.

BEYOND THE AWARDS IS THE COLD FACT THAT THE TOUGHEST JUDGE OF projects these days tends not to be loan committees, architectural juries, planning commissions or city councils, but rather the marketplace. It is just too bad that some bombs of buildings have to be constructed to prove how wrong developers, financiers, critics and public officials can be.

Actually, for the development community, these buildings are worse than bad.

Once scarred by a gross mini-mall, a ticky-tacky apartment house and an overscaled office block, local communities are not prone to look sympathetically at sensitively designed projects that just might serve them and their neighbors well.

The situation is often further exacerbated by private developers and public officials who consider the targeted local communities the enemy, to be manipulated, coerced or co-opted. In their short-term goals of ramming a plan or a project through, they don't seem to realize that the communities consist of users and voters, who, in the long run, have the last say.

As a result, private/public partnerships in these days of increasing community concerns over development teeter between self-interest and self-destruction, with the ULI trying to hold the line.

WHILE THE CONCEPT OF PRIVATE/PUBLIC PARTNERSHIPS MOST LIKELY WILL BE aired at the ULI conference, it is being put to the test in various forms and in various Los Angeles communities.

In Center City West, bounded by the Harbor and Hollywood freeways, Olympic Boulevard and Witmer Avenue, a coalition of commercial interests there, in cooperation with the city, is sponsoring the development of a compreshensive urban design and land-use plan. The coalition is at present rounding up the usual suspects to decide who will conduct the effort.

A little further west in the Wilshire Center area bounded by 3rd, 8th and Alvarado streets and Wilton Place, a coalition known as the Wilshire Stakeholders is sponsoring a more modest planning effort. It is being dutifully conducted by the Urban Innovations Group (UIG) out of UCLA.

Of concern is that funding of the efforts is coming mostly from the private sector, in particfular from commercial interests in the area that can substantially benefit from subtle shifts in zoning and land-use patterns.

This is somewhat like the situation that a few years ago sank a privately sponsored UIG plan for the Mid-Wilshire area, and, more recently, cast a shadow over Hollywood Redevelopment program, where major property owners loaned the city's Community Redevelopment Agency money to fund the planning effort.

While property owners have a right to act to improve their investments, whether directly through a zoning change or indirectly through a general plan, there is the question of the greater public good being pursued, if not simply protected. A dangerous precedent can be set if the prerogatives of public planning in the interest of expediency are turned over to the private sector, no matter how altruistic.

In the formula for private/public partnerships, the public must dominate. So far in the shaping of the Center City West effort the office of Councilwoman Gloria Molina seems to understand this and is holding the reins. We trust her grip will be strong.

The Stakeholders present a similar challenge to Councilmen John Ferraro and Nate Holden, and to the targeted residential community. It is hoped that they will be able to assert themselves in the planning process, for the sake of the credibility of the private interests involved, and of UIG, as well as the plan itself.

Oct. 4, 1987

THE INITIATIVE FOR THE DESIGN OF PUBLIC SPACE IN THE LAST FEW YEARS has shifted from the public to the private realm, in particular to the more imaginative architectural and planning consultants and enlightened developers. They realize well, even if the city doesn't, that the key to the success of any development of any size today is "place making."

The result has been such engaging downtown projects as the Seventh Market Place and the Japanese Village.

And engendering promise of "place" are the water terraces and stairway at the base of Library Tower, connecting Bunker Hill to the restored (we hope) west lawn of the rehabilitated (we hope) Central Library. There is promise, too, in the Showa Village proposal for Little Tokyo, if it isn't crushed by a compromised City Council.

Add to this list is the recently announced plan for the private development of nearly 14 acres of prime Ocean Boulevard frontage in

Long Beach, including the former site of the Pike amusement park. It was packaged under the name of Pike Properties by developer Wayne Ratkovich and a host of advisers and investors, including James Rouse of Festival Market fame.

The plan has a $1-billion price tag and calls for the staged development over the next decade of the now familiar and welcome mix of office towers, varied housing types, a hotel, eateries, retail outlets and convenience shopping—subject, of course, to the availability of financing.

What distinguishes the plan is the the emphasis is not on the buildings, but on the public spaces.

They will be developed first, in stages, not as afterthoughts, as they usually are; in effect, providing the basis for a "location" that will determine the form and orientation of the varied structures. That, in fact, is the way cities traditionally have been shaped.

The public spaces include an expanded and enhanced park along Ocean Boulevard and a series of landscaped courts, terraces, malls and walks within the development, edged with diversions designed to encourage pedestrian activity. Parking will be tucked under the development, yet easily accessible because of the 20-foot drop in the site from Ocean Boulevard to Seaside Way.

It is a relatively simple, yet sophisticated plan, taking advantage of the dramatic site and its views, while responding to the existing street grid of the city. Created is the potential for a distinctively picturesque and lively urban neighborhood, rather than the usual sterile settings of large commercial and residential efforts.

Long Beach certainly can use it to repair some of the damage done to its downtown over the last few decades by a perverted urban renewal program and a plodding city government.

The ambitious plan was fashioned by Stanton Eckstut, now of the firm of the Ehrenkrantz Group & Eckstut. Consultants in the design process included architects Charles Moore, Frank Gehry and Jon Jerde, and Richard Weinstein, dean of the Graduate School of Architecture and Urban Planning at UCLA. It is an interesting lineup, the kind that generates an award or two.

But frankly, the plan reads Eckstut, who was one of the principal designers of the much acclaimed Battery Park City in New York. The urban design elements focused on the public places that worked there are very much in evidence in the Pike Properties plan, and are welcomed. Hopefully, they can be instructive in other large planning efforts now under way, such as for Central City West adjacent to downtown Los Angeles.

As a public place, California Plaza has its problems; too isolated and too big, poorly edged and unfocused. That is what happens when politics wins out over design.

One of the things that might help inject a little life into the plaza and better connect it to the city is Angel's Flight, the funicular railway the Community Redevelopment Agency has repeatedly promised to rebuild.

However, its reconstruction has been delayed again. We hope

not for too long, and that a date be set and a schedule announced, and this time be met. If not, one of these days the funicular is going to leave the CRA standing at the station with mud all over its face.

—July 10, 1988

At this writing, we still await a timetable for the reconstruction of Angel's Flight. As for Showa Village, it was crushed by the Council. Pike perseveres.

Housing: the Good, Bad and Ugly

ALMOST EVERYWHERE YOU LOOK IN LOS ANGELES THESE DAYS IT SEEMS that an overblown apartment complex is being squeezed onto some site, like a size 14 trying, with embarrassment, to get into a size 10.

And even if some of the complexes are not necessarily out of scale, they tend to be over-designed, badly designed or out of place. An appropriate architectural adage to describe the situation might be that more is less.

For an example, take a look at Bundy Drive between Idaho and Ohio avenues, in West Los Angeles. There, a wall of apartment buildings in styles that include folksy, muted, clapboard-sided Cape Cod; stark, white Late-Modern with a touch of Italian tile, and soft, peachy nouveau-Spanish, elbow each other as if they were reaching for free hors d'oeuvres at a press luncheon.

While the views from the well-detailed, spacious apartments on the upper floors of the modernistic 1555 Bundy, designed by JCA Architects, are nice, the views from the sidewalk of the building and its neighbors are not. They fight each other, and the street, with everyone losing.

Such fortress-like housing, with no usable open space, no brething room for themselves or their neighbors, just a dark double-loaded corridor linking the garage to the apartments, seems to be the trend these days.

You can see these depressing hulks not only in West Los Angeles, but also in other multifamily residential pockets in Mar Vista, Westwood, the mid-Wilshire and Fairfax districts, Highland Park, Studio City, Sherman Oaks, and North Hollywood, among others.

So much for sympathetic siting and imaginative designs among some private developers, and conscientious design review by our public servants. In defense of such developments, they argue that the housing is needed.

THERE IS INDEED FOR HOUSING, BUT SENSITIVELY DESIGNED HOUSING, AS WELL as affordable, comfortable and convenient housing; reasonably priced near where people work or can work.

That, and not more street widenings and freeways, is the only way the region's growing traffic problem will ever be esed.

That, and not more flimsy shelters and frail excuses, also is one of the ways we might begin to meet the myriad needs of homeless families. The more housing built, even the overpriced and ostentatious, the more that will be available.

33

But the housing also should work for the surrounding neighborhoods as well as for those who will live in it. Certainly, developers want to preserve, indeed enhance, the character of the neighborhoods that I assume prompted them in the first instance to build there.

It can be done, and done well, as demonstrated by some select projects recently orchestrated by the Community Corporation of Santa Monica, the city's Community Redevelopment Agency and the City of Beverly Hills. That all of these projects were built within strict budgets to provide affordable units make the examples even more dramatic, and sweeter.

What distinguishes the recently completed 2207 6th St. in the Ocean Park section of Santa Monica is that, at first glance, it appears like most other small, stucco-clad apartment complexes in the area: boxy and boring.

Only when you look at the moderately priced six-unit rental development closer do you notice that behind the boxy structure with the flat roof is a second structure with a curved roof, separated by a courtyard, and further individualized with varying materials and detailing.

As designed by the firm of Koning Eizenberg and developed by the Community Corporation, the complexis a practical, imaginative update on an awkward sloping site of the courtyard housing concept that served Los Angeles so well for so many years.

Also developed by the same architects and the Corporation in the same mode is a six-unit complex two blocks away at 2400 5th St. There, to overcome the parking and setback requirements and create the desired private and communal spaces, the apartments were sited in two buildings served by a central deck. It seems to work and not overwhelm the site or the street. Another modestly scaled project by the team is nearing completion at 1427 Berkeley St.

Promising also to be both user- and neighborhood-friendly is a 43-unit low-income cooperative housing development now being constructed by the nonprofit corporation on five separate sites in a two-block area in Ocean Park. In response to concern raised in community planning workshops, the in-fill project was designed by the firm of Appleton, Mechur & Associates in a Craftsman aesthetic, reflecting the bungalow-type housing that marks the area.

WITH THE SAME CONCERN FOR A NEIGHBORHOOD'S SENSE OF PLACE THE LOS Angeles Community Redevelopment Agency a year ago blocked the demolition of three historic houses in the Pico Union area, and provided the financing and incentives to have them rehabilitated into nine low-rent apartments.

Designed in a colonial revival style fashionable a century ago, the houses at 1047-53 S. Bonnie Brae St., and 1851 W. 11th St. lend the struggling neighborhood some welcomed housing and a touch of class.

Whether it is called in-fill, or over-fill, the fact that the City of Beverly Hills could provide a convenient site for 151 units of affordable housing for senior citizens and the handicapped is praiseworthy. There is a desperate need for such housing today.

That the city, with the help of the Federal Department of Housing and Urban Development and the Jewish Federation, also could provide the site in combination with needed parking and an upscale supermarket on the edge of its central business district, a block from City Hall, is even more impressive.

You really have to look hard to see the housing at the corner of North Crescent Drive and Dayton Way, but it is there, above Mrs. Gooch's and an 877-space parking garage, in an inspired design by the former architecture firm of Kamnitzer & Cotton.

WHAT THESE PROJECTS DEMONSTRATE IS THAT APARTMENT COMPLEXES CAN be developed without requiring the demolition of existing, sound units to provide a site, and that do not degrade streets with unfriendly designs. Indeed, they demonstrate that new housing can improve neighborhoods, and lives.

—Feb. 14, 1988

Suburban Dreams

THE SUSTAINING DREAM OF MOST SOUTHERN CALIFORNIANS IS TO NOT LIVE in, or even near, a city. Just as when millions of young families flocked to the small farming towns on the fringes of a burgeoning Los Angeles after World War II, today people are seeking economically and socially homogeneous suburban neighborhoods. That doesn't mean the cookie-cutter tract developments of the '40s and '50s, however; today's suburban home buyers seek subdivisions with sensitive master plans that incorporate meandering bike paths and jogging trails, pleasant parks and pools, competent community schools and convenient shopping centers. In short, they're looking for a comfortable small-town atmosphere within commuting distance of a big city, an almost idyllic place to watch the kids, the grass, the real estate values and the equity grow while they pursue the American dream.

Across Southern California the population is expanding into spanking new suburban areas in Irvine, further south into San Diego county, east into San Bernardino, north onto the high desert and west toward Ventura. In 1987, this growth accounted for two-thirds of the region's population increase.

Southern California is, without question, the pacesetter for the design of the new, village-oriented, suburban America. "Ever since the sprawling [93,000-acre] Irvine Ranch was master-planned in the 1960s, we have been making pilgrimages there to check out the latest designs," remarks Nevada developer Mark Fine, who surveys residential developments in the United States as an officer of the Urban Land Institute.

"What you see going up in Southern California now is what you most likely will see going up in other suburbs across the country in the next few years," adds Fine, who has used these ideas in developing Green Valley, a successful 8,300-acre planned community outside Las Vegas. "The materials and architectural styles may be different because of the weather and local preferences, but the land-use concepts, floor plans and marketing concepts will be quite similar to what's on the rise in Southern California, generally, and in Irvine, specifically."

THE LATEST INNOVATION IN THE SHAPING OF SOUTHERN CALIFORNIA SUBURbia is what planners called "increased densification"—putting more housing on less land. In the '50s, the average density in a tract development was perhaps three or four homes per acre; today's developments artfully compact as many as 7.75—sometimes even more— homes on an acre. Significantly, developers have not only doubled the number of homes per acre, they've also doubled their size from an average of 900 square feet to an average of 1,800 square feet. But this does not necessarily mean that suburbia is being overwhelmed with cheek-by-jowl housing.

"If you can—with imagination—keep the amenities people want in suburbia, such as the backyards, the bike paths, parks and a sense of open space, increased densification is not bad," observes Santa Barbara-based architect Barry Berkus. "In fact, density can increase the desirability of a community by creating a friendly village atmosphere, not unlike in a Mediterranean country." Berkus was a pioneer of what are called planned-unit developments in Southern California—including the prize-winning Woodbridge Landing and Turtle Rock Highland neighborhoods of Irvine—and recently he has been experimenting with even higher densities, inspired in part by the ancient villages and towns of Italy and Greece.

Berkus' design of the new Leisure Village Ocean Hills retirement community, in the rolling hills of north San Diego County near Oceanside, is considered one of the most successful of the recent, higher-density developments, with 5.2 homes per acre. Architects and developers from across the country are also studying the Le Parc planned communities in El Toro, Chino, Simi Valley and Westpark in Irvine.

Westpark, designed by the architecture firm of Richardson Nagy Martin of Newport Beach, won a Gold Nugget Award for best site plan last year from the Pacific Coast Builders Conference. The Westpark plan was cited for creating "a distinctive architectural character and sense of community on a site devoid of natural or topographical amenities."

A collection of six neighborhoods totaling 4,500 homes, Westpark is being constructed over a five-year period. It focuses on homes for the "Young professional couple with a growing family" and "maturing professional families," according to sales literature. "Informal living" is stressed and, judging from the strollers and bicycles scattered in front of the houses along the gently curving streets, the developers targeted their market correctly.

What Westpark illustrates is how so much house can be finessed on to relatively small lots. In the case of the single-family Promenade subdivision, where houses average 1,800 square feet are selling for about $300,000, the developers achieved a density of 7.75 detached single-family houses per acre, equal to the densities of some of the attached townhouse developments in the area. Just a few years ago in Irvine, the density of detached·housing developments averaged about four to five per acre.

This successful higher density—which makes the site seem larger than it is—was accomplished by a clever technique known as the Z-lot plan, in which the lot and house are laid out diagonally to the street, forming a Z, with front and back yards at angles to the home. The front entrance, located on the lot line, can be better detailed and made more attractive, improving curb appeal. Compact yards become more usable, and the floor plan of the house both feels and looks more spacious than the old '50s boxlike tract model. Numerous windows brighten the interiors with natural light.

In the two-story Promenade model, designed by Walt Richardson, gated archways lend the front facade a pleasant focus and, not coincidentally, take your eye away from the double garage doors edging the street. The archway leads into a welcoming private courtyard. Once you step inside the front door, the living and dining rooms are arranged so that you can look diagonally through them into the rear yard. This see-through design, aided by large corner windows, lends the house an openness and makes it seem larger. The layout is an impressive architectural maneuver.

"The houses have a strong indoor/outdoor relationship that small houses can't do without," comments Richardson, who designed the houses in a fanciful, abstracted California style with vaulted chimney tops and half-round Palladian windows.

"Streetscaping" and landscaping, as well as security and maintenance, are stressed in the Berkus-designed 1,672-unit Leisure Village Ocean Hills development. Designed in the spirit of a Greek island village of attached houses and geared to the active older adult, Ocean Hills is being developed in stages. The most recent units range in size from 1,131 to 1,936 square feet and sell from $160,000 to $224,990. Of 1,636 homes, 960 have been sold.

Striding through his instant village, Berkus pauses every few yards to call attention to fragrant flowers in bloom, the use of classical forms such as arches and bell towers, the extra thickness of hand-finished walls and the patina of the red tile roofs to "hint at a certain architectural timelessness," as he puts it. He paid particular attention to the country club at the center of the property. "We wanted to create a place that was like a resort, where residents would want to get out of their houses and enjoy taking part in activities," he explains.

Although it is new, there is a real sense of place and a feeling of community at Ocean Hills. "People no longer just want shelter, a house with a back yard set off from their neighbor's, as they did when they first started flocking to suburbia in the 1950s," Berkus says. "Tract housing is out."

SUBURBAN DESIGN, BERKUS EXPLAINS, IS RESPONDING TO SHIFTS IN LIFE STYLES. "People who look at computer screens all day want to get out and walk, see what is happening up and down the street, maybe talk to a neighbor, take part in an activity," the architect says. "To achieve that feeling, higher densities actually help. Not only does it reduce the cost of housing and make it available to more people, but higher density actually makes for a friendly community and, in many ways, a more interesting design."

The delicate balance between the social and physical aspects of densities illustrated dramatically by the Le Parc projects, which were planned with first-time buyers in mind. Designed in a sprightly abstracted Modernist style by architect Johannes Van Tilburg of Santa Monica, the projects have densities of nearly 20 units to an acre and focus on central, communal recreation facilities.

Opened last year, Le Parc Simi Valley is the most recently completed of the Le Parc projects. It consists of 277 units in 22 clustered two-story buildings, accented by pastel colors, glass-block walls, metal pipe railings, curved patio walls, exotic plantings and both modern and rustic-styled foundation around the property. The feeling is playful: a bit of Marina del Rey northwest of the San Fernando Valley.

To keep costs down—units are priced in the $90,000 range buildings were designed with standardized layouts of 12 units each. However, to lend the buildings character, each unit was turned this way and that, levels created, landscaping varied, and each unit was given its own exterior doorway instead of a shared interior hall. The units also were lent individuality by the varying use of interior lofts, cathedral ceilings and skylights and, on the exteriors, by alternating private patios, balconies and roof gardens.

Like Berkus, Van Tilburg believes that the challenge of design in suburbia today is to shape developments that offer residents both a sense of place in their communities.

Or, as one happy Le Parc resident put it, "the price is right, the location is right, and, I think, about now the temperature of the water is about right." She then excused herself, rose, took two steps to the edge of the pool and dived in.

—Sept. 15, 1988

The Future of L.A. Is Now

THERE ARE VARYING LONG VIEWS OF LOS ANGELES THAT PICTURE IT AS THE ascendant capital of the Pacific Rim, a Third World city of the first rank, a collection of urban villages that are neither urban nor villages, or simply Lotus Land. Take your pick.

However one might perceive Los Angeles, defined here not as a city but a multi-centered, expanding grid of about 100 fiefdoms, the hard fact is that the long view is fast becoming the short view; faster than we like to admit, and faster than our floundering local governments can react to it.

Despite sewer moratoriums, slow-growth propositions, the lack of affordable housing, poor schools, shoddy municipal services, a crumbling infrastructure, pathetic public transit, polluted beaches and a bruised environment, Los Angeles continues to grow; the promise of a better life in a benign climate perseveres, a triumph of hope over reality.

This growth, promise and hope permeates the recently published report of the bipartisan, blue-ribbon Los Angeles 2000 Committee. I have tended to be wary of such efforts, labeling futurism an excuse used by public officials and private interests not to deal with the problems of the present and filing the reports away in an appropriately dusty cabinet.

But the report, labeled "LA 2000: A City For The Future," is an exception, much to my surprise and pleasure. After all, I live here and hope some day my four children and their families will also be able to, in their own houses or condos, as well as, among other things, swim once again in Santa Monica Bay, have confidence in a public education system, and enjoy and be enriched by the region's many cultural attractions.

Included in the report is a synopsis of the problems that have been caused by the region's phenomenal and haphazard growth; you've heard them here and elsewhere before. And then there is the obvious list of needs—not a "wish" list, but a "must" list, from cleaner air, water and beaches to more park, playground and cultural facilities and transportation alternatives, and better schools, hospitals, housing, urban design and job opportunities.

Where the report, for me, strikes a nerve is its recognition that these needs simply cannot be met by the existing government structure; that "while local governments struggle to control the identities and destinies of their own communities. . . . Glendale sewage ends up in Santa Monica Bay, South Bay industrial emissions help throw a pall over the San Gabriel Mountains, South-Central drug gangs move into Rialto near the outskirts of San Bernardino and an accident on the San Diego Freeway can make a Westlake [Village] resident miss her plane at LAX."

As stated here previously, the issue no longer is growth or no growth, but how can growth be best controlled and managed; that beyond the delivery of frail basic services, such as fire and police protection, and garbage collection, most governments aren't hacking it; that the region's Byzantine political structure has created a bureaucratic gridlock. The dream of a livable city has fallen into the cracks of a fractured metropolis.

The report, citing a RAND Corp. survey in which the public expressed their frustrations with local government, calls the situation a "crisis in confidence," and hints that it will get worse as the region grows and its need multiply.

Then, in my opinion, comes the ziner, buried in black-and-white on page 68, but, no doubt, to be colored purple, if not red, by civil serpents and others clinging to the status quo asit slowly sinks into a sea of self-interest.

"If we are to capture the future potential of the metropolitan area, we must find innovative ways to manage this growth, even in the face of an understandable reluctance to give up entrenched power or to accede to the reorganization of outdated structures," states the report. "To do nothing will have serious long-term consequences, leaving Los Angeles in the 21st Century with endemic ills that are beyond any solution."

The report then recommends, in particular, two new regional government agencies to manage growth and the environment; agencies that have the potential for broad powers to set policy and possibly enforce implementation. We are talking here no less than reshaping home rule to create, among other things, a better balance between jobs and housing, and transportation and land use.

At the same time, the report suggests that to achieve its myriad goals of a livable city "different relationships between government functions" may be needed, as well as ways "to open the way for greater participation at the neighborhood or community level."

And warming this heart, it specifically calls for the city to establish a "streets for people" program to encourage pedestrian activity, conservation districts to protect architectural and design landmarks, an expanded urban forestry program and how public lands and existing rights-of-way may be used as greenbelts or open space.

Though there are some inherent contradictions in the recommendations and some hard questions about accountability that must be answered, at least we have at last a basis for a serious dialogue. This is a report that should not be buried, but rather heatedly debated, indeed decorated in festive colors and waved in the front of politicians and bureaucrats, and used as a guide to the future.

That future is now.

AT THE NEWS CONFERENCE WHERE THE "LA 2000" REPORT WAS RELEASED, I was confronted by a usually mild-mannered, even-tempered city official who was angered by recent columns in which I challenged him and his department to follow through on a variety of promising proposals.

If only that anger somehow could be directed at the problems of homelessness, the lack of affordable housing, the poor urban design that is scrring our streets and the transportation mess, among others. That is anger I would understand, and respect.

For me it was a sad footnote to the release of the report, and an indication of some of the problems its implementation faces within the existing political structure.

—Nov. 27, 1988

II

WHOSE CITY
IS IT,
ANYWAY?

Waking up in Westchester to the buzz of power saws cutting down a row of graceful shade trees so a street can be widened; wandering out in Studio City to buy milk and getting stuck in traffic; watching oversized office buildings balloon up over Burbank; wanting to go to Westwood for a movie, or to the Redondo Beach Pier, but deciding not to because of the hassle of parking; wondering while stuck on the Santa Monica Freeway what happened to the dream of a low-key, low-scale, lush Los Angeles with the ocean, the mountains, shopping, work and play never more than 20 minutes away from wherever—these concerns are ricocheting across the diverse Los Angeles landscape, generating confusion, anger and protests.

But the same concerns have prompted a new spirit that is making residents ponder what they value about living in and around Los Angeles and how they can protect it. In recent years, the number of resident associations in the city of Los Angeles alone has doubled to about 300, say community activists and campaign consultants who monitor such trends. And, they add, the groups are not simply one-time, one-issue committees but seem to be digging in to prompt major changes in the city politic.

"No question about it," observes Dan Garcia, who for the last 10 years has presided over the city Planning Commission, "communities are more organized, more likely to oppose projects, more likely to file a lawsuit than ever before. It is no phenomenon anymore. It's a fact—the most dramatic thing occurring in the city today. And while some of it is parochial and negative and some of it is reasonable and well intentioned, the total is getting louder and more forceful."

From San Pedro to Sunland, from Boyle Heights to Venice, across dinner tables and back fences, at supermarkets, shopping centers and gas pumps, on the job and at the beach, the weather is no longer the prime topic. It has been replaced by such issues as traffic, planning and zoning, and whether Lotus Land is disappearing in a cloud of exhaust fumes or in the shadow of a high-rise.

A direct result of this apprehension is Proposition U on the Nov. 4 Los Angeles city ballot, the so-called slow-growth initiative, which, if approved as expected and not diluted by political manipulations, would cut by half the size of commercial buildings in Los Angeles. The measure would restrict growth in areas covering about 85% of the city's commercial properties, most of them bordering single-family neighborhoods. As Election Day nears, the City Council has been trying to exempt select properties from the restrictions, to the chagrin of neighborhood activists.

Though some would have preferred that the initiative be more radical and sweeping, it was embraced by most of the city's resident groups, who gathered 105,000 signatures, substantially more than needed to qualify it for the ballot. Reflected in support for the measure is the fact that discontent with the shaping and misshaping of the city is taking on an increasingly militant tone.

"It is a very frustrating and also exciting time, for we have finally realized if we don't take some control of the growth, it will very shortly overwhelm us," says Charles Rosin of the Carthay Circle Homeowners Assn. At a recent meeting in the livig room of Rosin's Spanish Colonial bungalow, neighbors echoed his determination, ticking off their particular peeves, which included crass billboards and the destruction and defacement of landmark buildings.

FOR THE CARTHAY CIRCLE GROUP, TAKING CONTROL HAS MEANT DEVISING traffic-management programs and lobbying for their implementation, pressuring developers to pay for community improvements such as street landscaping, monitoring requests for zoning changes, testifying at Metro Rail hearings, and generally looking closely over the shoulders of their elected representatives. Recent victories include designation of some local streets as one-way and installation of barriers to discourage through traffic. Rosin says that it took nearly two years of badgering the city to get the changes approved and to persuade the developer of a nearby office tower to pay for them "as a gesture to the community." But, he adds, it was worth it. "The streets are so much more quiet now, and safer. And they are a wonderful demonstration of what a community can do if it organizes."

Increasingly heavy traffic spilling off congested Wilshire Boulevard is a concern for the neighboring Miracle Mile Residential Assn. For homeowner and resident associations in San Pedro, Wilmington, Highland Park, North Hollywood, Van Nuys, Sunland and Tujunga, the major worry is a rash of uncongenial apartment houses.

According to Peter Mendoza of the Wilmington Home Owners Assn., who has lived in that South Bay community all of his 45 years, "it seems everywhere you look in L.A. the quantity is going up and the quality is going down." What the Wilmington association has done, as have groups in Westwood and in the Valley, is to pressure their City Council representatives to get the city to impose a limited building moratorium on apartment projects. "It is not that we are against growth," Mendoza says. "We just want to get a handle on it."

"I've been in Los Angeles since 1937, worked in real estate in the 1940s and 1950s, and have lived almost everywhere in the Valley, and loved it," says Sylvia Gross, a guiding force in the Sunland-Tujunga Area Residents Assn. "There were problems back then, too. But what I am seeing now—the trees coming down, the hills bulldozed and the cheap apartment houses and stores going up, with no regard for the surrounding neighborhood—breaks my heart. That is why we are organizing and getting more members. While the developers and politicians may not care what they are doing to Los

Angeles, we do. We live here and will be living here long after they are gone."

For Diane Alexander of Highland Park, what moved her community to action was "the bulldozers knocking down the fine old California Craftsman-styled bungalows here to put up those cheap, three-story, ticky-tacky stucco apartment houses, as if this community didn't have enough problems as it is." So last year Alexander and her neighbors formed a group known as Residents and Others for Highland Park to protest what they consider "overscaled" development.

"In 1776 it was taxation without representation that stirred the population. In 1986, in Los Angeles, it is development without representation," says Patrick McCartney of the Westchester-based Coalition of Concerned Communities. An umbrella group for 19 resident associations in areas between Santa Monica and the airport, the coalition's main worry these days is the impact of commercial growth on neighborhoods. "We need housing and we're getting offices," McCartney says.

The coalition sends representatives to almost every city meeting or hearing at which matters that might affect the area are brought up. It also is quick to issue statements to the press, criticize the votes of local representatives and file lawsuits to block or at least frustrate proposed developments. In addition, the coalition puts out a newsletter to keep members informed and fired up.

Such efforts command attention. Among the proposed projects the coalition has had a part in altering is the ambitious $1-billion Playa Vista, a combined commercial, retail and residential development between Westchester and Marina del Rey. The project subsequently has gone through numerous revisions to meet local objections.

Proposed developments in Westwood are also being monitored by resident groups. "When we moved here from New York [in the 1970s], Westwood was a pleasant college town," says Laura Lake of Not Yet New York, a citywide coalition of the more ardent resident groups. "But every time we'd go away on a trip and come back, there was some landmark being ripped down, a crane out in the middle of the street blocking traffic, and another office tower going up. Now, Westwood is a place to be avoided, ringed by high-rises that do not contribute to the community. Our quality of life, everybody's quality of life, just the things that made L.A. so attractive, is being ruined. And then some politician asks why we are so angry, why we want to change the system so it can work for residents as well as it works for developers."

IT IS A LAMENT THAT HAS BEEN HEARD FOR A CENTURY, EVER SINCE IMMIgrants tired of the cold and crowded cities of the East and Midwest started flocking to Los Angeles to make growth·the city's biggest industry.

Los Angeles is not expanding as voraciously as it did in the boom years of the 1880s and 1920s or the 1950s and '60s. But it is growing—steadily in population, sporadically in residential and commercial development, and haphazardly in location. At last count, the city's population was about 3 million, the county's nearly 8 million. According to studies by the Southern California Assn. of Governments, the population of the six-county L.A. metropolitan area could, if its current rate of growth continues, reach 18.3 million in 2010.

The nature of the growth is changing too, observes Councilman Zev Yaroslavsky, whose Westside district is a ferment of community action. "The actual increase in the population in my district has been slight. For the last 11 years, the district has remained at about 200,000. What has changed dramatically is life styles. L.A. used to be more private, with people entertaining at home, living more modestly. Now people are going out more—to restaurants, to shop, to theaters. Businesses and services also have increased, with the result that the city has become more urban, and that means congestion. The growth can't be stopped. It's what makes the city tick. But it can be controlled and shaped better."

He adds: "It's like L.A. was a popcorn maker with a couple of cups of kernels in it. After slowly being heated up, all of a sudden the kernels have begun to pop—a few at first and now all of them—like crazy."

The explosion in part prompted Yaroslavsky, along with Planning Commission President Garcia, Councilman Marvin Braude, architect Mark Hall and former Tarzana Property Owners Assn. President Irma Dobbyn, to sponsor Proposition U. "We are just trying to give some direction to a very strong neighborhood sentiment," says Braude, who started his political career as head of a homeowners association in the 1960s. "Back then, the groups were relatively unsophisticated," he adds. "Today they are much sharper and stronger."

The initiative is seen by many of the community groups as the first ringing volley in a war over the future shape and style of Los Angeles. "The system now is stacked for developers in a way that forces communities into an adversary position," Laura Lake explains. "Not Yet New York is not anti-growth. We are for reasonable growth that takes the affected community into consideration, lets it play a responsible role in the development process. As it is now, residents are frozen out." While supporting the initiative, the coalition is also pursuing legal action to contain development and is studying with others the establishment of community planning boards.

.THE TONE OF THE RESIDENT GROUPS WORRIES THE CITY'S DEVELOPMENT COMmunity, which is concerned that slow-growth efforts will turn into no-growth efforts. "Citizen involvement is essential to the planning process, but it has to be in concert with the political leadership and professional urban planners," says Edward Helfeld, former director of the city's Community Redevelopment Agency and now a private developer and professor of architecture and urban planning at USC. "You canoot expect good planning by election initiatives, such at Proposition U. You may prevent the worst, but you cannot get desirable, livable communities out of the ballot box. That must come from a more reasonable and less emotional process, with all involved over a period of time, than what is happening in many communities today."

But citizen groups argue that they are shunted aside in the planning process. "Trying to keep up with the proposals now is like being the proverbial boy with a finger in the dike," says Alexander Man of Pacific Palisades. For the last 12 years, Man, as head of the Federation of Organizations for Conserving Urban Space (FOCUS), has monitored city projects that he feels threaten the ambiance and ecology of neighborhoods.

On occasion, he has gone door to door, like Paul Revere, to alert residents about, among other things, proposed street-widening projects that would destroy trees. The last-minute actions of Man and others saved the rows of magnificent, mature palms that had been planted along Highland and Hollywood boulevards to commemorate the 1932 Olympics. Man says that the trees were to come down for a street widening, proposed in part, ironically, to ease traffic that was expected for the 1984 Olympics. The tactics included threats by resident to chain themselves to trees, appeals to the news media for coverage, gathering signatures on petitions, and letter-writing campaigns.

Victories are rare, Man says, because it is hard to get information. "The administrators, bureaucrats, engineers and architects all have vested interest in the developments and look upon citizens as an annoyance." He contends that, time and again, residents have learned about projects too late to do anything except become more frustrated and alienated. "And if you take off a day [from work] to go to a meeting," he says, "it is the bureaucrats and lobbyists that get all the courtesies and are allowed to speak on and on, and the poor, affected citizens are made to wait. Yet, it is the residents who actually own the streets and for whom the bureaucrats work."

"Downtown just takes us for granted," complains Sheila Cannon, who recently organized the Concerned Citizens for South-Central Los Angeles to protest the location of an incinerator in her neighborhood. "Just because we are a low-income, minority community, the city thinks it can use us as a dumping ground. Well, it is time for us as a community to play a role in our own future and stop being treated like a plantation."

Though frustrating, the increasing confrontations with "downtown" have actually stiffened the resolve of communities to grab hold of planning policies. "We have by necessity become tougher," says Brian Moore, head of the Federation of Hillside and Canyon Assns., a coalition of 49 homeowner groups.

"I was not a joiner. But one morning in 1978 I woke up to witness the landmark house next to mine, which had been owned by Francis X. Bushman, being bulldozed without a permit. It made me so angry that I am still feeding on it after all these years. For me it was the Bushman house; for others it is the views, the hills, the ambiance that they see being destroyed. People are waking up to what is happening."

—Oct. 26, 1986

Prop. U was approved by a two-thirds vote, but as the following columns indicate it was a long time coming, and a fight.

Hamilton Goes, 15 Fiefdoms Stay

A FTER MORE THAN A YEAR OF WHISPERS OUT OF CITY HALL, THE WORD AT last has come from Mayor Tom Bradley that Calvin Hamilton will be resigning as planning director. No one can ever accuse the mayor of acting impetuously.

But typical of Bradley, he equivocated as to when Hamilton will be leaving. It seems it will not be before April so that Hamilton can host an American Planning Assn. national conference here—an association presently investigating Hamilton for alleged violations of its code of ethics.

We now can look forward to having a lame-duck planning director.

Actually, Hamilton has not been much more these last few years, given his numerous trips abroad as a consultant to other cities, his leave of absence following the disclosure of a conflict of interest and the resulting loss of credibility so vital to being an effective planning director.

But Hamilton's failure as a planning director was not all of his making. Contributing also was the City Council and the mayor himself. They have combined—sometimes by neglect, other times by intrusion—to make planning in Los Angeles at best an afterthought in an often nasty development process.

Good planning in the form of good design to create pleasant places to work, live, shop and play has popped up here and there in Los Angeles. But most of these places have been created, not because of the city's planning review process, but rather often in spite of it and by sheer luck or persistence.

For instance, Melrose Avenue flowers *despite* its trees being cut down and its sidewalk being narrowed. But imagine how much nicer the serendipitous street could have been with wide, tree-shaded sidewalks, letting cafes spill out onto them, a bench here and there for people watching, if not just resting one's feet. It almost makes me cry to think of the urban design opportunities Los Angeles has fumbled away.

As for Hamilton, there were in his 20 years in office—in addition to his occasional lapses of judgement—flashes of insight, unabashed enthusiasm and the ability to recognize a good idea. This included the concept of focusing high-density, mixed-use development in satellite centers across the city, which his staff developed and Hamilton embraced and promoted.

Much of the problem of the city's planning process is the city's convoluted political system, which divides the city into 15 fiefdoms. It is tough enough being a planning director accountable to one mayor, but having to be in effect 15 planning directors accountable to 15 council members is really beyond any one person's ability. No wonder Hamilton liked to go on so many trips.

Barring an unlikely revision of the city's charter (no one in any political system can be expected to be enthusiastic about giving up power), what is going to be needed to bring sensitive planning practices to Los Angeles is a commitment by the mayor in more than just an occasional speech.

But to be sure, the commitment must be to the planning practice, not necessarily the planning director, a mistake Bradley seems to have made in his protracted support of Hamilton. While the so-called Hamilton affair has dragged on and on, the city's already weak planning process has been weakened even further.

AGGRAVATING THE SITUATION HAS BEEN THE BRADLEY-APPOINTED PLANNING Commission that, despite sporadic statements by chairman Dan Garcia, has not offered any real leadership in recent planning controversies.

This is unfortunate. The city is in desperate need of some planning, what with its varying degrees of frustrating traffic, pollution, haphazard development, bad design, poor housing, and threatened landmarks.

However, the planning should not be on a grand, regional scale, replete with thick studies and multicolored maps presented at a seemingly endless series of seminars and conferences presided over by pedantic professors and babbling bureaucrats. We have had enough of those efforts for awhile.

What is needed is planning on a practical, block-by-block, neighborhood level involving those who will be affected. It is time for fewer reports to be filed away in some cabinet and more sensitive plan reviews, perhaps even a suggestion of an amenity or two, such as tree plantings and street furniture.

With an end in sight to the Hamilton debacle, it is time for city planners to be assertive and involve themselves in the urban-design process, to turn off their computers and desk calculators, to rise from their encrusted desks and to get out of their cars to walk the streets of the neighborhoods of their concerns.

As a matter of fact, it wouldn't be a bad idea if all city officials involved in the planning process did the same.

Perhaps then they would not be so quick to approve a street widening, a demolition of a landmark or the construction of some out-of-scale, out-of-character project. Perhaps then they would begin to understand how planning can, if carried out on a human scale and with those affected in mind, can make a good city great.

—July 28, 1985

Neighborhoods Strive for Common Link

NO ONE REALLY LIVES IN LOS ANGELES.
They live in Silver Lake, Echo Park, Downtown, Hollywood, North Hollywood, Mt. Washington, Boyle Heights, Studio City, Beverly-Fairfax, Westwood, Venice, Encino or one of the dozens of other distinct communities scattered across the cityscape.

Whether recent transplants or natives, most Angelenos do not identify with that amorphous, arbitrary, political mass known as Los Angeles. Instead, they identify with their community or, on a smaller scale, their neighborhood, however disorganized and seeming anonymous to all but realtors, developers and planners.

What Los Angeles has become as it has grown in spurts is really a sprawling collection of villages, some urban, many suburban and a few exurban, tied together at best by a mesh of crowded freeways.

The result is a parochialism that, while encouraging a healthy pride among the growing groups of residents trying to improve their neighborhoods, also tends to isolate them.

Too late do they find out that the road-widening project destroying the trees and ambiance of a bordering neighborhood is going to hit them next, or that another neighborhood is suffering similar problems as theirs because of poor planning.

Missing is a network through which neighborhood groups can share common experiences and interests, help each other monitor the city's arcane planning and development process and perhaps join together to act on broader regional issues.

It was with establishing such as network in mind that a smattering of scattered neighborhood groups gathered in Westwood last weekend. As such meetings go, it was a good beginning.

There were, of course, too many speeches, but at the end, after the lawyers stopped talking, plans were discussed for a newsletter, a hotline and another meeting.

Though the effort is a positive one, the tentative name the formative group has given itself, Not Yet New York, is, I think, quite negative. There are many aspects about New York that are quite desirable, such as its cultural attractions, shopping, select street life and neighborhood spirit.

Indeed, if such a spirit existed here and was channeled through community planning boards of the type that are in New York, many of the problems the group in Westwood expressed concern over could begin to be solved.

But, perhaps I just read the name of the group wrong, and that the emphasis was not on the *NOT* in Not Yet New York, indicating disapproval, but on the *YET*, and consciously or subsconsciously, the members have established Manhattan and its environs as a model to strive for.

Whatever, there was at the meeting a sincere expression of frustration over the city's lack of responsiveness to the needs and goals of neighborhoods and a desire for residents to assert themselves more in the planning process. It is a worthy goal, despite the name.

—May 19, 1985

Citizens Want a Hand in Zoning

BEING CIRCULATED THIS WEEK ARE THE FIRST OF THE PETITIONS FOR A PROposed ballot initiative this fall to limit commercial development in select areas of Los Angeles.

Better late than never.

Better also that for a change the public will have an opportunity to redefine zoning—albeit for now through the ballot box—

rather than fumbling city planners, finagling politicians and finessing developers and their lubricious lobbyists and lawyers.

And better too broad than too narrow: The initiative chops in half, from three times the buildable area to one and a half times allowed in the "Height District One" zoning designation of the city's municipal code.

While the designation sounds mild enough, developers have been able to manipulate it with the help of inventive architects to create such sore thumbs as the office buildings towering up to 21 stories in West Los Angeles and along Ventura Boulevard in the San Fernando Valley and the colorful, over-scaled and overwrought Westside Pavilion.

The district presently covers about 85% of commercial properties in the city, almost all bordering on single-family neighborhoods. Yet, it is obvious that the recent abuses of the district have been for the development of regional retail and office facilities, not for neighborhood services for which the designation was originally created.

By limiting development to neighborhood needs in the District One zones, perhaps the regional needs will be directed to, and better met in, the designated city centers.

To be sure, those centers, such as downtown, Los Angeles International Airport, Century City and Warner Center, need fine tuning. But before the fine tuning comes the overhaul, which is what the initiative sets in motion.

Of course, this is what the city's general plan outlines and what citizens working on community plans for decades have been urging. But despite the urgings, public lawsuits and the best intentions of the city's Planning Department, the zoning needed to give the plans teeth never has caught up with the reality of development.

The initiative will lend the city's sluggish zoning reforms a burst of needed speed. And certainly, it is a recognition by its principal sponsors, Councilmen Zev Yaroslavsky and Marvin Braude and city Planning Commission President Daniel Garcia, that residents of impacted neighborhoods are angry.

As development has nibbled away at their quality of life, casting shadows and spilling traffic into neighborhoods, residents have been growing more and more frustrated with the city's planning process, or what they prefer to call a lack of process that favors developers cum campaign contributors.

"The initiative should give residents a stronger voice," commented Braude. Some of Braude's colleagues on the council are not happy over the prospects of stronger citizens input, while a few neighborhood groups, particularly those in the fledgling coalition labeled Not Yet New York, want more of a voice.

Before the initiative for a commercial zoning rollback was announced, there was serious talk in the neighborhood trenches about a more radical initiative, something that would take the development approval process out of City Hall and put it in neighborhoods through the creation of local planning boards—with teeth and with staff.

Perhaps in time that will come, as it has in other cities. But for now, there is "the initiative for reasonable limits on commercial buildings and traffic growth," as the petitions are labled.

While it is a conscientious attempt to control and direct growth, the initiative can't but help raise the city's design consciousness and whet the appetites of communities to play more of a role in shaping their future.

THE INITIATIVE AND THE TALK OF ESTABLISHING LOCAL PLANNING BOARDS have resulted from the failure of the will of professional planning in Los Angeles, and, ironically, coincides with the conference here of the American Planning Assn. It opened Saturday and will run through Wednesday.

Hampered by the indiscretions and lack of leadership of city Planning Director Calvin Hamilton—who will be leaving shortly—public planning in Los Angeles is at its nadir.

It did flourish for a time and for a limited degree, however arbitrary, under Redevelopment Director Edward Helfeld. But he was recently and unceremoniously dropped for being, among other things, too opinionated. It is hard not to be when you care about the city.

And to be sure, there are planners within the city government who, like many planners elsewhere, are intelligent and well-meaning, sensitive to urban design issues, zoning incentives, public-private innovations, community concerns and the whole grab bag of the latest planning catch words, concepts and tools.

But like public planners elsewhere, when it comes to taking an initiative and implementing an idea, or simply supporting one, they seem to disappear behind a pile of printouts and projections, or the excuse that they are blocked by a convoluted and, sometimes, corrupt political process.

While public servants are indeed subject to the local political process, it would be nice, once in a while, if they stood up and be counted for what they say they believe in: better planning for a better life for all.

Instead, they appear with wan smiles to rationalize bad design, rubber-stamp abusive development proposals and defer to politicians seeking favors for contributors.

Then they wonder why planning—so popular a course of study and as a career for 20 years—now is so friendless. Times and values do change, and so do professions.

And they also wonder why local journalists, concerned with the shape and direction of the city, will not be hanging on every word spokena the conference. No guts, no glory.

Welcome to Los Angeles, planners. R.I.P.

—April 6, 1986

The Battle Over Prop U.

LINGERING DOUBTS OVER THE NEED FOR PASSAGE OF PROPOSITION U FADE with each frantic action by the city to weaken the slow-growth initiative.

The latest in a series of legally questionable maneuvers initiated by the City Council is scheduled for Thursday when the City

Planning Commission will hold a public hearing on whether to exempt thousands of properties from the designated zones that would be affected if the proposition is approved.

But don't expect everyone to testify, especially not the opponents of the subterfuge, for the commission most likely will follow the council's example and stack the speaker list to favor vested and special interests.

Neighborhood persons who have attended zone-change hearings in the past involving one insensitive proposal or another know the pernicious procedure well—one of the reasons why some 105,000 signatures were gathered with relative ease to get Proposition U on the ballot.

It is really too bad, because the council's actions, taken with the blessings of Mayor "I-know-who-butters-my-bread" Bradley, just reinforce the view from the neighborhoods that planning in the city is a cozy Monopoly game being played by politicians and their campaign contributors—and they're playing it badly, judging by the city's dwindling quality of life.

One can only hope at this stage of the farce that the Planning Commission will somehow assert its independence, intelligence, respect for the prerogatives of the electorate and faith in a damaged planning process by rejecting the Council's actions.

And where has our new, squeaky-clean, stand-tall planning director, Kenneth Topping, been during this farce, other than signing the pay sheets for the overtime his staff put in to mail a record 56,000 public-hearing notices to owners of property to be affected?

By taking a stand against the obvious zoning subterfuge, the commission, Topping, and his staff would be doing the council, as well as themselves, a favor and would restore some credibility to the city's convoluted and crumbling planning process.

Certainly, the commission, the council, the mayor and the powers-that-be must recognize that the lack of credibility in the process was what prompted the drafting and avid support of Proposition U, and why it most likely will be overwhelmingly approved by the voters.

FOR THE PAST FEW YEARS, NEIGHBORHOODS HAVE BEEN SENDING THE CITY A very loud and clear message that they are fed up with insensitive, out-of-scale development and the resulting traffic mismanagement, and want some changes in the planning process.

But the city has not been listening. Instead, it has been retreating further into the recesses of its chambers and back offices to manipulate the planning process.

And so now we have Proposition U, the first volley in what amounts to a residents' revolt.

The proposition might be a meat-ax approach to planning by the public, as it has been characterized by opponents. But that is better than the present stiletto approach of the city.

Actually, as an advocate of a sensible planning process to better direct and shape growth to the needs of both residential and commercial communities, I had worried, when the initiative was first proposed, that it indeed was too sweeping.

Planning exercised properly is much too much of an art to be broad-brushed.

In addition, too often in the past planning by ballot box has had a negative cast, catering to economic and racial prejudices and creating as "us versus them," time-to-lift-the-drawbridge situation.

(Certainly Proposition 13, which in its way was a planning initiative, has over the years created more property-tax inequities than it originally might have corrected, to say nothing of the damage it has done to public services.)

I much prefer a sensitive process geared to the neighborhood level, where an open forum involving advocate planners and local residents can rationally review development proposals within reasonable guidelines.

In my continuing optimism, there is the hope that properly orchestrated and designed growth can actually create a better quality of life for all, providing needed housing, services and amenities.

Density does not have to strangle a city. When shaped with care and coordinated with transit, it can energize a city.

But it is apparent that a rational planning process does not work in an irrational political system that has been hardened over the years by a short-sighted council, a fumbling planning commission, a self-serving civil service system and a weak mayor.

More than a sweeping zoning change, or an initiative, Proposition U is, in my view, a message of public discontent with the direction in which the cityscape has been drifting. It also is a challenge for the city in concert with communities to begin focusing on the city's waning quality of life.

If not, we can look for more such initiatives in the years to come as a dissatisfied citizenry comes to grips with a stumbling public sector.

—Oct. 19, 1986

Three weeks later Prop. U. was approved.

Hope for Local Planning Boards

THE BATTLE TO SAVE LOS ANGELES FROM ITSELF CONTINUES.
    In reaction to a planning process that over the last few decades has misshaped the city, a citizens' committee has called for some fundamental changes, principally the establishment of community planning boards.

If not corrupted or manipulated by development interests, pandering politicians or civil *serpents*, the boards hold the promise of a planning process more sensitive to the needs and desires of the city's diverse neighborhoods.

The committee's report should at least receive a respectful, if cautious hearing by the city's planning establishment, coming as it does on the heels of the overwhelming passage of the slow-growth initiative, Proposition U.

THE ESTABLISHMENT, HEADED BY MAYOR TOM BRADLEY, THE CITY COUNCIL and the Planning Commission, had in various ways attempted to defeat or subvert the proposition. What they did accomplish was to expose their insensitivity to the dissatisfaction welling up in the city's changing neighborhoods.

More than specifically reducing the size of new buildings in select commercial zones in a "meat ax" approach, the proposition was an expression by voters of frustration with the city's present planning practices, anger at insensitive development and the desire simply to be heard.

And, of course, if the citizens' committee report is pigeonholed or watered down, like so many other well-meaning volunteer efforts in the city's checkered past, it could always form the basis of yet another proposition. Indeed, it just might take a proposition to properly implement the boards.

In these days of besieged neighborhoods, one does not need a weatherman to point out which way the winds of change have been blowing. Certainly, Councilmen Zev Yaroslavsky and Marvin Braude and city Planning Commission President Dan Garcia did not need one before they chose to sponsor Proposition U last spring.

And it was no coincidence that soon after that the commission president prompted the formation of the citizens' advisory committee, charging it to evaluate the city's so-called centers concept, developed in the 1960s, and aimed at concentrating development in select prime pockets across the region.

While the concept was reasonable, the reality was that the city experienced rapid development, not only in the centers, but haphazardly elsewhere. And more often than not the fragmented development was badly planned and designed, creating chaotic traffic situations, overwhelming adjoining residential neighborhoods and infuriating homeowners.

The citizens' committee quickly realized that the problem went far beyond the centers concept and involved the entire planning process. (The move reportedly put off Garcia, who was then having second thoughts about Proposition U and the waning prestige and power of *his* commission.)

The committee nonetheless pushed forward. As co-chaired by Dan Shapiro and Allan Lowy and including among its members architects, planners, developer types and community representatives, the committee's efforts were commendable and impressive.

Quite specific, and sensible, is the recommendation that the Planning Department assume the function of transportation planning, which is now gridlocked in an archaic Transportation Department.

It has been long apparent that the Transportation Department lacks the leadership, imagination and will to do much more to solve the city's traffic problems than cut down trees, widen streets and paint yellow lines.

Declaring that the centers concept was "no longer the single valid planning tool for the 1980s and beyond," the committee recommended a new, comprehensive planning concept called "Targeted Growth Areas."

It is an interesting concept that deserves further exploration, particularly the call for a more active role by the city to encourage good urban design.

BUT BY FAR THE MOST INTERESTING, POTENTIALLY EXCITING AND DELICATE concept proposed by the committee is the recommendation to establish community planning boards in 35 districts.

As proposed by the committee, the boards would revise community plans, review proposed projects, hold public hearings and make recommendations, specifically regarding projects requiring so-called discretionary approval. Their role would be purely advisory.

However, given their format, and with the proper fashioning, the boards could be an extremely effective force. Such boards in other cities and over time have gown in prestige to a point where their recommendations have taken on the power of ultimate approval and disapproval.

To help them get established, the committee has recommended that before the city plunges ahead, a pilot program be launched in three diverse planning districts for a trial period of not longer than two years.

Key to the credibility and effectiveness of the boards will be their membership.

The committee has recommended that each board be composed of 15 "citizen" members, with some appointed by the City Council and the Planning Commission and the balance elected. The exact number to be elected and appointed has not yet been determined.

There are problems with both the processes of election and appointment. Elections tend to cost money, and that money usually comes from special interests, principally development interests. Limit the amount that can be spent, and some lawyers and campaign consultants will always get around it.

Elections also become nasty, especially if development interests and local demagogues get involved, as no doubt, they will. The results could turn the boards into a farce, scaring away the more responsible and knowledgeable persons in the community concerned with planning and development.

The appointment process also has flaws, especially if controlled by the local council member through his or her office, or through a compliant Planning Commission. The temptation would be to appoint cronies or straw persons, and turn the boards into a buffer group or a puppet troupe.

Bear in mind, the concept of the local boards was prompted in part by the failure of the present planning process, dominated by the commission and the City Council. Letting them appoint the members could have the effect of letting the fox into the chicken coop.

To be credible, and therefore effective, the power of the boards is going to have to come from the bottom up, with its members nominated out of the present web of civic and resident groups and local institutions, and not from the top down. And the process must be open, for all to see.

Too much is at stake to leave the process hidden in the back room. That is how the city got into its present planning mess.

—Nov. 23, 1986

Mayor's Speech 5 Years Too Late

P RESIDENT REAGAN HAS THE IRAN/*CONTRA* SCANDAL AND MAYOR TOM Bradley has planning and development. Both are tangled messes that can't be dismissed by slick speeches.

With insensitive development scarring many communities, traffic growing worse daily, and the city's quality of life diminishing, the mayor finally got around to addressing development issues recently, albeit not before a planning group or a neighborhood forum, but a safe gathering of American Telephone & Telegraph Co. employees.

It would have been a great speech—five years ago.

Among other things, the mayor called for "vigorous and fair enforcement of Proposition U," new limits on mini-malls and hillside development, establishing neighborhood planning councils and re-organizing the Planning Department to stress long-range planning.

I would hope that there will be vigorous and fair enforcement of slow-growth Proposition U, considering that 70% of the voters approved it last year, despite the mayor's opposition.

As for Bradley's call for stricter controls on mini-mall and hillside development, it is welcome. But for many communities the restrictions are grievously late, if not after the fact. When it comes to pressing planning issues, Bradley, unfortunately, often is an after-the-fact mayor.

The restrictions would have been much more welcome years ago when mini-malls began trashing the city's streetscape and new housing sites were being gouged out of the hillsides.

Actually, the attack of the mini-malls was reported here three years ago, along with a call for quick city action, while the restrictions on hillside development were proposed 11 years ago.

No one can ever accuse the mayor or the City Council of acting precipitously when it goes against a development community that includes some of the more generous contributors to local election campaigns.

With mini-mall construction slackening, what is now of more concern to communities is incompatible housing and commercial development. If only the mayor had said something about that, focusing in on specific, egregious projects, such as in the Mar Vista and Wilshire districts, and adding that he was actually going to do something about them, besides talk.

And not a peep out of Bradley about the most recent bureaucratic bungle, the Board of Education's block-busting, neighborhood-wrecking land grab.

Letters and copies of letters keep pouring in here, calling attention to ill-considered school expansions, and the utter failure of officials to involve affected neighborhoods and explore alternative sites and facilities. It seems the Board of Education bulldozer is running amok.

As for Bradley's blessing the concept of neighborhood planning boards, that was suggested in this column three years ago, pressed by community groups two years ago, and proposed by a citizens advisory group last year. The issue now is not whether we should have them, but in what form and how soon.

Most pathetic is Bradley's call for reorganizing the Planning Department to stress long-range planning, just when neighborhoods and logic are urging short-range, so-called micro-planning.

Now is not the time to spend bureaucratic energies rearranging offices, appointing advisory committees, holding all-day conferences and producing ultimately useless reports and multicolored area maps. That, in part, was what led to Calvin Hamilton's demise as planning director.

Instead, it is time for planning to get down to the street level, explore on a block-by-block basis with the help of residents how neighborhoods can be stabilized, sound housing preserved and streets improved with vest-pocket parks, in-fill development, sensitive landscaping and the diversion of traffic.

Welcome to L. A. and 1987, Mister Mayor.

—April 5, 1987

Little Tokyo Wary of Big Plans

S OMETHING SMELLED FISHY IN LITTLE TOKYO, AND IT WASN'T THE SUSHI. Quick and concerted action by a proud and involved community there appears to have located the offense and put it out with the garbage, but it has made local leaders wary about the future planning and design of the area.

The situation once again involved the north side of 1st Street between San Pedro Street and Central Avenue. The community, through petitions, statements and meetings over the years, has made it quite clear it wants the strip preserved.

The block is the last vestige of the original Japanese community downtown and includes the distinctive Hongwanji Buddhist Temple, the Japanese Union Church and a very urban mix of stores with housing above. The total conveys a unique sense of time and place, as well as lending the street an inviting pedestrian scale.

For these reasons, the community proposed that the block be designated a state and national historic district and the churches be named local landmarks. And it also supported a broader Community Redevelopment Agency proposal for the area, in large part because it specifically called for the preservation of the block's fronts.

Though the agency succumbed to the mindless need of the city Department of Transportation by agreeing to chop off two feet from the north sidewalk, the plan was a reasonable mix of housing, office and retail development. Most of it was to go behind the 1st Street frontage on city-owned property. "Everything was going well," recalls Toshikazu Teraswa, president of the Japanese American Cultural and Community Center.

But this spring, the city's administrative officer took exception to the CRA plan, declaring in a memo to Mayor Tom Bradley that the proposal would not give the city "an adequate return on its assests."

The terse memo made it sound as if the future of Little Tokyo as a viable community was up for sale to the highest, and not particularly most responsible, bidder—and that the balanced plans developed over two years with maximum citizen input be damned.

If the city is so concerned with adequate returns in the area, perhaps it should look at the retail and office potential on the north side of 1st Street, between San Pedro and Los Angeles streets. There, an ugly two-level parking lot destroys the street's frontage, and cuts Little Tokyo off from the Civic Center to the west. It could be a wonderful strip for stores or stalls, especially if the street was narrowed.

The memo was (coincidentally?) issued at about the same time Councilman Gilbert Lindsay was sitting on the community's proposals for landmark designation while he talked about a marvelous proposal for the area by developer Jerry Snyder.

The proposal included violating the 1st Street frontage, possibly and presumptuously relocating the Temporary Contemporary Museum and developing a mixed-use cluster dominated by high rise office towers.

While possibly satisfying the city's avarice, the package is not what Little Tokyo, or downtown, needs; certainly not its projected 1 million square feet or so of new offices.

What the community and the marketplace have been receptive to is more housing, such as the recently completed Tokyo Villa condos. The attractive, 128-unit project is the most successful housing downtown, in large part because of its location adjacent to the restaurants, stores, community facilities and cultural attractions of Little Tokyo.

The real value of Little Tokyo is that it is just the type of thriving, mixed-residential and commercial community that needs to be reinforced to give downtown balance, color and vitality.

But it is just that ambiance an over-scaled commercial project as outlined by Snyder would destroy, and what the city administrator's office does not seem to be able to calculate in its financial projections.

Also disturbing to the community was that the city openly touted Snyder's plan, without even putting out a so-called RFP, a request for a proposal, to give anyone else a chance to come forward, not even from the community. With Lindsay aide Sal Altimirano running interference, the councilman's office laid out a very nice table for Snyder.

Therefore, it was no wonder that when the plan was presented at a recent community meeting, it was met with such hostility. With its many fine restaurants featuring seafood, Little Tokyo has a good nose for the condition of fish, no matter how it is wrapped and who is delivering it.

The protests seem to have been very effective. Lindsay has, in the aftermath, reaffirmed his support of the community's desire to keep the northside frontage intact and its preference for the CRA plan.

Snyder has gone back to the drawing boards to incorporate the community's concerns, with a spokesperson adding that he will respect the RFP process. And the landmark designations once again are moving forward.

But the course Lindsay laid out has left a lingering odor in Little Tokyo, putting the community very much on the alert to what next might be served.

—April 13, 1986

ALERT: THE CITY HAS ISSUED A CALL TO DEVELOPERS FOR PROPOSALS FOR AN area known as "north of 1st," in Little Tokyo, adjacent to the Temporary Contemporary Museum. Being greedy and short-sighted, the city wants to see the area developed to the maximum for office towers.

Aside from the question of whether more office space is needed in Little Tokyo, downtown or anywhere, the site begs for a well-scaled, sensitively designed multi-use development, with emphasis on housing—something the community has been discussing with the CRA for years.

But with the CRA these days, unfortunately, showing signs of backing down in the face of City Hall and special interests, the community and its friends are going to have to assert themselves. At stake is no less than the future of Little Tokyo.

—April 26, 1987

Back to the Nitty-Gritty of the City

RECENT COLUMNS BY ME DISCUSSING THE AESTHETICS OF ARCHITECTURE with a capital A have prompted letters and calls from a range of readers expressing concern that I am retreating from the more pressing issues of urban design.

"On (a recent) Sunday you wrote about the city as though it existed simply as a dreamscape for a gigantic architectural display. Usually what you write makes approximate sense," concluded Jane Adler of Santa Monica in a particularly pointed letter.

Cornering me one morning in the Farmers Market, Charles Rosin of Carthay Circle added that while the style of isolated buildings was interesting, of more import was their siting, their effect on the street and cityscape, or whether they should be built at all.

"More crucial to the future of L.A. than the look of some high-rise going up downtown or some trendy restaurant opening up on the Westside, is such issue as the outrageous proposal to widen Fairfax Avenue that the City Council passed without really examining viable alternatives," snapped Rosin.

"If you would have written about that instead of the competition downtown between three 'name' architects," or yet another piece on Frank Gehry, added Rosin, "maybe you could have stopped the widening, or embarrassed the powers-that-be to come up with a plan that was sensitive to the neighborhood."

A caller from North Hollywood was more blunt. "Have you sold out to the architects and their fat-cat clients?" she asked. "What about the slow-growth movement you used to write about; the neighborhood planning boards you proposed and how the city has watered them down? Let the art critic babble on about architecture. Urban design is what's happening."

In reply, I have always felt that there should be a strong connection between architecture and urban design; architecture being a practical and visual art that encloses a space to serve a human endeavor, and urban design a more ambitious weaving of that architecture, combined with a healthy dose of practical planning, to take into consideration broad environmental issues that shape a larger part of a city.

However, I do recognize that over the last decade that connection has been seriously weakened by the increasing emphasis in the theory, practice and promotion of architecture on style and materials; in short, on the look and image of buildings rather than impact on those who work in and around them.

Architects may talk about urban design, but whether out of frustration with the political and planning process, or whether simply succumbing to the role of the exterior decorator of zoning envelopes, they have done little about the issue. That is why so many of our recently designed buildings appear to be dueling each other with colors, shapes and materials, while seemingly adrift on an alien planet.

And while I feel the image of buildings is important to a city and should, on occasion, be commented on, I do agree with what some of the readers of this column have expressed: That a more pressing issue is the raw fact that Los Angeles has become more dense and urban, sprouting high-rises, spewing mini-malls and being submerged in a flood of traffic; and that if we don't control and shape better, the hope of the good life on which it is based will soon flow into ocean.

Then, it won't matter how some house in Venice or downtown office tower is styled and if its architecture is hailed and honored by the design community. No one would want to live or work in it.

So it is back for awhile to the nitty-gritty of urban design, beginning with the competing plans for the First Street North project in Little Tokyo that the City Council is scheduled to consider this month.

Of the various schemes submitted, showing most promise to serve the city's economic and expansion needs, the burgeoning local community and, most importantly from my perspective, a vision of a vibrant, pedestrian-oriented mixed-use district, is the so-called Showa Village proposal.

Designed by the team of Johannes Van Tilburg & Partners and Gensler & Associates for the Janss Corp. and Peck/Jones partnership, the proposal creates an attractive, serpentine streetscape lined with shops, stores and restaurants, topped by housing and anchored by the existing Temporary Contemporary museum, a new office building and hotel. Saved to be recycled into a museum and a theater, respectively, is the Nishi Hongwanji Buddhist Temple and the Union Church.

Some refinement is needed. The architecture, as indicated by the renderings appears to be overstyled, sort of like putting too much sugar into the recipe for Dutch chocolate. But the urban design—the creation of a place through sensitive programming and planning—seems right on target, and the housing above the retail just what the city needs more of.

In addition to providing desperately needed units and lending life and security to the street, such housing also offers an antidote to our increasing traffic mess. Simply put, more affordable housing in burgeoning neighborhoods like Little Tokyo ust might encourage more people who work downtown to live there, leave their car in the garage and walk to their job.

—March 6, 1988

WHAT MIGHT BE, OR LET'S HOPE SO, IS SHOWA VILLAGE, A PEDESTRIAN-oriented, mixed-use proposal for the area known as First Street North in Little Tokyo, designed by the team of Johannes Van Tilburg & Partners and Gensler & Associates and packaged by the Janss Corp. and the Peck/Jones Partnership.

Consisting of an imaginative blend of office, hotel, residential and retail uses, streetscaping and the recycling of two local landmarks, the proposal evolved out of a conscientious planning process to become the preferred scheme of the local community. And this despite local Councilman Gilbert Lindsay lobbying for other schemes over the years.

But it seems Lindsay is not done yet, and has been delaying the various votes of the City Council which the scheme needs to move forward. One of these days it would be refreshing for Lindsay to make a decision based on the design of a project instead of its politics. Then, perhaps, downtown, which is everyone's disctrict, not just Linday's, will begin to look and function like a central city, not a political fiefdom.

—May 15, 1988

ALERT: THE BATTLE FOR THE FIRST STREET NORTH PROJECT IN LITTLE Tokyo continues, with the development team of the Barker scheme favored by Councilman Gilbert Lindsay expanding to include a number of politically well-connected minority members.

But whatever color the Barker scheme is wrapped in, black, brown, white, or green, like in money for campaign contributions as other indulgences, the fact remains that the Showa Village scheme is the better scheme, and should be approved by the council and the mayor without further delay. It is the city's procrastination in the matter that has allowed the selection issue to ripen, and begin smelling.

The Showa Village scheme has been endorsed by the community and recommended by the City's Administrative Officer, and, from my perspective, has the promise to create an engaging, mixed-use urban neighborhood that would add some glue and interest to the downtown fabric. At stake also is no less than the credibility of the city's planning and development policies.

Let us hope the city does not bow to the pressure of Lindsay and other special interests, as it did on Bunker Hill when it had the opportunity to create something exciting in the Grand Avenue proposal orchestrated by developer Robert Maguire and instead opted for a well-greased but bland design. And then people wonder why downtown Los Angeles looks the way it does.

—June 5, 1988

It was politics as usual a few weeks later when the City Council voted 8 to 5 in favor of the Barker scheme. Showa R.I.P.

The Hope For a Livable City

"A CITY MUST BE SO CONSTRUCTED THAT IT MAKES ITS CITIZENS AT ONCE secure and happy. To realize the latter aim, city building must be not just a technical question but an aesthetic one in the highest sense."

So wrote Camillo Sitte 100 years ago in his classic "City Planning According to Artistic Principles," in which he urged those shaping cities to pay more attention to the creation of public spaces, in particular squares.

Sitte felt it was such spaces that generated a sense of place and community; that buildings, in addition to being functional and decorative, should be thought of as backdrops for places where people can meet, stroll, see and be seen and, generally, take part in the life of a city.

What Sitte, in effect, was urging was the creation of an inviting place with an identity, be it a sense of history or style. This concept is known in current real estate terms as "location," or "an address," a hard-to-define factor that investors correctly consider the key to a successful development.

It also is a concept that planners in the public employ talk about a lot, and do little, especially in Los Angeles.

Unfortunately, city planners here under a timid Ken Topping and under constant pressure from politicians seem to have abandoned their roles as urban design innovators to become sort of glorified zoning police, parking space attendants and traffic counters.

Los Angeles begs for a planning department, indeed any public agency, that can take the initiative as advocates for sensitive urban design, sympathetic in-fill housing, more parks and playgrounds, pedestrian-friendly streets, accessible neighborhood shopping, responsible citizen participation and, generally, a more livable city.

One wonders what city employees are putting themselves on the line for these days—what they believe in and are prepared to fight for—other than their own jobs, medical plans, parking privileges and retirement benefits.

And we are not talking here about reams of planning studies that end up on dusty shelves, but employees willing to walk the streets, listen to residents, help them develop positive programs for their neighborhoods and confront the powers that be downtown.

Just how long can the municipal government here wallow in a 1950s mind-set, treating communities like subversive cells and urban design like a disease to be quarantined and studied?

—July 10, 1988

"AFTER 23 YEARS, POOREST REGIONS TO GET ECONOMIC BOOST," declared a headline of a recent story in the Metro section of this newspaper reporting that a large swath of ailing South Central Los Angeles had been targeted for redevelopment by both city and county agencies.

What the headline should have read, or course, was, "Planners and other Bureaucrats to Get Economic Boost, Poorest Regions Maybe."

This is not to question the good will of the agencies involved and the need to aid South-Central. The area can use all the help it can get, and more, and that before stumbling forward those involved should have some sort of community understanding and renewal strategy to guide the effort. It is the least we can ask for when scarce public funds are involved.

But those funds should be used to generate real projects, like needed housing, vest pocket parks, street scaping, not just for salaries of bureaucrats downtown, grants to pandering consultants, or subsidies for well connected real estate speculators, as has happened in the past.

Though redevelopment programs tend to be well intentioned, too often they seem to get stuck in an uncharted bureaucratic bog infested with civil serpents. Indeed, some government workers have spent careers there, up to their waists in a paper-based muck, perfecting the art of evasion.

It is not that they don't care, they say to anyone who asks. And then they go on and on indignantly telling you why something can't be found, or can't be done, or why they can easily do it, but won't. It is sometimes amazing to me that anything gets done in government.

I just hope South Central is not in store again for some grand macro-planning efforts, centered in a cluster of offices in the bowels of the civic center, to be dragged out over a number of years, at the end of which a stack of reports will be released, heavy with statements of the problems, weighted by charts and multi-colored maps, but light on recommendations and implementation. In short, full of sound and fluff, signifying nothing.

But far be it from me to sacrilegiously score the ancient administrative rites focused on the "in" and "out" basket and weaken the ranks of the civil service. However, while the long range planning effort for South Central inexorably moves forward, like some elephant in mud, it would be refreshing if there also could be some short-range, so-called proactive micro-planning demonstrations.

If anything, such demonstrations should thicken the ranks of planners, involving intensive resident participation in a door-to-door, block-by-block exploration of what type of industry, commerce and housing is needed; where it can be best sited; how neighborhoods can be stabilized; housing preserved, and streets. Schools, security and, generally, city services improved.

And while the planning process continues, implementation should begin as soon as possible, even if it just a street closing or streetscaping. For most neighborhood residents, planning is not real unless they can touch a result, be it a traffic barrier, or a housing project. Until that time planning is considered a polite subterfuge, something to divert concerned communities while special interests huddle with politicians to make the real decisions downtown.

To be effective, planning is going to have to be a process that begins in the neighborhood, from the bottom up, starting with a modest project, and moving from person-to-person, house-to-house, block-by-block, hopefully to generate a success that will breed more successes.

That is how communities are renewed, not by bureaucrats and politicians rearranging offices and furniture downtown, appointing advisory committees, holding all-day conferences, commissioning studies, issuing reports, and arranging press conferences. It is time for planning, to use a South Central colloquialism, to get down.

And talk about studies, reports and multi-colored charts, I am curious to see what will be issued at a press conference this week by the Los Angeles 2000 committee, a citizens group organized by Mayor Bradley to help guide the city's development in the 21st Century.

Being a literal minded journalist, faced with periodic deadlines, I tend to be wary of futurism, thinking of it as a way to avoid dealing with the myriad problems of the present. Such preoccupations might titilate the academic community, but they have harmed the credibility of planners, reinforcing an image of timidity.

When I used that phrase last July to describe city planning director Ken Topping in an column wondering what his staff was doing other than to secure parking privileges and other benefits for themselves I received a detailed letter from the department outlining a variety of programs aimed at making the city "a more livable urban place."

According to the letter signed by Topping, the programs include community plan revisions "getting underway," advisory committees "being established," a new urban design unit that "will be formed," antiquated, redundant mapping "being replaced," and "for the first time in years, a work program is guiding, prioritizing, and scheduling a longstanding heavy overload of planning projects requested by the City Council."

In addition, the letter stated "a neighborhood planning division has been designated to focus attention more directly on important local issues," and "a fledgling citywide planning program centering on transportation, growth, air quality, urban form and waste management, is rising from the ashes of Prop 13."

It all sounded fine, But I wanted to know what indeed had been accomplished, or simply how have all, or one, of these activities made the city "a more livable urban place," better yet made one block more livable by controlling traffic, reshaping the streetscape, or forcing the construction of a more neighborly project.

"Don't tell me," I asked Topping at a subsequent meeting with him and his staff. "Show me."

A lot of arrows are being shot into the air these days by the planning and development community. The hope here is that a few will hit their targets.

—Nov. 13, 1988

III

STRIP MINING
THE URBAN LODE

L OTUS LAND IS TURNING INTO A WASTELAND, AT LEAST ACCORDING TO
many of the increasing telephone calls, letters and comments received here.

They charge, in so many words—and with varying passion—
that the lack of sensitive planning, sympathetic design and conscientious development are chipping away at the livability of Los Angeles.

That they are concerned with the shaping of the Los Angeles
cityscape is heartening. From downtown north, south, east and west,
across the sprawling valleys, there seems to be a rising consciousness
that planning and design are critical ingredients in the social and
economic health of the city.

What is disheartening is that this consciousness is being
prompted by bad planning and design in numerous proposals and projects that citizens feel are threatening their homes, businesses, neighborhoods and life styles. And they are getting angry, as evidenced by
the tone of community meetings and by recent lawsuits.

I T WOULD BE A MISTAKE TO SIMPLY DISMISS THE PROTESTS AS THE SELFISH
rantings of no-growth advocates. While a few obviously are, more
seem to stem from a reasonable desire that developments be humane
and better serve the long-range interests of their communities.

What many of the protesting groups and individuals simply are
asking is that they be allowed to play a legitimate role in the development process, have their questions answered with civility, be shown
viable alternatives and not be cavalierly dismissed or buried under a
costly pile of slanted studies.

After all, it is the communities that will have to live with the
projects, be they street widenings, shopping malls, office towers,
cultural and entertainment centers or housing complexes, not the
sponsoring developers or bureaucrats or the compliant council
members.

Though the portrait they paint of Los Angeles is not as apoc-
alyptic as, say, Tod Hackett's in Nathanael West's "Day of the
Locust," a recent sampling of concerns witnessed across the city and
received here raises some provocative planning and design issues.

There was the mayor's Little Tokyo Community Development
Advisory Committee expressing concern about how the federal government was locating facilities downtown, "a coalition of concerned
communities" questioning the impact of various developments in the

Westchester area and a North Hollywood resident protesting the massing of new apartment complexes rising near his house.

Also outraged by complexes "destroying the flavor and scale" of their communities were residents in Sherman Oaks, Topanga Canyon, South Pasadena and Highland Park. And a Brentwood homeowner wondered why the Getty Trust has to build its art center in the 'Santa Monica Mountains, "damaging the environment and aggravating suburban sprawl," and not on a more accessible and urban site.

MEANWHILE, A VENICE RESIDENT WANTED TO KNOW HOW THROUGH TRAFFIC in the alley behind her house could be discouraged because "it has become quite dangerous during the rush hour." And in Santa Monica, a builder was bemoaning that city's lack of imagination and will to address the housing problem there. "All they do is talk, and talk," he said.

There also were "urgent" calls about proposed street widening and sidewalk-narrowing projects, replete with the destruction of trees, front lawns and neighborhood ambiance. Included was one concerning the fate of the singular Ship's diner at the northwest corner of Washington Boulevard and Overland Avenue, a 1950s delight that lends Culver City a rare sense of history, and patrons a sense of place.

It seems the local redevelopment agency wants to knock down the thriving Ship's so Overland can be widened and, not incidentally, provide an adjacent smear of a shopping mall a few more parking spaces. So much for an agency dedicated to the eradication of blight and deterioration.

Happily, the public hearing held on Martin Luther King's birthday was continued until May 5, thanks in part to the pleas of the vigilant Los Angeles Conservancy. This, hopefully, should give the opponents of this sacrilege time to rally the forces of reason and the city to reexamine the plan.

—Feb. 2, 1986

The Culver City Ship's was spared.

BARNSDALL PARK, FOR YEARS, HAS BEEN LESS OF A PARK THAN A BUreaucratic jungle, with a variety of city agencies squabbling over whose turf it is.

Often stumbling over themselves and each other have been the departments of Recreation and Parks, General Services, Cultural Affairs and Public Works and the city's administrative office.

The bureaucrats have been guided, as usual, by the Catch-22 macro ecopolitical mathematical formula:

Promises = megalomania ÷ paranoia = inaction.

TYPICAL OF GOVERNMENT, NO AGENCY HAS WANTED TO TAKE RESPONSIBILITY for seeing the park and the facilities maintained, let alone improved. Instead, all wanted to keep their thumb in the operation and take credit for whatever there was to take credit for. And, of course, no one wanted to take the blame for nothing being done.

Meanwhile, the historic park, with its landmark Hollyhock House, designed by Frank Lloyd Wright, the Municipal Art Gallery and Junior Arts Center, views and open space have suffered. And though the facilities have been functioning, thanks to a dedicated on-site staff and volunteers, their potential as a marvelous resource for the East Hollywood community and the city at large remains frustrated.

But there is hope that at long last the park and its facilities will be getting the attention they need and deserve.

Prodded by a persistent mayoral task force, the Friends of Hollyhock House and other volunteers, the city has selected a design team to develop a restoration and maintenance program for the landmark structures.

There is also the promise of some funds from the city and the hope of more funds from the state, depending on what is developed by the team of Mark Hall of Archiplan and preservation architect Martin Eli Weil.

THIS COULD BE AN IMPORTANT START IN THE PROCESS THAT WILL LEAD TO THE fulfillment of the spirit of the Aline Barnsdall's dream 70 years ago, to develop the area then called Olive Hill into an egalitarian art center. It was the oil heiress Barnsdall who gave Frank Lloyd Wright his first commission in Los Angeles to design for her a home on the hill as a centerpiece in a cultural complex. Eventually, the property was turned over to a reluctant city for a park.

But if the process is going to avoid falling into the trap that undermined similar past efforts, a broad and imaginative master plan will be needed to establish the framework and goals for the restoration and maintenance programs.

Many of the park's current problems, including difficult access, lack of parking and inadequate facilities, stems from the failure in the past of the city and others to be able to embrace the greater potential of this rare public resource.

Still needed to guide the effort is the good will, good works and good ideas of the task force and persevering others who hold dear the dream of Barnsdall and Wright.

—Sept. 21, 1986

Westwood Village Woe

ONE ONLY HAS TO DRIVE THROUGH THE NORTH WESTWOOD NEIGHBOR-hood to see why residents there have demanded a building moratorium.

The rolling, verdant, squaremile area bounded by Gayley, Veteran and Le Conte avenues is pockmarked by vacant lots recently cleared of buildings, buildings marked for demolition and new, over-scaled and ostentatious apartment complexes.

According to Bob Breall of the neighborhood association there, within the last year about 30 apartment buildings have been demolished and an estimated 900 persons displaced to make way for a wave of oversized and overpriced apartments.

Of course, if developers want to construct overpriced apartments—and there are people who want to rent them—that is just fine. The entire Los Angeles region needs housing in all price ranges.

But developers should pursue the market with infill projects, on vacant land, with imagination and sensitivity, not at the expense of existing housing and the character of a neighborhood, particularly a stable one.

Ironically, it is the pleasant character of the north Westwood neighborhood—a mature, multiunit area that has long provided a housing resource to the adjacent bustling UCLA community—that no doubt attracted the latest rash of avaricious speculation and insensitive development.

And, if the development is allowed to continue unchecked by a moratorium, in time, no doubt, it will destroy the very character of the neighborhood that initially made it so attractive to the speculators.

But by then most of the speculators probably will have "cashed out" and moved on, repeating what has occurred in the past in other neighborhoods.

What we are witnessing is a sort of ugly urban strip mining, in which sound, well-scaled structures providing needed housing are being demolished for a short-range gain.

One can also see examples of this insidious practice along Ventura and Wilshire boulevards and in pockets of Hollywood and West Los Angeles, as well as in north Westwood.

What is needed, of course, is planning. Planning, and the zoning that gives it muscle, are supposed to protect the residential character of a neighborhood, hopefully improve it.

Planning is not supposed to provide incentives for developers to demolish sound structures so they can build oversized buildings. But that is what is happening under the present zoning for the north Westwood neighborhood, and for this we can thank those who drafted the Westwood Community Plan.

And until that planning and its resultant zoning can be corrected in a new plan to serve the area, and control and shape development, a moratorium is a necessity.

A moratorium may be an imperfect and at times unfair tool, but it can provide the time necessary to repair the planning process and help the community before both are buried under a pile of construction debris.

—Aug. 25, 1985

THE QUESTION THESE DAYS IN AND AROUND THE FAST FOOD, FAST SALES and fast forward entertainment district of Westwood Village is whether a proposed, so-called specific plan can make a difference.

Prepared for the city by Gruen Associates, the plan recommends a sweeping down zoning, reducing buildable footage from the present four times the lot size to twice the lot size, setting height limits, increasing parking requirements and putting a lid on the current number of movie seats.

At the same time, the plan, through a system of building bonuses, encourages the preservation of structures of historic interest and the development of stores that provide neighborhood services. The latter would include drug and hardware stores and groceries, as opposed to yogurt parlors, pizza stands and T-shirt emporiums.

The plan also calls for a variety of pedestrian amenities, including, at long last, the widening of sidewalks, a sensitive selection of street furniture and plantings, and encouraging sidewalk cafes.

Better late than never.

Though the plan will not turn the clock back to a time when Westwood Village was, indeed, a village in style and spirit, it will control the growth somewhat and may even make the area a pleasant place for a person over 30 to stroll through on an occasional evening.

Despite the bonuses for the neighborhood service, Westwood Village most likely will continue in the evenings to serve the region's adolescent and post-adolescent population as a big, uncovered mall and "the place to go to when there is no other place to go."

As such a "place," the village has been very much a success, and relatively free of unpleasant or gang-related incidents. It is nice to have such a neutral area where young persons can be entertained and socialize, of course, as long as it is not in your backyard or down the block.

What is unfortunate is the traffic this generates. When added to the traffic generated by the office buildings along Wilshire Boulevard and what is coming and going from UCLA, and nearby Century City and Beverly Hills, Westwood is a mess from early morning to late at night.

That the Westwood Village plan allows for even more development, however controlled and shaped, is not going to help. Controlling traffic is much harder than controlling growth.

Even with the plan in place, nearby intersections are just going to get more jammed, with traffic overflowing onto side streets. And the wider the streets are made, the more traffic they will generate. Traffic abhors a vacuum.

In addition to controlling and limiting traffic in the village, the plan is going to do the same for adjoining residential streets. By creating cul-de-sacs and one-way streets, limiting parking and enforcing restrictions, the adjacent neighborhoods are going to have to be isolated or in time they will be overrun worse than now.

The city's prosaic Department of Transportation has traditionally opposed such measures, arguing that they only shift congestion to other residential streets and neighborhoods.

Of course, if it is planned correctly, those other streets and neighborhoods also can be protected and the traffic channeled to commercial streets. There, traffic becomes its own control; that is to say, if it jams up and there is no place to go, people will start finding other times or ways to travel.

And who knows, that could be the start of a rational transportation system that has so long eluded Los Angeles.

—July 19, 1987

Renovating Houses, And Rent Control

A DEDICATION CEREMONY WAS HELD A FEW WEEKS AGO IN THE OCEAN Park section of Santa Monica for a sensitive and sensible renovation of a Craftsman-styled bungalow of some historic interest.

The well-detailed bungalow at 2302 5th St. dates to 1913, but in recent years had been battered by rent control, trashed by tenants and neglected by owners to become a sorry eyesore at the southwest corner of 5th and Strand Street.

Then, last year, the innovative nonprofit Community Corp. of Santa Monica stepped into the picture to save the structure from further humiliation and probable demolition by recycling it into six apartments.

In keeping with the housing corporation's philosophy, the largest and more desirable of the apartments will be rented at market rate, estimated at $1,200 a month, with the money going to help reduce the rents of the five other units so they can be made available to eligible low- and moderate-income families.

OF COURSE, TO DO THIS THE 5TH STREET PROJECT HAD TO BE EXEMPTED from rent control.

That is no easy task in Santa Monica. Rent control there stands with God and motherhood in the pecking order of, if not the universe, the tenants who make up the vast majority of Santa Monica's voters and who are subsidized by the system, whether they are in need or not.

(Most tenants are not, but this does not stop them from enjoying artifically low rents, which, in effect, are being subsidized by landlords. It is no wonder that apartments in Santa Monica are so desirable and generate sizeable finder fees.)

Nevertheless, the corporation won the exemption. It was granted on the basis that the project would have been economically infeasible if rents had been limited to the so-called maximum allowable established under the restrictive guidelines of the rent control board.

(That the rents of most units in Santa Monica are limited to these maximums says something about the economic feasibility of owning and operating an apartment house there.)

NO DOUBT HELPING IN THE DECISION FOR THE EXEMPTION WAS THE CORPORATION's noble effort to creat affordable housing for senior citizens and families. Not coincidentally, one of the purported goals of rent control is to maintain such housing.

However, the respective efforts have had quite different results.

While rent control, as administered in Santa Monica, ironically and sadly has diminished housing, the community corporation has been saving a modest amount and creating more. One has to be impressed with the corporation's efforts, especially in this Reagan era of housing subsidy cutbacks.

After a slow start hampered by too much talk and too little action—a common Santa Monica malady—the corporation with each new project has been gaining credibility. So far, it has projected 144 new and rehabilitated units, with construction to start soon on 47 more in a series of in-fill projects imaginatively designed by the young firm of Koning Eizenberg Architects.

"Our success, in part, I think, is based on our ability to walk the thin line between the cliche images in Santa Monica of, on one side, the greedy developer/landlords, and on the other side, the crazed tenant activists who protest anything that might raise their rents more than $1 a month," commented Neal Richman, the corporation's executive director.

Richman's candor and humor, as well as obvious ability, also has helped the corporation overcome some major obstacles in Santa Monica, not the least of them the well-intentioned City of Santa Monica itself.

As someone who was a renter in Santa Monica and is now a landlord/occupant of a small rental property there, I have had a close, if prejudiced, view of the obstacles. And in no place are their effects more in evidence than in my former neighborhood of Ocean Park, where I still walk and bicycle regularly.

Pushed and pulled by the convoluted politics of Santa Monica, Ocean Park seems at times to be going in two directions at once.

While heartening improvements in the form of new and reno-vated housing, such as the 5th Street and similar projects are on the increase, so is disheartening disinvestment in the form of scattered, deteriorating and vacant apartment complexes and houses, and garbage-strewn vacant lots.

The new developments generally are being encouraged by the community's prime location near the beach and freeway and its grow-ing array of upscale restaurants and stores, and nearby entertainment.

The deterioration is being accelerated by a perverted rent con-trol system that caters in the extreme to tenants, while discouraging and, in effect, penalizing owners who try to maintain their buildings.

As for the oddity of vacancies in a place where, and at a time when, apartments are in great demand, some owners feel that it is less expensive and less troublesome to leave units empty rather than have to repair them and be unable to raise the rents to cover costs. Of course, a few hold out the slim hope for vacancy decontrol, which would allow them to make the repairs and pass on the costs to new tenants.

In the rent control board's zeal to serve existing tenants, and, not incidentally, pad its own bureaucracy, it says it is doing so to preserve the social and economic diversity of Santa Monica. So much for rhetoric.

The reality is that it is apparent that in its modest way the community corporation is doing a much better job of it.

And, unlike the rent control board, the corporation is not in the process of subsidizing the rents of those who do not need or deserve them, and it is certainly not promoting housing deterioration.

In renovating the 5th Street bungalow for a range of needed housing out of the bonds of rent control, the community corporation

71

has preserved a piece of Santa Monica's proud past and given it a hint of a better future.

—Feb. 1, 1987

Land Use Abuse Continues

YOU WOULD THINK THAT WITH THE PASSAGE OF SLOW-GROWTH PROPOSItion U and the variety of other recent citizen protests of land-use abuses, the powers that be would understand that the major issue in the city is now neighborhood stability and quality of life.

But no.

While the rhetoric of some developers and their fawning politicians and bureaucrats may have changed somewhat to include phrases like "design compatibility" and "traffic mitigation," a nightmare of egregious projects continue to be processed.

No matter how architecturally *au courant*, how sensitively detailed and how well painted in the latest and most fashionable pastels and earth tones, the projects, by any other design or name, would smell the same. And they are not coming up roses, except perhaps for the real estate speculators, bureaucrats and politicians involved.

FROM SUCH DIVERSE COMMUNITIES AS MAR VISTA, LONG BEACH, LINCOLN Heights, East Hollywood, North Hollywood, West Adams, Pasadena and in the Mid-Wilshire area come reports of out-of-scale and out-of-character apartment complexes being shoehorned onto sites, or worse, gobbling up existing housing.

Better late than never, the City of Long Beach has had drawn up for it a set of desperately needed design guidelines for multifamily development. The package put together by the consultant firm of Sedway Cooke Associates, addressing issues of scale, livability and aesthetics, makes sense and is well recommended. That Pasadena also is exploring such guidelines is welcome.

However late, the time has come for cities to make zoning more prescriptive and allow planners to be more creative, and not to waste them as simply plan checkers and paper shufflers.

As usual, Los Angeles lags behind. That the city has yet to find a way to somehow stop or scale down such horrors as the apartment complex proposed by the Homestead (read "homebash") Group for Detroit Street, says something about its lack of fortitude and the utter failure of the zoning process.

If allowed—and there is still time and ways for the city to stop or at least scale down the project—the Detroit Street debacle could set a dangerous precedent for the abuse of other, similar architecturally and socially stable areas. This could possible touch off depressing waves of blockbusing speculation and accompanying deterioration.

Such projects that try to milk the last allowable square foot out of dated and inadequate zoning codes also make it just that much harder for more reasonable and sensitively designed housing proposals to gain community acceptance.

Will the Homestead horrors be the housing mini-malls of the late 1980s?

72

In the continuing battle to stablize communities, one, unfortunately, has come to expect that most developers will be greedy, insensitive and shortsighted, but not the Los Angeles Board of Education. Schools are supposed to stablize communities.

However, the board's announced plans for expanding various schools west of downtown are as bad as any recent rape of a neighborhood. If the board has not has enough recent troubles with busing, now it has added blockbusting to the list.

The plans, as they now stand, literally drive a stake through the hearts of a struggling half-dozen vest-pocket neighborhoods. These include, among others, clusters of well-scaled houses in the vicinity of Whitehouse Place and Vermont Avenue, Queen Anne Place and Pico Boulevard, Berendo Avenue and Olympic Boulevard and West 8th Street and Wilton Place.

Some of the houses are of historic interest, but more important, most of them are owner-occupied and well-maintained, lending a desperately needed stability to the struggling neighborhoods.

And making the possibility that the houses will be bulldozed, the lives of the occupants convulsed and the neighborhoods torn asunder, even more outrageous is that they need not be—if the board and its bureaucrats would just exert a modicum of common sense and imagination.

That, of course, is a big "if."

Even assuming that the board's calculations are correct on how much new and expanded facilities are needed to handle present and projected overcrowding in the area schools, there is much that can be done to ease the impact on adjacent neighborhoods.

A tour of the schools slated to be expanded reveals that there is on the present campuses much space that can be better utilized. They all need not be junior college campuses, composed of clusters of classrooms, inefficient recreation areas and parking lots sprawled over acres, as if located in some semi-rural county.

Before it starts wielding eminent domain as if it were peanut butter in a school lunchroom, the board's building committee should sit down and read the studies conducted a few years ago by the Ford Foundation-supported Educational Facilities Laboratories. In them are a variety of imaginative ways overcrowding and expansion has been dealt with efficiently and relatively inexpensively by other school districts.

The tour also revealed in the adjacent neighborhoods what one would consider soft spots. These included vacant lots, parking lots and obviously underutilized and deteriorated commercial properties, the taking of which, no doubt, would have a less disruptive effect on individuals and areas.

What most of the proposed takings indicated was that the board and its bureaucrats just didn't do their homework.

For what the board and its bureaucrats have done, and the grief they have caused in numerous households and in the affected neighborhoods, one feels compelled to grade them:

In *civics*, for the lack of citizen involvement in the planning process, *F*.

In *economics*, for wasting thousands of dollars in time and studies to come up with a costly and inefficent expansion plan, *F*.

In *planning*, for demonstrating no imagination in the use of present facilies and land, *F*.

In *conduct*, for trying to intimidate those who question their plans and behavior, *F*.

The grades total up to a resounding failure, and automatically place the board on probation. One hopes that there will be a decided improvement in the next marking period.

—March 15, 1987

Schools Fail to Justify Home Grab

WHEN 53 HOMES WERE DESTROYED IN THE FIRE THAT SWEPT BALDWIN Hills in July, 1985, it was a major tragedy, with the anguish of the families prompting public concern and news for weeks.

But just imagine if that fire had not been controlled after it had destroyed nearly 2,000 homes and displaced 5,000 persons, what the magnitude of the tragedy, and response, would have been.

Well, that is the estimated number of homes that will be destroyed and persons displaced under the ill-conceived expansion plans of the Los Angeles Unified School District.

And beyond the obscene numbers, it is a far greater tragedy than the Baldwin Hills fire for the reason that much of it could be avoided with a modicum of common sense, public courtesy, conscientious planning and imaginative design.

Some takings may be necessary to meet future school needs. But so far, the district has shown little compassion and less imagination in developing viable alternatives to blockbusting and bulldozing.

The taking of homes should be considered only when all other possibilities to accomodate the expansion have been exhausted.

That the school district, reacting to an initial wave of community protests, reduced the number of its proposed expanded and new sites from 42 to 30 is a clear indication of the arbitrary planning process of the agency. Were those 12 sites really needed in the first place? Does that mean if there had not been protests the houses there would have been condemned and demolished? Why were they spared and not others?

This has led to further questions, such as what really are the district's expansion needs? What are those needs based on? How come the district—that a few years ago was closing dozens of schools—now needs to expand so precipitously?

Between February, 1982, and June, 1984, the district closed 22 schools. And here it is, a few years later, and the district is scrambling to assemble new sites. That does not engender confidence in the district's planning process.

One hopes the current scrambling is not just because the state has made available a few hundred million dollars of construction funds, the use of which could nicely pad a bureaucracy from periodic budget cuts.

Could much of this plan be motivated not by the projected educational needs of the city's children, but by the nefarious need of bureaucrats to justify their own existence and an ambitious construction program to pay off some political debts?

The targeted communities also have been asking questions, such as why homes must be taken for school playgrounds, which are often used for parking for teachers and administrators, when streets could be closed during school hours for the same purposes?

Also, why can't the district utilize existing facilities better through renovations, sensitively designed additions and redistricting, or by the imaginative recycling of commercial and industrial structures?

There have been reams of excellent questions by various concerned community groups and local representatives, in particular Councilman Michael Woo and State Sen. David Roberti (D-Los Angeles), but few answers by the district.

Also starting to ask questions about the expansion, as well as they should, are the city Planning Commission and Planning Department. The district's proposed construction program has ramifications far beyond education that should be of deep concern to the city's planners, as well as others involved with shaping the city.

IN RESPONSE TO AN EARLIER COLUMN IN WHICH I ACCUSED THE DISTRICT OF not doing its homework in coming up with a projected increase of 75,578 students to justify the need for new expanded schools, I received from a consultant firm identified as Criterion Inc. a thick demographic study it had done for the district.

Along with the report came a letter in which the Dallas-based firm declared "we are willing to schedule a meeting with you so we can discuss our methodological approach in detail."

Not particularly anxious to be sandbagged by bureaucrats and their hired guns, but wanting an objective opinion, I asked a respected educator who recently retired as a senior administrator after 30 years with the New York City Board of Education, to review the report.

While declaring that the demographic analysis was interesting, he said it lacked perspective and raised more questions than it answered, such as the basis of the mathematical formulas used to project the statistics into hard figures in the future. "You really can play games with that to serve the interests of those paying for the study," said the educator.

He noted that in making projections, the study did not appear to take into consideration shifting family structures and values, such as the birthrate among Latinos most likely declining as their socioeconomic status rises, or the placement of their children in private or parochial schools.

He also said the report ignored the possible effect on projected facilities of changing educational theories and practices, such as developing work programs for dropouts instead of their being carried as students, and the fast tracking and special needs of, say, the growing number of Asian students.

Among items he wanted to know more about was the present utilization of facilities, as well as the basis of projected housing patterns. "I think it is important to know if they took into consideration such factors as proposed transportation systems and anticipated zoning changes," he said.

Similar questions have been asked by community groups.

"The report is two-dimensional, and not the sort of document on which I would want to base a decision that effects thousand of persons," he said. The educator added it certainly would not float in New York City or, for that matter, in Beverly Hills, where education and community groups are more coalesced.

Asked to grade the report, the educator gave it an "I," for incomplete. Once again the district has flunked its responsibility to the city.

—Aug. 2, 1987

A half year later the School District disclosed that the projections had been miscalculated, and that it was amending its planning and building program accordingly. Almost all the sites were withdrawn. No apologies were offered the residents.

Museum Ventures Into Real World

THE ANNOUNCEMENT BY THE MUSEUM OF CONTEMPORARY ART THAT IT IS planning a major architecture exhibit exploring the legacy of the so-called Case Study Houses is exciting—and worrisome.

Though the exhibit at the museum, and an accompanying off-site housing demonstration, is two years off, the ambitious effort raises issues quite pertinent to the drift today of architecture into the art world here and elsewhere.

In addition, there also are problems that, if not resolved by the museum soon, will in all probability be quite embarrassing to it when the exhibit and demonstration are scheduled to open in late 1989 (and which has been funded by the National Endowment of the Humanities to the tune of $350,000).

For those who might not know, the innovative Case Study Houses program was conceived in Los Angeles in the wake of World War II to illustrate how modern design might meet the then pent-up need for both affordable and attractive housing.

However, the program, rooted in the social and service tradition of architecture, was not just another one of those well-meaning efforts that never goes much beyond the discussion stage at some design conference.

As organized by the then crusading "Arts & Architecture" magazine, actual sites were purchased and a host of mostly local architects were commissioned to develop plans and to supervise construction. About 28 distinctively modern homes were produced, most of them during the 1950s.

In addition to providing shelter for 28 families, the designs pioneered various structural and design concepts, garnered numerous awards, attracted national and international attention, reinforced the reputation of Los Angeles for innovative design and generated considerable builder and buyer interest.

That the program should be the first architecture exhibit mounted by MOCA is quite appropriate. The Case Study Houses program is considered by many to have been Los Angeles architecture's finest hour, and with its strong social purpose, deserves to be explored in a public format.

But an architecture exhibit in a museum poses some real problems, especially if the subject matter is so recent. An example of this problem can be seen in the Machine Age exhibit now at the Los Angeles County Museum of Art.

Fragments placed behind plexiglass or scattered out of context and photographs of something that was so pervasive in its time just do not convey the spirit of the age.

Perhaps, if the entire exhibit had been placed in a replica of a 1939 World's Fair pavilion it would have been more effective. Appropriate also would have been a streamlined circulation pattern.

Architecture, and, to some extent industrial and interior design, is, in my opinion, treated too preciously in museums. While sculptural, they are not pieces of sculpture, but something that was designed to serve a function, be it to provide shelter and comfort, or to sit on, or sharpen a pencil. That is the essence of their aesthetic, and therefore, somehow, should be presented alive, not placed in coffins.

A problem in architecture today is that many designers seem to be primarily worried about what sort of statement their buildings make instead of how they work; indeed how they might photograph and perhaps find their way into a magazine and, eventually, into a museum, to be catalogued, discussed on docent tours and toasted at receptions.

For too many architects, being "arty" has become a form of escapism, conscious or subconscious, from the social responsibility of their profession, or worse, an excuse for a design that just might not work. For these architects, being different and attracting attention appears to be more important then being good.

Playing to this self-absorption among architects have been a number of architecture schools and museums. While architecture is indeed a legitimate curatorial subject in these institutions, the pressure to be *au courant* has taken its toll in exhibits, their designs and, generally, the intellectual bent of the profession.

Art in these instances has given way to advertising, and fashion to fad, with museums, perhaps unwittingly, lending credence to commercial ventures and suspect careers.

It would be a shame if MOCA was co-opted by a few favored architects who, somehow, want to arrogate the program's mantle of innovation for their own grandiosity, just as the liberal "Art & Architecture" magazine was resurrected a few years ago, to end up serving a biased clique and, sadly, self-destructing.

But then again, given MOCA's emerging respect in the art world, perhaps it is best that the museum lead the architecture profession out of its current self-absorption. Certainly, it doen't seem that the American Institute of Architects is capable or ready to do so, worrying as it does more about image than issues.

The museum also has going for it the sincerity and community concerns of director Richard Koshalek and design curator Elizabeth Smith, and the aid of architect Craig Hodgetts. This just might be enough to mount an inventive exhibit within the museum, paste together a catalogue and stir some waters in the art and architecture world.

BUT WHETHER IT WILL BE ENOUGH TO PULL OFF THE HOUSING DEMONSTRAtion project is another matter. Without question, the demonstration involving the commissioning of six architects to design prototypes of affordable multifamily housing is the most ambitious and exciting element in the exhibit.

After all, when it comes to architecture, the city itself is really the museum and the buildings the exhibits.

But these are very real problems with the proposed demonstration. MOCA has identified only one potential building site, a CRA parcel in Hollywood draped in red tape. Desperately needed are more sites, preferably owned by enlightened developers.

Then there are the problems with the cast of architects selected: Craig Hodgetts and Eric Moss of Los Angeles, John Hejduk of New York, Adele Naude Santos of Philadelphia, and Itsuko Hasegawa and Toyo Ito of Japan.

Ray Kappe of Los Angeles was selected as the coordinating architect, but it is not clear what will have to be coordinated. Unfortunately, Kappe is the only one with demonstrated local experience in the development of user-sensitive multifamily housing.

Well-intentioned as they might be, Hodgetts and Hejduk are known more for their architectural philosophizing than their few buildings. (And it is not as if Hodgetts did not have enough to worry about as co-curator and designer of the exhibit, and Hejduk as the dean of Copper Union.)

As for Moss, his work has appeared more intuitive than socially and culturally responsive.

Santos, Hasegawa and Ito have designed multifamily housing, but not in Los Angeles with its varied building codes, climates and cultures. If these projects are to be innovative in their response to changing housing needs and building technologies, they cannot be designed or built via Federal Express.

There also are concerns of how the architectural programs will be developed; whether they will be drawn from the involvement of the potential residents and neighbors and their needs, or imposed by a design elite.

It is clear that MOCA is going to need a lot of help and luck turning the impressive rhetoric of its proposal into reality.

May MOCA and the spirit of the Case Study Houses persevere.

—Sept. 13, 1987

Horray, We Hope, for Hollywood

FOR THE LAST HALF-DOZEN YEARS HOLLYWOOD HAS BEEN THE SCENE OF some of the more heated battles over planning and redevelopment in Los Angeles.

To this observer, it is obvious that Hollywood desperately needs a plan to deal with the current chaotic commercial construction and tangled traffic there, as well as to guide the development of needed housing, more and accessible parks, public services, and sensitive streetscaping to bind neighborhoods.

Various plans and revisions attempting, in part, to deal with these issues have been floating around Hollywood for the last year or so, orchestrated by the city's Community Redevelopment Agency (CRA), with the Planning Department and the office of Councilman Michael Woo acting as a sort of a chorus. The resulting tune has been quite discordant.

Unfortunately, as has been pointed out by Hollywood Heritage and others, the plans seem to have some gaping holes in them, enough so that a developer could ram some high-rise office towers through them with little difficulty and aggravate the scale and traffic of the community even more than it has been in the last few years. The result is that the plans have not been particularly well received.

Compounding the situation is Hollywood's history as a sort of ball of Play-Doh, to be capriciously mauled by politicians and real estate interests, a mold it found itself in during the tenure of former council member Peggy Stevenson. It is no wonder that residents were wary when the CRA waded into the muddied waters there, welcomed by Stevenson and funded, in part, by a host of commercial property owners.

However well intentioned the CRA might have been then, it really should have gone much further to embrace the broader community, including the growing confederation of neighborhood and preservation groups there. Instead, like so many other governmental bodies, its collective ego got involved, and it retreated into an advocacy position, dealing with residents as if they were, in effect, the enemy, to be manipulated and pacified.

What obviously is needed now is for the community to lower its voice and for the CRA to listen harder; for those in the planning process to come up not with edicts or vague guidelines, but a host of alternatives and an honest study of consequences.

The planning of Hollywood should not be thought of as another notch in a bureaucrat's belt, or a line in some resume, but rather a democratic process leading to the goal of a more livable community.

THIS BRINGS ME TO THE ISSUE OF THE CITY-OWNED LOT IN HOLLYWOOD AT the northwest corner of Franklin and La Brea avenues that has been proposed as a site for a housing demonstration project sponsored by the CRA and the Museum of Contemporary Art (MOCA), and blessed by Councilman Woo.

Presumptuously trying last March to force feed the proposal to the community, as if it was a classroom of fawning students, was a self-described avant-garde clique. It had been christened by MOCA to carry out the demonstration in connection with an exhibit scheduled for October, 1989, exploring the legacy of the Case Study Houses program of the 1950s. Under that program, a series of houses were built in Los Angeles to demonstrate how modern design could produce both affordable and attractive housing.

A year ago, MOCA, with much fanfare, called for the commissioning of six architects to design prototypes of affordable multifamily housing. But the lack of sites and funding, and questions by the development community of the competence and commitment of those involved, prompted a cutback. The only site identified was the one in Hollywood, the design of which would be the subject of a limited competition among three of the surviving architects, Adele Naude Santos of Philadelphia and locals Craig Hodgetts and Eric Owen Moss.

When the architects, accompanied by the CRA and Woo, went before a community meeting last March they were booed. In addition to not being enthusiastic about the housing and perferring instead a park, most of the residents made it clear that they were tired of being lectured to, and not being involved, in the decision-making process shaping their neighborhood.

While the community grumbled, MOCA and CRA went ahead with the competition, which was won by Santos. The six-member jury that included only one community representative, declared the Santos design of the 40-unit complex as the most site-sensitive and innovative, being set like individual houses in a hillside garden, featuring sunlit parking areas and a series of inviting pedetrian-oriented spaces.

Though I take exception to the way the program was handled and presented, and also think there should have been a few more residents on the jury, after reviewing the submissions myself, I agree with the verdict.

There can be no denying that the Santos design represents a welcome departure from the raw monolithic housing projects mooning the streets of Hollywood and Los Angeles. It deserves to be built, with the hope that it will not only enhance the Franklin and La Brea neighborhood and provide needed housing, but also raise the design expectations of other communities.

THIS IN NO WAY LESSENS THE CRITICISM OF THE CURRENT PLANNING PROCESS and, I feel—under the circumstances—the concerned residents who came to the March meeting, deserve a sincere apology from the officials involved.

But it would be a shame if the Santos scheme is not realized. Being innovative and not the usual ticky-tacky decorated slab, it is going to need all the help it can get, from the neighborhood as well as from Woo, MOCA, the CRA and the city.

Also deserving to be built somewhere is Hodgett's scheme, consisting of modular blocks of flexible units centered around a courtyard. The Moss design features individualized units in a raised building mass oriented to three interlocking courtyards. All three schemes were very much in the tradition of the original Case Study

Houses, demonstrating how innovative design can meet changing user needs in a changing city.

While the MOCA Case Study program might have gotten off to a shaky start, the housing designs it has produced seem to be on firm architectural grounds. Certainly, their promise of a comfortable residential environment serving both user and community exceedes much of what is being built in Los Angeles today.

—July 31, 1988

Better Design for Better Housing

THE CONSTRUCTION OF OVERBLOWN APARTMENT BUILDINGS ON UNDERsized lots is one of the major complaints I receive here from residents and groups concerned with the general deterioration of their neighborhoods, and Los Angeles.

They note with proper outrage that the unfriendly scale and strained styles of the buildings, along with their sidewalk-level garages and parking areas, severely damage the frail residential quality of the surrounding streets.

The interiors also tend not to be attractive. Typically, the garages are Stygian dungeons, the building entrances inhospitable and the long, double-loaded corridors institutional, the result of which is that most apartments have limited views and no cross ventilation. The total is, in a word, schlock.

To see these insensitive, elephantine designs shoe-horned into a block of single-family houses or courtyard complexes is to understand why neighborhoods are so opposed to any multifamily housing proposal, no matter how well-intentioned or packaged a rare few might be.

The architects, developers and politicians involved should understand that the continued production of this schlock makes it just that much more difficult for quality housing to be built; for once taken advantage of and abused, community groups naturally tend to be wary.

This is a shame, for as reams of studies have told us, and the overcrowding of existing units and the homelessness has demonstrated, there is, at present, in the Los Angeles region a desperate need for housing, particularly affordable housing.

And having learned from the planning mistakes of the past, we know this housing must not be developed as mega-projects, but rather carefully woven into the fabric of established neighborhoods on socalled in-fill sites, convenient to work, schools and shopping.

Also, by gently increasing density, the city in this manner can ease the development pressure on our environmentally sensitive outer suburbs, reduce home-to-job commutes and make mass transit a more feasible alternative; and thus begin to untangle our traffic mess.

But first is the critical element of encouraging multifamily infill housing that is sensitively designed, modestly scaled and detailed and generally user and neighborhood friendly.

OFFERING SUCH A HOPE, I FEEL, IS THE WINING PROPOSAL FOR A 40-UNIT housing demonstration project at the northwest corner of Franklin and La Brea avenues in Hollywood. It is sponsored by the city's Community Redevelopment Agency (CRA) and the Museum of Contemporary Art (MOCA), and courageously supported by Councilman Michael Woo despite local opposition prompted, in part, by an insensitive presentation.

As I commented in a previous column, the design by architect Adele Naude Santos of Philadelphia presents a welcome departure from the raw monolithic housing projects mooning the streets of Hollywood and Los Angeles, and deserves to be built.

The project design was described in the proposal as a "deliberately romantic, small-scaled and inhabitable setting," with the character of a small town featuring a series of courtyards and play areas linked by ramped walkways, arches and a garden path.

There is a hint in the drawings of some engaging pedestrian spaces, the type that, with the right balance of resident involvement and management concern, can generate a sense of place and community so needed in our increasingly anonymous and alienating residential developments.

The housing itself will include a variety of unit types, grouped into 10 structures not unlike private homes in a clustered, pedestrian-oriented subdivision, with each unit having an individual entry, its own outdoor space and cross ventilation. Parking will be tucked under each structure to limit its visibility, while providing easy access to the units above. The focus of the project will not be on the parking, but on the open spaces.

There is the promise in the Santos design of demonstrating that affordable housing also can be attractive housing; indeed, that it can serve as a model for other in-fill projects, be they publicly or privately funded. It now remains to be seen whether the CRA can demonstrate the needed flexibility and resolve to make the project a reality.

ALSO ATTEMPTING TO DEAL WITH THE ISSUE OF HOW MULTIFAMILY HOUSING can be better designed to serve the resident and enhance the surrounding community is the City of Pasadena. It initiated a study last year to explore "an entirely new kind of zoning ordinance" that would permit high-intensity development in a way that would be in keeping with the city's heritage.

Aiding the effort was the San Francisco-based architectural firm of Daniel Solomon, which has designed some imaginative multifamily projects, and the Center for Environmental Structure, headed by planning theorist Christopher Alexander. It was Alexander who in his last book, "A New Theory of Urban Design" (Oxford University Press), declared the single overriding rule of that theory is that "every increment of construction must be made in such a way as to heal the city."

The resulting draft report is, happily, unlike any other zoning document I have ever read, focusing on the element the authors feel distinguishes Pasadena, and that should be the prime consideration of any building standards. That element is the garden in the various forms of landscaped courtyards, generous lawns, lush plantings, street trees, flower beds and gardens themselves.

The draft report goes on to comment that this garden character of Pasadena has been harmed in recent years, in large part, by the planning and development process being concerned more with accommodating the automobile than with maintaining the residential integrity of neighborhoods. The result is that parking and asphalt has been allowed to dominate the streetscapes, leaving "no coherent open space which people can use and enjoy."

To remedy this situation, the draft proposes a set of ordinances in which the garden "plays a role as important as building volume and parking layout in shaping development."

In these observations and recommendations, I feel, are the seeds for a more livable Pasadena that with hope can spread to communities elsewhere.

—August 7, 1988

IV

ARCHITECTURE,
FOR BETTER OR WORSE

ARCHITECTURE, ANYONE?
There has been an echoing lament from who else but architects that this column pays an inordinate amount of attention to planning and preservation issues and not enough to architecture.

My contention, of course, is that planning and preservation issues are architecture issues, and if architects don't address them, they will soon find themselves in a small corner of the design world.

Actually, from my vantage point, that corner is getting quite crowded, something the American Institute of Architects should be concerned about.

TOO MANY ARCHITECTS APPEAR TO HAVE DESIGNED THEMSELVES INTO IT IN their preoccupation with the look and symbolism of their structures, rather than with their functions and social and cultural context.

No doubt their efforts titillate peers and editors of regressive and indigestible architecture magazines, but in the larger scope, purpose and import of design as a social art, they tend not to be particularly important, or worthy of review. There will be no jumping on the fish truck here.

In the perfidious pursuit to become a superstar, these self-appointed serious architects (SASAs) seem to work as hard at promoting or trying to explain their projects as designing them. There is talent out there, but to what end is at question.

Still, architecture in the Los Angeles area appears to be very much alive, if not altogether well.

—Oct. 26, 1986

THERE IS A LOT MORE THAN MEETS THE EYE AT THE ARCHITECTURAL EX-hibit entitled "The Critical Edge" closing next week at the Newport Harbor Art Museum.

Because of the rush to judgment that plagues critics, I did not read a book based on the exhibit until after I had written my review that appeared a few months ago. Actually, to avoid being prejudiced, I tend not to read books, catalogues and reviews of exhibits (as well as projects) before recording my own observations.

For those who have not yet seen the exhibit, it displays models and drawings of 12 controversial projects constructed in the last 15 years. They were selected, not by a poll of critics, academics or professionals, but by the amount of printed commentary they inspired.

Beyond prompting viewers to draw their own critical conclusions concerning the merits and demerits of the projects, the exhibit and the book entitled "The Critical Edge" (edited by Tod A. Marder and published by the MIT Press of Cambridge, Mass.), raises the issue of the role of the professional and popular press as arbiters of taste.

Particularly provocative is an essay by Martin Filler, an editor of House and Garden magazine and a respected architectural writer and critic. He decries "the lack of informed public discourse on the direction of architecture in our country today" and blames both the popular and professional press for that situation.

Among the many pertinent points Filler makes is the tendency that for the press to rush into print when a building is completed, prompting hasty evaluations.

"What ought to be a central component of the critical analysis of a building—how well it does its job and how it enhances the lives of the people who use it—is thereby either ignored or left to the twilight zone of innuendo and hearsay." Filler adds that the practice "rather neatly exempts publications from having to delve into potentially uncomfortable areas of investigation, thereby perpetuating the celebratory tone in what generally passes for architectural 'criticism.' "

It is an excellent point, and makes me consider undertaking some post-occupancy reviews. But I should add that the problem is prompted in part by architects and developers anxious for publicity and playing favorites ("I'll let *you* see it first") in hopes of a favorable review that will lead to other favorable reviews.

Filler also discloses how architects, when dealing with trade publications, attempt to control which photographs are used, veto writers of whom they don't approve and review manuscripts by dangling the promise of an exclusive showing, sweetened by providing their own costly photographs. (I became aware of this nefarious practice as a contributing editor to Architectural Forum and Architecture Plus in the early 1970s, and have resented it ever since.)

And then other architects wonder how a select few peers always seem to get good plays replete with cover photographs in certain publications. Meanwhile, those so blessed take their clippings and proclaim their international fame in hopes of attracting clients, while trying to intimidate local critics to promote their projects, however mundane and inane.

These are what I call the hype architects, as in hype artists, who seem more concerned with marketing themselves than any particular design skill, or serving their clients. And if a critic displays any resistance to being used as a public relations tool, to rush out and praise the project and interview the architect, then he or she is condemned as a Philistine. I found that these architects do not want their projects critiqued. They just want to be quoted.

Contrary to rumor, the real pressure on critics does not come from publishers, but rather from peers and social contacts. As indicated by the inclusion in the book of excerpts from various reviews, frantic free lancers parading as critics and attempting to be trendy, tend to dig deep into obtuse psychological theories to justify their fawning and perhaps win favors from select architects and obtain more assignments from sycophantic publications.

Filler calls for tougher critical critieria, such as applied by art publications, with the hope that there by more controversy concerning architecture, no less. "We need analysis, judgment, and above all, moral teaching in its least restrictive and most liberating sense," he concludes. Powerful stuff that many in the coddled architectural community may not like.

A problem that Filler does not go into is how the prejudices of the editors of the East Coast-based professional publications looking for "something different" from Southern California, prompts architects here to do "something different" to gain attention.

The process tends to be a vicious circle that has produced some particularly bad architecture, such as punk designs that, at a high cost, pervert low-tech materials in the name of art. But it also has produced some weighty publicity for the architects involved yearning to be superstars.

It is a process that I don't want to be party to, preferring instead to explore how design affects people; will it improve or harm their quality of life, and quite secondarily, does it advance or set back, any new theory, style or technology, not personality?

If anything, too much is said about architectural superstars, which I admit the press has had a role in creating. Perhaps it would be better if the architects remain anonymous, and their designs speak for themselves, with the reward for having done them well being the pleasure of the users, and not getting photographed in front of one of the projects or having it included in an exhibit such as "The Critical Edge."

—Sept. 15, 1985

Design for Future Schlock

When we build, let us think that we build forever.
—JOHN RUSKIN, 1849.

THERE WAS THE FAINT HOPE THAT IN TIME THE BLACK- AND WHITE-STRIPED mini-mall at the southwest corner of La Cienega Boulevard and Melrose Avenue just might disappear, like a bad mirage, or that it might be softened by sensitive landscaping or in a heavy rain, its colors would run into a silky gray.

Unfortunately, it hasn't. The mall, designed by the firm of A. C. Martin for the Olympic-Barrington partnership, exudes tackiness, a very clumsy attempt to make a trendy architectural statement.

There is nothing wrong with designing an architectural and commercial calling card, something distinctive that in an eclectic funky-punk context, such as Melrose Avenue, stands out and announces itself to all the world. except that it better be good.

Instead of taking advantage of the prominent corner, the massing, styling and detailing of 8500 Melrose Ave. detracts from it. A notched second floor crushes a column below, pushing it into a planter full of angry firethorn bushes, making sitting on the ledge a masochistic act. Like the architecture, the landscaping is not very friendly.

THE CORNER COLUMN ALSO DESTROYS WHAT COULD HAVE BEEN ONE OF THE best exposures in the city for a display window. Not helping either are the badly scaled window mullions. And the effect of the second-floor windows, accented by the forced striping, is to press down on the ground floor and overwhelm the sidewalk and street.

As for the entry through a central court, it is overwhelmed by a spiral staircase, made all the more awkward by the pipe railing painted a sultry pink. The high-tech touch lends the building that little extra confusion of styles it certainly doesn't need.

The black-and-white marble cladding, which works so well on the facade of the 14th-Century cathedral in the Piazza del Duomo in Siena designed by Giovanni Pisano, just doesn't make it on Melrose Avenue. Somehow, as applied here, it looks very much like wallpaper. Cheap.

A. C. Martin appears to have a very bad case of facadism, and Melrose Avenue has another bomb of a building. Those responsible in the firm for design should do some serious reexamination of their own intellectual and aesthetic pretenses before foisting them on others. Unlike a newspaper column, architecture cannot be easily discarded.

A much more successful attempt at a mini-mall is the Boulevard, at 8611 Santa Monica Blvd. Designed in a modest high-tech style by the architectural firm of Herbert Nadel & Partners, the two-story structure, if anything, is too self-effacing.

The mall addresses the street with a well-scaled and massed uniform facade, reinforcing the sidewalk and encouraging pedesrian life. The facade is punctured by a broad stairway leading up under a glass atrium to second floor offices and an open rear parking lot. Though concealed from view from the street, the parking is quite convenient.

Unlike 8500 Melrose, each of the 11 street shops in the Boulevard has its own front door, creating a very neighborly feel to the sidewalk. Indeed, what makes this mini-mall so attractive is that it doesn't appear like a mall at all, but a block of attractive shops.

The effect is urban, yet accessible, a rare and welcome combination.

MOST DEVELOPERS OF MINI-MALLS WANT THE STORES SET AS FAR BACK FROM the street as possible, putting the parking adjacent to the sidewalk where those driving by can see it. The effect often is to destroy what little pedestrian life there was on the sidewalks and to weaken the street.

These are not developers who are building for the ages, as Ruskin had urged. And if an architect in their employ protests too much, one can be assured he or she will not be employed for very long, and that the developer will seek a more compliant associate.

If a developer insists on the parking in the front, the challenge then for architects who want to pay back their student loans, or simply pay their rent, is to somehow design the mall to at least be more attractive.

Whatever their situation, architect Don Barnay and landscape architect Laura Saltzman have done an admirable job, lending some style and sensitivity to the Serrano Center on the north side of 6th Street between Serrano Avenue and Hobart Boulevard.

WHILE UNDER CONSTRUCTION, THE CENTER LOOKED AS IF IT WAS GOING TO BE another mini-mall of the type that has been defacing the city-scape.

However, the recently completed one-story stretch of stores is modestly scaled and detailed in a clean, Art Deco style, replete with peach pastel awnings. Helping also are the struggling palms and the other frail plantings.

Though Ruskin, were he to pass through Los Angeles, no doubt would not write home about the Serrano Center, or the Boulevard, they appear as conscientious attempts at architecture within the constraints of reality. After all, most architecture of retail spaces is really the art of effect, and if the effect is good, then the architecture is good.

—Jan. 19, 1986

A Contest for Self-Congratulation

LOS ANGELES' DIVERGENT ARCHITECTURE COMMUNITY IS RESTLESS. IT wants to be noted, quoted and loved.

Once a focus of international attention for innovative design, a testing ground for new technologies and styles to serve a burgeoning, optimistic population, it seems to have become over the last few decades a relatively minor force on the shifting design scene.

The promise of the architectural traditions of such designers of the past as Greene & Greene, Gill, Goodhue, Parkinson, Wright, Schindler, Neutra, Ain, Ellwood, May, Lautner, Eames and Jones somehow have been submerged in the city's sprawl and the profession's self indulgences.

There have been a few recent exceptions: an isolated building here and there by Pelli, Lumsden, Moore, Meyer, Kappe and Gehry. When not catering to the cliche visions of Los Angeles extolled by professional publications, and not blinded by the flash of photos and fawning peers, each in his own way has perpetuated the promise.

And then there also was, a few years ago, an inspired team effort (including Myers, Moore, Halprin, Pelli, Gehry, Contini, Legorreta, Kennard, KDG and Pfeiffer) orchestrated by Robert Maguire and the late and lamented Harvey Perloff, to give new life to Bunker Hill downtown with an urbane redevelopment scheme.

What could have been the city's variegated version of New York's Rockefeller Center, and a model for an urbanizing world, was, unfortunately, rejected by the city's Community Redevelopment Agency. Its board ignored the recommendation of Edward Helfeld and his staff and instead selected a safe, slick reworking of a typical urban renewal solution by a team headed by Arthur Erickson.

So much for history.

Now, in an apparent effort to garner anew some international attention, the local chapter of the American Institute of Architects has announced the establishment of a biennial competition for something labeled the "Los Angeles Prize," replete with an award of $10,000 and a bronze trophy.

With a theme this year of "visions of architecture in the year 2010," the competition "will address the future of human habitat, terrestrial and extraterrestrial new materials and systems as well as new uses for existing materials and systems." Judges will be architects Erickson, Richard Meier and Hans Hollein and novelist Ray Bradbury, all of whom are traveling at the moment in their own orbits quite above the mob.

If anything, the competition should help to reinforce the prejudiced views of professional peers from around the world of spaced-out architectural concerns in Los Angeles. This is just the stuff that the waves of visiting architects, educators and critics searching for materials for lectures and articles thrive on. It's blast-off time for punk architecture in El Lay.

More pertinent and damaging, the competition also should reinforce the general public's view, at the moment, of an irrelevant archicture community, seemingly constantly congratulating itself and its friends.

What the public perceives is a community dominated by an odd combination of would-be artists drawing funny pictures and building funny little funky expensive houses, and corporate types fronting for developers who want to pave over neighborhoods and build a commercial cathedral or a mini-mall.

And heaven-forbid that a critic raise questions concerning these creations, trying to put them into a broader perspective rather than concentrating on the play of shadows on overwrought materials.

Though obviously established with good intentions by professionals of good will, the competition appears to be yet another attempt by the local architecture community at self-aggrandizement. A pity.

If architects want to prompt publicity and gain the interest of the public—if they want the public to "value architecture," a recent national theme of the parent AIA—then perhaps they should take a lesson from Los Angeles' rich architectural history.

What attracted so much attention to architecture here in the past, such as in the 1950s, was the effort of the designers then to address current problems. And by trying to serve the public—trying to make a difference—they served themselves by demonstrating their relevancy. The acclaim simply followed.

An example was the Case Study program, sponsored by a then-inspired Arts & Architecture magazine to illustrate how modern design might meet the need for both affordable and attractive post-war housing. The program generated an enormous public interest in architecture, while also establishing Los Angeles as a world center of innovative design.

But the effort that attracted such attention was not like the kitsch or the bad art masquerading as architecture that some of our more vocal, local designers at present crank out when they snare a naive client—and for which they feel they should be venerated.

Rooted in the concern of architecture as a social art, the effort "did not encourage heroics," declared Esther McCoy in her definitive monograph of the program. "What it asked for was service."

If the Los Angeles architecture community wants attention, then, to paraphrase a popular television commercial of a few years ago, they should do it the old fashion way: earn it.

—March 16, 1986

Seeing Light in the Dark of Garages

TURNING, TURNING, TURNING RECENTLY UP WHAT SEEMED AN ENDLESS ramp of a cavernous garage; searching, searching, searching for a space for my car, and then waiting, waiting, waiting for someone to back out of one, my thoughts naturally turned to parking structures.

They are essential to life in Los Angeles; we must drive almost everywhere, including places where we like to walk, and when we get there, park.

Yet as ubiquitous as they are, garages tend to be architectural afterthoughts. Most are awkwardly stuck on to, under and above buildings, or squeezed into or behind shopping streets.

Talk about experiencing architectural schizophrenia: There is nothing like approaching a well-detailed, welcoming commercial complex, only to descend into its stygian subbasement to have to park your car.

THERE THE SCHIZOPHRENIA DEEPENS AS ONE MUST STEP GINGERLY OVER OIL-stained concrete slabs, weave in and out of a maze of gritty vehicles, and through a poorly lit, dented, dirty steel-encased doorway to finally get to the usually sparkling, marble encrusted elegant lobby. So much for interiors.

As for parking structure exteriors, particularly offensive are those that line the sidewalks and out of which poke the front and rear ends of cars. In addition to being simply unattractive and discouraging pedestrian life along the streets, the garages also consume some very valuable retail frontage.

But some light is creeping into the darkness of garage design, and into the garages themselves.

That is what the architectural firm of Welton Beckett & Associates did by creating atriums in the garage at Colorado Place office and restaurant complex at Colorado Boulevard and 26th Street in Santa Monica. There the light and the plantings of the atriums orient visitors parking in the garage to the attractive glass-enclosed elevators that serve the complex above.

A most elegant garage entry can be found at the Rodeo Collection, designed by Olivier Vidal, at 431 N. Rodeo Drive. There a patterned brick-paved ramp curves past potted plants, sculpture pieces, and attentive parking valets, setting the mood for the stores above.

Beverly Hills, in fact, has been a trend setter in developing municipal garages that not only serve the need for parking, but also include shops at street level. This preserves the pedestrian ambiance of the sidewalk while generating a healthy income through rents to the city. Particularly successful is the dual-use garage at 461 N. Bedford Drive, designed by Gensler Associates.

MORE AMBITIOUS IS A MULTI-USE GARAGE IN THE LAST THROES OF CONstruction a few blocks away on Crescent Drive. Designed by Kamnitzer and Cotton with the firm's usual concern for budget and aesthetics, the structure includes parking for 877 cars, 20,000 square feet of gound floor commercial space, and about 150 units of senior citizen housing above.

Also pursuing the concept of multi-use and better-designed garages is the city of Pasadena. Nearing completion at the southeast corner of Union Street and Fair Oaks Avenue is a garage combined with a retail arcade than in scale and tone form a pleasant and needed addition to the surrounding so-called Old Pasadena historic district.

Recognizing that such multi-use garages are most likely going to become more common as Los Angeles becomes more urban, Arthur Golding had his students at the USC School of Architecture recently devote a semester to studying the potential of such structures.

"Garages are a fact of life in L.A. and I think we have ignored them for too long as a design problem," commented Golding as he and assorted guests reviewed an imaginative array of solutions by the students.

Unfortunately I missed the first few presentations, for I had a hard time finding a parking space and had to eventually wend my way up to the roof of one of USC's high-rise garages. The view was spectacular, prompting me to think that it would make a nice site for some apartments.

—Jan. 3, 1987

Post Mortem on Post-Modernism?

IN BESTOWING THE COVETED PROGRESSIVE ARCHITECTURE MAGAZINE awards reviewed here a few weeks ago, the jury made some telling and noteworthy remarks about Post-Modernism and its embrace by the architectural profession.

"All four of us were distressed by the great number of mediocre Post-Modern submissions," said Bernardo Fort-Brescia, a Miami architect who served as a juror, along with architectural historian Thomas Hines of UCLA and architects George Hoover of Denver and Ricardo Legorreta of Mexico City.

"If Post-Modernism was supposed to come here and save us from the uniformity of Modernism, it certainly came more uniform than what it was replacing," add Fort-Brescia. "It's almost as if there were a dictionary of architectural cliches telling us about a machine-made history. It was scary."

The architect said the jury worried about finding winners, and when they did, "it was as if we had returned to unpretentiousness and innovation. It was a return to buildings that are designed not only because the architect knew history, but because the architect is talented and has good intuition about volume, space, light and sculptural form.

"Post-Modernism did awaken architects, and that was good, because today we look at Modernism with different, and I think improved, eyes," Fort-Brescia concluded.

Hines generally agreed with Fort-Brescia, and added that the first day, when the submissions were initially culled, "was the most interesting, educational, and, at times, depressing day I've had in along time. It was a Post-Modern Sweet's catalog; it was the school of Graves, the school of Jahn and some of the work of the masters themselves."

In an interview later, Hines estimated that of the nearly 700 submissions, perhaps 450 to 500 were what he called Post-Modern cliches.

"It seems that architects have gotten the word that Post-Modernism is in and have become true believers, playing with their designs mindless, suffocating and depressing games," he added. "It's definitely a backwash that is making Modernism look good again. But that is not to say we should make the mistake and abandon Post-Modernism the way Modernism was abandoned."

Hines called attention to remarks he made concerning the award to an expressionistic constructivist-styled concrete batching plant in Oakland: "However tired we may get of the late International Style, and however tired we get of a certain Post-Modern silliness, there is something about this that one cannot get tired of when it's well done."

He explained that in selecting winners, the jury based its preferences on designs that had a certain, indefinable freshness, no matter what their style. They were designs that "seemed to suggest things and even to teach us things we had not thought about in quite the same way," Hines said.

The jury's struggle with the submissions, its disappointment with the drift of Post-Modernism and its search for freshness also stirred my memories of shirting styles back in the bad old days when Modernism reigned.

Once embodying the promise of a better, brighter world, the sleek Modern style by the mid-1960s had become oppressive. It was the architecture of the establishment, giving form to alienating, cookie-cutter high-rise housing projects and anonymous, slick corporate office towers.

The heavy-booted march of these monoliths in the wake of federal bulldozers plowing through communities made may of us then involved with cities yearn for a design style more in the vernacular and more humanistic. Instead of solving the ills of the city, Modernism seemed to be exacerbating them, creating alien environments.

For me, Modernism hit its nadir when, in 1966, as downtown urban renewal director of New Haven, Conn., I reviewed with others a moderate-income housing scheme the city had commissioned Modernist master Mies van der Rohe to do. I remember remarking at the time that the proposed project looked like one of Mies' exquisitely structured glass and steel north-shore Chicago apartment houses, laid to rest on its side, cold and rigid.

Mies was politely dropped, and the city hired the then new dean at the Yale School of Architecture, Charles Moore, whose designs at Sea Ranch in Northern California hinted at what we were seeking in our Church Street South project: not just another anonymous housing complex, but a neighborhood.

MOORE, WITH THE AID OF OTHERS, FULFILLED THAT PROMISE, INCORPORATING into a lively, well-scaled and modestly detailed housing design, stores, small plazas and winding pedestrian street. Though the project was not without problems, its use of time-tested Italianate urban amenities and colorful supergraphics and playful shapes generated hope for a more congenial community.

What we were seeing at the time in Moore's fanciful design was the beginnings of the later misnamed Post-Modern movement, and most of us concerned with cities took heart. Architecture had, in our opinion, gotten pompous, corporate and cold, and needed a jolt of something to remind it of its history, social purpsoe and aesthetic potential.

A jolt it did get in the 1970s in the select designs of the talented Moore and Robert Venturi, soon followed by some interesting efforts by a than aspiring Michael Graves and Robert A. M. Stern. All eventually were blessed by supersalesman Philip Johnson and chronicler Charles Jencks.

In the process, the bright, populist promise of Post-Modernism as an antidote for the elitist Modernism became for many a faddish exercise, its potential for art and humanity giving way to mimicry, self-indulgence and self-promotion. Being different did not necessarily mean being better.

SO MUCH FOR ARCHITECTURAL REVOLUTIONS, AND BEWARE THOSE WHO MIGHT question and deviate, for they run the risk of being ridiculed by disingenuous cultural arbitrators and being cast out of the temple.

This is all not to say that many Post-Modern-styled buildings weren't an improvement over the severe Modern style. When competently handled and not overdone, they certainly make for a more interesting skyline and cityscape.

It is just to say that there once was the hope that Post-Modernism would be something more than a pastiche pasted on a building or a witty massing, and by using history, would better serve architecture's social purpose and aesthetic potential.

Perhaps the singular designs cited by the Progressive Architecture magazine jury will give the Post-Modern movement a needed jolt to get it back on track, just as Post-Modernism a decade ago gave Modernism a needed jolt.

—March 8, 1987

Dull Skyline in for a Change

THE DULLEST SEGMENT OF THE POPULAR TELEVISION SERIES "L.A. LAW" has to be the opening tease that offers glimpses of the city's downtown skyline.

The sad fact is that the architecture of most of the office buildings that form the downtown skyline is uninspired, and not what one would expect for a city the size, stature and, especially, the spirit of Los Angeles.

Of course, Los Angeles was never meant to be a city of highrises, but rather a horizontal collection of small towns in a grand Arcadian dream. Indeed, during the first half of the century when gloriously sculpted skyscrapers were rising in New York and Chicago, structures here were limited to 13 stories, with the exception of the City Hall and the Federal Building.

And when that limit was lifted in the 1950s and the skyline started to grow, it was in the severe Modern-style mold: boxy and boring, cold and corporate. Not helping was a city ordinance requiring flat roofs to accommodate helicopter landing pads.

While a few of the recent additions to the skyline have been more sophisticated—notably the red-granite, polygonal Crocker Center complex designed by the San Francisco office of Skidmore, Owings & Merrill—the bland, conservative look that we see in "L.A. Law" dominates.

But that look, happily, may be changing as indicated recently by the dedication of one building and the ground breaking for another.

DEDICATED EARLIER THIS MONTH WAS 1000 WILSHIRE, LOCATED JUST EAST OF the Harbor Freeway between Wilshire Boulevard and 7th Street. The 485,000-square-foot structure was designed by the New York-based firm of Kohn Pederson Fox, in association with the Los Angeles firm of Langdon Wilson Mumper Architects.

Working with the Reliance Development Group, headed by a relentless Henry Lambert, the architects have fashioned a building that, in a welcomed contrast to its bland neighbors, lends the skyline some verve.

Whatever the style might be called—it has been arbitrarily labeled Post-Modern—the structure makes the most of its site by presenting a provocatively clad and shaped facade, an engaging entrance gate and plaza, and an elegant lobby detailed in marble.

The light-gray granite facade with accents of black granite and black glass form articulated fenestrations in varying combinations from different perspectives to provide the 21-story building a distincitve rhythm. And though the banding of the building seems to this eye a bit heavy, it is striking, particularly at night, when among other things, the classical style penthouse is lit up.

As for the sign on the building, even though it was chiseled into granite and not stuck on in the form of a billboard, I still think it is tacky, like putting labels on the rear of jeans. You would think the building's architecture was enough of a signature for Coast Savings.

PROMISING TO BE THE SIGNATURE BUILDING FOR ALL OF DOWNTOWN IS Library Tower, the ground for which was broken last week at 5th and Hope streets. The 1.5-million-square-foot structure was designed for the Maguire Thomas Partners with elan by Henry Cobb and Harold Fredenburgh of the firm of I. M. Pei & Partners.

Certainly, the tapered, crown-topped circular structure, clad in a pale rose marble and rising 1,017 feet (73 stories) in a series of setbacks, to be the city's tallest—indeed the tallest in the West—promises to provide the Los Angeles skyline a stylish focal point it has long lacked.

As with so many other designs by the prolific Pei office, there is nothing modest about the tower. It makes a bold statement, and whether the windows and fenestratins might be too monotonous and the scale too much for the site, judgment must await the project's completion, scheduled for late 1989.

But even more exciting and potentially affecting more people and the city's image is a stairway following the western curve of the base of the office tower from Hope to 5th streets. Designed with a flourish by landscape architect Lawrence Halprin, the steps will be graced with a cascading water garden, and marked by terraces providing space for outdoor cafes, lounging and people watching.

The steps also will provide a vital link in a proposed pedestrian network unifying downtown from Bunker Hill to South Park. Critical to this marvelous concept is the development of the library's west lawn.

Unfortunately, the plan for the lawn has been dropped from the first phase of the renovation and expansion of the Central Library, which is tied to the development of the office tower in a complex financial package involving the transfer of air rights.

The lawn was squeezed out by an excessive program embraced by the library and an excessive scheme fashioned to accomodate it by the architectural firm of Hardy Holzman Pfeiffer. Both the program and the scheme need to be reduced, in the interest of the budget, the scale of the landmark library as originally designed by Bertram Goodhue, and the lawn.

This is no time for the library board to get greedy or the architects vain. No one wants to delay the library project, but at the same time no one wants to see mistakes made that will haunt it and the city for generations.

—June 28, 1987

Fox Plaza: Nice Style, Poor Design

THE RECENTLY COMPLETED FOX PLAZA OFFICE TOWER IN CENTURY CITY already has become an architectural focal point on the Westside.

What makes the building at the southwest corner of the Avenue of the Stars and Olympic Boulevard stand out in addition to its not immodest 34 stories is its distinctive form and style.

Not another boxy, boring building in the severe International style, the Fox Plaza is clad in pink-toned granite and gray tinted glass and tilted and angled at the upper floors to subtly reflect light.

The building, styled by R. Scott Johnson of Pereira Associates in a updated Moderne fashion, looks good, especially at a distance and when compared to most of the other office towers in the area. Even

95

the garage with its banded concrete block and arched entry is distinctive looking.

But looking good doesn't necessarily mean being good.

The closer I looked at Fox Plaza on a tour there recently the less impressed I was, and it illustrated for me the increasingly misunderstood difference in architecture between style and design; style generally being how something is expressed—the look of it—and design generally being the plan for a function—how it works.

Most disappointing was the entry. The two central sections of the broad stairs off the Avenue of the Stars lead directly into a bulky column; not a particularly gracious gesture in front of the entrance of a public building, or any building. The entry off the court, where most people pass through, also has a column dividing it.

And while the lobby is tastefully detailed in granite and Moderne-styled light fixtures, the columns blocking the natural light cast a pall over the space and makes it feel oddly claustrophobic. The unattractive facade of the Merrill Lynch office in the lobby does not help.

Disappointing also was the landscaping, which on the street side with its lawn, looked more appropriate to a suburban split-level house than an office tower aspiring to be urbane. The rear motor court has a view, but little else. The offices being private and of varying functions were not toured.

IN PLANNING A BUILDING, ONE OF THE FIRST THINGS TO BE CONSIDERED IS THE circulation system—how people enter, move through and leave a structure. It is the key to the functioning of a building, and often the key to the building's design. Then comes the styling, which might express the design, hide it or ignore it.

That is the usual order of the architectural process. But in these days when some architects, and critics, consider the look of the building—its so-called statement—more important than its function, that process can become convoluted.

As for Fox Plaza, it gets high marks for style and low marks for the design of the public areas. The architecture was a grandstand play that didn't quite make it.

A MORE EGREGIOUS EXAMPLE OF THE GAP BETWEEN DESIGN AND STYLE, AND what might be called architectural grandstanding, is the California Aerospace Museum in Exposition Park. I selected the museum because it is a public building that has received considerable publicity and praise.

As styled by Frank Gehry contends, the museum is a sculptural collision of forms and materials: a plain stucco box with a metal-clad polygon, separated by a glazed wall and topped by a windowed prism and a metal sphere. An F-104 Starfighter jet is a nice touch of advertising to the billboard building.

Gehry being a master of architectural showmanship, there is much in the styling to catch the eye and generate interest.

The design of the museum is another matter. To see the problem, you only have to stand to the south and watch people searching for an entry trek up long, raw exit ramps or cluster at the service entrance beneath the jet—and bang on doors.

Eventually they wander, with difficulty, around the structure to a small entryway that has been tucked between the museum and the old armory to the north, usually to be confronted there by hordes of children exiting. The space does not read well and is at best awkward. The interior circulation is not much better.

We have been told that museum officials wanted the entrance there, as a logical connection between the museum and the neighboring armory, the latter eventually to be renovated for additional exhibition space. That, no doubt, created a perplexing planning and architecture problem.

Solving such a problem by designing the building to both work and read well is what makes great architecture; succumbing to the problem to play with forms and materials to make a statement about style does not.

The style of the museum may say something about the building and its setting, as Gehry contends, but it won't help the teacher with 20 or so 9-year-olds in tow that I observed recently trying to keep order while searching in the hot sun for the entrance.

—Sept. 20, 1987

A Plus and Minus for Civic Center

THE PRIME CONSIDERATION IN THE RECENT APPROVAL BY THE COUNTY Board of Supervisors of a proposal for a private office building in the Los Angeles Civic Center was economics.

Simply put, RCI (Raffi Cohen Industries) and WCC (Westinghouse Credit Corp.) offered the county, in partnership with the state and the city, the best deal if it allowed them to develop the vacant 4.6-acre site on the north side of 1st Street between Broadway and Spring Street for a $125-million office building.

Such a basis for approval is unfortunate, for the county also has an obligation to see than land under its aegis is developed to benefit the public aestheticaly as well as financially. After all, government is not supposed to be a bottom-line operation, but a public trust.

However, given the bent these days of the country board and other public bodies, good design tends to occur, not becuase of government but despite it.

Happily, a case in point is the RCI and WCC proposal. While the board's decision was based primarily on economics, the scheme designed by Helmut Jahn of the Chicago firm Murphy/Jahn for the 21-story structure shows promise of lending the Civic Center some needed architectural verve.

The scheme calls for a bold structure set back from 1st Street, with the south and north facades accented by a super grid of cross bracing, covering what appears to be in the model a smaller grid of floor to floor scale. The facade is punctured by a 12-story-high opening, forming a monumental entry to the building and a gateway to a mall linking Broadway to Spring Street an an axis with City Hall.

Topping the high-tech geometric concoction like a small hat on a broad-shouldered giant robot made from an erector set is a four-story pyramidal-shaped frame echoing the pyramidal top of City Hall. The shape is repeated in the glass and steel tops of the four food kiosks on the mall and the retail arcade proposed to line the 1st Street facade.

Not indicated in the scheme is the coloring of the building, which is a concern, for Jahn in other such buildings has leaned to a brash and unappealing Crayola look. It just doesn't go well with his lyrical machine imagery. And definitely in need of some sophistication and sensitivity is the landscaping, which, in the model, appears hard and harsh.

But these items can be corrected relatively simply. What is important, and welcome, is the scheme's urbanity. With its base of retail shops and restaurants, places to eat outside, and a child-care center, the office tower, if developed as indicated, should lend the Civic Center new life. Certainly the architecture will give it a boost.

NOT VERY URBANE IS THE 1,400-SPACE GARAGE PROPOSED BY THE LOS Angeles Times on the site of its present parking lot, between Broadway and 2nd, 3rd and Spring streets.

According to the model of the proposed garage, it is a nondescript structure, connected by pedestrian bridges to The Times guilding to the north across 2nd Street and to an existing garage to the east across Spring Street.

As someone who works on occasion in The Times building and parks in the open lot, I sympathize with the need for the bridge over 2nd Street. It will be convenient, relieve some of the crush in the building's present elevators and not visually impair an already raw side street.

But the proposed bridge over Spring Street is another matter. The street is a major corridor leading into and through a struggling historic district. A bridge over it would be a distraction, and not very neighborly.

If security on the street is a problem, it will not be solved by abandoning the street, but by encouraging more activity there. That is why the lack of stores, restaurants or food stands on the ground level ont he Spring Street and Broadway frontage of the proposed garage also is disappointing.

While the cluster of stores and stands wrapping around the southeast corner of 2nd Street and Broadway will be saved, more such sidewalk activity is needed, not less, as will be the result of the ill-conceived Spring Street pedestrian bridge.

The garage, as proposed, shows little imagination and is not a particularly friendly gesture toward downtown.

—Sept. 27, 1987

THE DESIGN COMPETITION BETWEEN THREE WORLD-ACCLAIMED ARCHITECTS for a major downtown development that I wrote about with enthusiasm a few months ago turned out to be something less.

This is a problem these days with so many architectural competitions across the country vying not only for the best design solution for their particular project but also for the biggest names and headlines.

What I found so exciting about the competition here was the location and program of the proposed project—a mixed-use development of 2 million square feet on nearly 5 acres just east of the Harbor Freeway at 9th Street. I felt that in the combination was the potential to fashion a superstructure to lend the downtown skyline some needed identity and the streetscape, verve.

And making the competition, organized with much fanfare by the Parkhill Partners, even more attractive was that it pitted Michael Graves of Princeton, N.J., and of Post Modernist fame, against high-tech advocates Helmut Jahn of the Chicago-based firm of Murphy/Jahn, and John Andrews of Australia.

As one would have expected from the three architects involved, there was a spirited presentation of distinctly varied schemes. Andrews proposed a futuristic high-rise composed of clusters of pods; Jahn, three slick towers encased in an exposed structural grid, and Graves, two pairs of twin towers clad with his trademark cookie-cutter collage of classical elements. I preferred the scheme by Jahn.

A decision was promised by Parkhill within days, but when the days became weeks and the weeks a month, I began to worry that once again we had been a witness to less a design effort than a public relations effort to test the real estate waters.

Eventually, came word that Graves has been selected as the architect and that he was radically altering the scheme he had proposed. It appears the decision of whom to select was not particularly based on the schemes but on which architectural firm was most accommodating. So much for private design competitions.

But competitions and corporate conveniences aside, we can be grateful that the original scheme by Graves was, in effect, abandoned. As I had written in the original column on the competition, I felt the style, palette and materials proposed by Graves combined to create a classical cartoon of his award-winning Humana Building in Louisville, Ky. We already have enough recycled designs downtown.

More promising is the design by Graves indicated in the photograph of the study model of his latest scheme for Parkhill. However, before expending more ink on the project I will wait until it seems more real than a model and a press release.

Meanwhile, the project and its potential to create a more architecturally engaging downtown persists.

—May 1, 1988

A Heaping Portion of Fish Shticks

BEING OFFERED AT THE MUSEUM OF CONTEMPORARY ART DOWNTOWN ARE some choice architectural tidbits artfully presented and a heaping portion of fish shticks.

The fare is the long-awaited retrospective of Los Angeles-based Frank Gehry, whose guileless exploration of symbols, shapes and materials in a range of diverse designs has blurred the traditional lines between art, architecture and kitsch.

Though he is yet to design a major building, Gehry's singular efforts defying easy categorization (post-modern? punk? petulance?) and his penchant for publicity have made him one of the world's more prominent and honored architects.

And just as many of his didactic buildings have challenged the way we experience architecture in the shifting setting of the city, Gehry in the limited confines of MOCA has designed an installation that expands our experience of an architecture exhibit.

It is what one would expect from a show mounted by Gehry, especially in a museum he had yearned to design but did not. (That commission went to Japan's Arata Isozaki, while Gehry got to do the Temporary Contemporary on a much more modest budget.) Assisting in mounting the Gehry show was MOCA architectural curator Elizabeth Smith.

In addition to the usual montage of models, drawings and photographs, featured in the exhibit are four striking constructions that present a sort of architectural language with which Gehry designs. They include a towering ziggurat of dark-stained Finnish plywood, a pair of brightly polished copper and gray lead-coated copper clad rooms, a house fashioned out of honeycombed cardboard, and a structure in the form of a fish.

The fish, replete with sheet-lead scales, dominates the first gallery and invites you to experience the structure. Inside, giving off a weak light, is a translucent lamp sculpted by Gehry in the form of a fish. What this apparent fish fetish has to do with architecture is explained on a panel on a nearby wall that describes a proposed office and apartment complex that Gehry has designed for a site in Dallas.

"The interesting thing about all the fish studies for me has been the ability to capture movement in a built form," states Gehry. "The movement of the scales of a fish is something I'm trying to transmit into architecture," he says, noting in particular that the office building for the ambitious Turtle Creek Dallas project comes out of the fish form.

You have to look very hard at the model to see the form and the connection, and harder still to accept it as a major design determinant, or even as a whimsical metaphor, particularly from someone like Gehry, who in his early years so valiantly confronted and incorporated the issues of context, materials and shape.

The fish form is very much evident in the scheme Gehry designed for a waterfront restaurant in Kobe, Japan, and that is presented in Gallery B in an exquisite model, excellent photographs and weak drawings. But in the design, the towering copper-clad fish sculpture of chain-link mesh is simply and, to be sure, effectively used as an advertisement, not as a form giver in the rich Los Angeles tradition of programmatic architecture.

As for the squiggly and sketchy ink and pencil drawings, in addition to being, frankly, not very good, their selection also indicates Gehry's preoccupation with form, that is, how the structures look as volumes playing against each other or by themselves.

Missing are floor and space studies, or perspectives examining circulation patterns and how the structures actually might work.

While architecture is usually identified by the way space is manipulated, it is what happens in that space that really defines architecture.

An example, displayed in the South Gallery, is the Norton House, which Gehry describes as his "pride and joy." Here again, the emphasis is on the project's sculptural integrity, with the only hint of how the occupants might experience it a photograph taken from the living room looking out toward the beach. The view is not of the beach, but of the rear of a playful tower Gehry had erected as a gesture to the owner, who once was a lifeguard.

Also in the South Gallery is the plywood ziggurat and copper-clad rooms, the play and contrast of which I think dramatically suggest the sculptural effect Gehry is striving for, particularly in his later, more sophisticated and less financially constrained projects. These include the Winton guest house in Wayzata, Minn., and a house for a sprawling site in Brentwood, both of which are displayed.

There is no mention or hint of fish or whims in Gehry's comments concerning the Brentwood project or, for that matter, his design of a laser laboratory for the University of Iowa, even though it is located on the Iowa River; for a speculative office complex focused on water gardens adjacent to the Santa Monica airport, or for a residence for the Yale Psychiatric Institute in New Haven to house 60 adolescent schizophrenics. It seems Gehry, when not playing the role of architecture's aging *enfant terrible* or pretending to be a carefree artist, can be almost commercial.

Also revealing of a more sober Gehry are the displays of his design for the Loyola Law School and, with artists Claes Oldenburg and Coosje van Bruggen, Camp Good Times. Gehry seems to have viewed both projects as a response to the people and places involved, rather than as a puzzle to be cleverly manipulated into a statement about art and architecture. It is no coincidence that these are his best works to date.

Displayed in the cardboard house and hung from the wall of a passageway leading from the South Gallery to Gallery D is a collection of Gehry's cardboard furniture. They look raw, cheap and awkward, something for the kids to play with and on, but not too near the fireplace.

Though the cardboard seems like fun, and the snakes and fish fashioned out of Colorcore displayed in Gallery D are cute, it seems to me to be not art or architecture but, respectively, low-grade and high-style kitsch. They are also not a particularly inspiring or representative display with which to end the exhibit. You might want to return to the first gallery, take another look and leave from there.

While Gehry's investigations of forms and materials have been mixed, weakened, I feel, by his shticks, they have expanded the experience of architecture as an art. His sculptural essays cannot be compared to, say, Labrouste's building of a lightweight cast-and-wrought-iron infrastructure over the reading room of the Bibliotheque Nationale in Paris, or Brunelleschi's dome over Santa Maria dei Fiore in Florence. But, as demonstrated by this exhibit, it is significant, if only for its promise and the inspiration of future generations of architects.

—Feb. 21, 1988

On display at the Museum of Contemporary Art downtown is an exhibit of the work of Los Angeles architect Frank Gehry, whose idiosyncratic designs have catapulted him to international fame.

The exhibit, mounted by Gehry, includes about 250 drawings, photographs and scale models of his architecture, as well as furniture, furnishings, stage designs and odd pieces of art he has fashioned.

As an illustrative supplement to the exhibit, a short tour of Gehry's projects that have been built locally is very much in order. After all, for the best display of the art of architecture, there is nothing like seeing and experiencing the actual projects.

The projects Gehry has designed over the last two decades cannot be categorized as, say, Post-Modernist, Constructivist or Minimalist,or explained as self-promotion, genius, or simply archtectural anxiety. They have been too varied, and their results, as architecture that serves the user and the surrounding community, too mixed.

Gehry's earlier designs, in which he often used exposed and misshappen raw materials, such as plywood, corrugated sheet metal and chain-link fencing, have been interpreted as inspired attempts to capture the drama of the construction process. They also have been described as bold challenges to accepted architectural "norms," and brazen statements about the use of the structure and its setting.

Perhaps the most dramatic example of this phase of Gehry's career was the design of his own house at the southwest corner of Washington Avenue and 22nd Street in Santa Monica. Here, in 1977, he took a modest pink, nondescript, two-story house, exposed portions of the framework and wrapped it all in an expanded shell of odd-angled metal, plywood, glass and chain link.

According to Gehry, the design explored the collision of materials, their geometry and their layering to create a tension between the old and new house, not to mention the house·and its surroundings. Though the remodel and expansion were completed 10 years ago, the unfinished, raw materials make the house appear that it is still under construction, or deconstruction, an effect the architect says he wanted to achieve.

Other residents Gehry designed in this mode and which can be seen from the street are the Spiller House, a corrugated-metal-sheathed duplex at 39 Horizon Ave., and three attached artist studios at 326 Indiana Ave. Both projects are in Venice and very much at home there.

Each studio in the Indiana Avenue complex is clad in a different material; green asphalt, unpainted plywood and blue stucco, mimicking the tone of the eclectic neighborhood. Check out the windows. Because of some confusion over the survey, site and plans, all the windows that face south were supposed to face north.

Also in Venice, at Ocean Front Walk and 25th Street, is Gehry's Norton House, a chaotic stack of varied building materials, including logs used as a sun screen. The materials look as if they were washed up onto the beach to form a structure focused on a lifeguard tower. Though the tower does not work particularly well as a study, which it is supposed to be, and blocks part of the view of the ocean from the house, it has become a landmark.

The Norton House represents Gehry's more recent architectural explorations, in which he breaks down each of his projects into various elements, leaving them to stand seemingly at random, attached or detached, to create a fragmented, sculptural set piece. Different materials are used in some of the projects to further accent the pieces.

Varied examples include the Cabrillo Maritime Museum, 3730 White Drive in San Pedro; the Frances Howard Goldwyn Library at 1623 Ivar Ave. in Hollywood; the Loyola University Law School, 1441 Olympic Blvd. in Pico Union.

The most successful of the four projects, in my opinion, is Loyola, where the fragmented structures, hinting at a raw classicism, form a modest, street-wise campus. More confused is the Aerospace Museum, where trying to find the main entrance is an adventure. As for the awkwardly sited Cabrillo Museum, I find the excessive use there of chain link fence, a Gehry "trademark," hostile and not particularly user-friendly.

—Feb. 20, 1988

Architecture as Sculptural Objects

DECONSTRUCTIVISM, ARCHITECTURE'S NEW WAVE, WASHED UP ON THE shores of New York's Museum of Modern Art (MOMA) here recently as a heralded exhibit, depositing what looks like fragments of shipwrecks and a dead fish or two. And as such detritus tends to do after a few weeks, it smells.

But the smell is not of rank decay. Some of the projects exhibited under the ill-defined banner of deconstructivism display a range of personal architectural and artistic interpretations that exude the *Sturm und Drang* of the design process and its multiple aesthetic considerations.

Rather the smell is of a sweet corruption that comes when sincere, if obtuse explorations of theory more suited to design studios, sculpture exhibits and graduate theses are scooped up by a fading dilettante desperate to be *au courant*, and declared the next "look" in the increasing fad-conscious world of architecture.

Immodestly promoting this modest exhibit is Philip Johnson, who in the past has ridden in the curl of the International Style, as director or architecture at MOMA in the early 1930s, of fascism as a commentator for a right-wing journal in the late 1930s, of Modernism as a MOMA benefactor and sometimes architect in the 1950s and '60s, and of Postmodernism, as the salesman, with design partner John Burgee, of some of the more fanciful corporate cathedrals of the last decade.

Having finessed his way to the position of architecture icon, Johnson now has taken it upon himself to promote deconstructivism, which, oddly, is a rejection of the frills and historicism of Postmodernism that he so recently championed. If anything, it is a strained, self-conscious reworking of Modernism, where structure is skewed, columns collide, walls tilt and roofs float away.

According to a wall panel in the exhibit, deconstructivism is "an architecture of disruption and dislocation, of displacement and distortion," in which pure form has been "contaminated" and transformed into "an agent of instability, disharmony and insecurity, of discomfort, disorder and conflict." In sum, a pie in the face, or L.A. after the Big One.

Concerning the label, a subject of some debate at present, it is rooted in the Russian avant-garde art scene known as Constructivism that flourished at the time of the Russian Revolution in 1917. To emphasize the link, a sampling of this art is displayed in the first gallery of the Deconstructivist show.

As a promoter, Johnson usually has been a little late picking up trends, and when he has, tends to associate with an idea man. For Modernism, it was with Henry-Russell Hitchcock and Alfred Barr and the mounting of the famed 1932 show, which came very much in the wake of Schindler, Neutra and the Bauhaus; for fascism, Father Charles Edward Coughlin, in 1939, when Germany already was on the march, and for Postmodernism, embracing Michael Graves after Robert Venturi and Charles Moore had stirred the waters and Charles Jencks had bottled it.

Helping the 82-year-old Johnson mount and explain the Deconstructivist exhibit was Mark Wigley, an architectural historian out of the University of Auckland, New Zealand, who lectures at Princeton. You can almost always count on an academic trying to define and label any architectural blip, no matter how arbitrary and obscure.

As for the timing, the exhibit comes no less than 10 years after Frank Gehry "deconstructed" his Santa Monica house, exposing wood framing, using bits and pieces of raw materials in an expansion and, generally, playing games with forms and perspectives. This very personal experiment, which generated considerable publicity for Gehry, was, in time, sanctified as a melding of art and architecture, or at least something different to debate.

The Gehry house, of course, is included in the exhibit. Of particular interest is that the model used indicates that a substantial addition is planned, including what looks like three outbuildings of varying forms and materials, related but connected to the original house, a lap pool, a cluster of leaning telephone poles and a large canopy in the form, I presume, of two cleaned and fileted fish. The proposal looks as if it will need a zoning adjustment and, no doubt, will generate some debate.

The only other project of the 10 displayed in the exhibit that at least, in part, has been built, is a striking, fragmented and distorted collection of structures by Bernard Tschumi for a park on the outskirts of Paris. Others include plans for a research center of varying and conflicting forms by Peter Eisenman, an expressively complex housing complex by Daniel Libeskind, a more formal and subtle housing project by Rem Koolhas, studies of a chaotic rooftop studio and a stylized skyscraper by the Viennese firm of Coop Himmelblau and a competition entry by Zahaj Hadid for a gravity-defying mountain-side club.

Unfortunately, most of the projects are treated as sculptural objects, with few hints at how they might function as habitable space, if they can, or how they relate, if at all, to their sites and surroundings. For example, while the Himmelblau rooftop studio is an exquisite construction, there is no indication how it will be used, what style or how high, or where the building it sits on is.

What seems to have been put aside in these diverse, challenging projects awkwardly assembled and arbitrarily stamped "Deconstructivist" by Johnson and Wigley is, what I feel should be architecture's prime concern: creating a compatible space for a human endeavor; a space that also does not mock or ignore its context, but improves it, indeed, heals it.

However interestingly and imaginatively these and similarly styled projects deal with such issues as mass, scale, materials, expression, and construction, I believe that if they are not founded on the social import of space it is not architecture but sculpture.

Though architecture can be sculptural, it differs from sculpture in that it is a social art, with hope serving the user, and the environment. If not, then it belongs in a museum where, when the fad fades, it can be packed up and put away.

—July 24, 1988

A World-Class Housing Need

"We require from buildings, as men, two kinds of goodness," wrote 19th-Century architecture critic John Ruskin. *"First, doing their practical duty well; then that they be graceful and pleasing in doing it."*

If ever there was a need in the Los Angeles area for the broad support of an imaginatively operated, sensitively designed affordable, in-fill housing program it is now; a program that is both practical and pleasing.

The pernicious cutbacks in federal assistance, the stringency of rent control, the continued demolition of low-cost units, accelerated by the need to comply with new seismic codes, and the gentrification of select neighborhoods, have in varied ways cut deeply and disastrously into the region's affordable housing.

Not helping either has been the retreat on all levels of government of a bloated development bureaucracy into paper-lined shells, the avarice of some landlords, the greed of speculators and, generally, in our planning and architecture schools, the inability to address social concerns.

The result has been an estimated shortfall in Los Angeles of nearly a quarter of a million affordable housing units. Not even the increasing, unsafe and unsanitary conversion of garages and backyard sheds into illegal apartments, nor makeshift recreational vehicles, the overcrowding of tents in the region's campgrounds, or the homeless shelters or the cardboard boxes under the freeways, can keep up with the demand.

In this respect, Los Angeles is turning into a world-class city in the way Calcutta, Rio de Janeiro and Manila are world-class cities, with a growing underground population. To be sure, there are no sprawling hillsides here of steamy squatter shacks—yet. Our homeless and ill-housed population is harder to see. Like our region, it is fragmented, but it is there (and should get worse this winter when the snowbirds arrive).

Meanwhile, our design consciousness is focused on the monster mansions being overbuilt here, the pricey, over-designed restaurants where the owners of the mansions, and their friends and followers, overeat, and the overtly promoted social events where they promenade.

And let us not forget the overpriced, self-congratulating architectural conferences, such as the one this weekend where for an entry fee of $350 one could have heard a select group of architects and academicians with an Eastern orientation discuss the development of Los Angeles in the 20th Century. The event that also included tours of local landmarks was sponsored by the national AIA, which because of its pronounced programmatic prejudices, is becoming known as the Atlantic seaboard Institute of Architects.

DESPITE WHAT SEEMS TO BE THESE DAYS A DECIDED PUBLIC AND PROFESSIONAL bent in design for the banal, a few desperately needed housing projects are being produced. However modest, they are to me much more important than a trendy play by an architect of symbols, typology, metaphors or materiality in some new boutique, eatery or house, offering as they do, some rays of hope for more humane and livable city.

The projects include in Boyle Heights, a transitional shelter for the homeless; in West Hollywood, the rehabilitation of a 28-unit apartment house; in Torrance, two new senior citizen projects; in Pico Union, an 18-unit courtyard complex, and in Santa Monica's Ocean Park, a scattered-site cooperative development. What a few might lack in style, a result of stringent budgets, they compensate with spirit.

Making the Chernow House Shelter dedicated last week in Boyle Heights particularly pleasing is that not only will it provide a transitional facility for homeless families with children, but that it also saves a historically significant Moderne-styled structure that adds a sense of style and stability to the street.

Located at 207 N. Breed St., the building had served as medical offices before being vacated and slipping into disrepair. Then along came the L.A. Family Housing Corp., an innovative, nonprofit corporation that for the last few years has been quietly, and efficiently, developing relatively modest in-fill affordable housing projects.

Instead of demolishing the structure, the corporation, under the indefatigable direction of architect Arnold Stalk and with the aid of the city's Community Redevelopment Agency and others, undertook a sensitive, adaptive reuse. The result is a a modest, 20-unit, 80-bed facility that respects the users and honors the memory of Alex Chernow, a former insurance executive for whom the facility is named.

This is the third and most ambitious transitional facility the corporation has completed; the others being a conversion of a motel and restaurant in North Hollywood, and a vacant apartment building in the Wilshire District. It also has developed three permanent, affordable housing projects, and is working on three more, including a modest eight-unit one next door to Chernow House, to be called Irmas Village.

THE IDEA IS THAT CHERNOW HOUSE IS A TRANSITIONAL FACILITY, WHERE families can live up to six months while receiving social services, looking for jobs and, generally, getting their lives back into shape. The long-term solution is for the families to break the cycle of hardship and move into affordable housing.

There are other problems to be solved, but obviously, housing is a major one, especially for families with children. That there are an estimated 10,000 children among the estimated 50,000 homeless in Los Angeles prompts one to wonder why there are not 100 Chernow Houses, and 1,000 Irmas Villages?

Perhaps that question can be addressed by the architects meeting at the design conference today, where they are scheduled to take up the question of whether there should be "a new set of standards for America's quintessential 20th-Century city," according to an AIA press release. Perhaps we all should try to address the question.

—Nov. 6, 1988

Competitions: Risk and Rivalry

THE SELECTION OF THE ARCHITECT FOR MOST PROJECTS IS AKIN TO A closed-door, shades-drawn, back-room poker game, with the players limited to the politically, professionally and socially well-connected. But in the last few years, both invited and open design competitions increasingly have become fashionable, especially for public and high-profile projects, putting the architecture profession into a sharper light. In effect, competitions are the wild card in architecture today, changing some of the rules of the game, stirring' risk and rivalry, and chance and controversy.

Few weeks go by without the announcement of a design competition across the country and abroad, be it for an affordable-housing project in Colton, Calif.; a war memorial on Long Island, N.Y.; a vision of a futuristic Milwaukee; a park in Paris and an array of facilities for a host of schools.

Under way at present in the Los Angeles area are at least a half a dozen competitions in various forms and stages. These include the Walt Disney Concert Hall downtown, a symbolic gateway to the city bridging the Hollywood Freeway and a cultural arts park in the San Fernando Valley. Just concluded was one for the urban design of Olympic Boulevard in West Los Angeles, and in the Beverly Hills Civic Center, the result of another is nearing the completion of construction.

Whatever their respective merits, the differing designs of the four finalists in the limited, by-invitation-only competition for Disney Hall, scheduled to be unveiled soon, is sure to generate debate. Because only one of the four will be chosen, either Gottfried Boehm of West Germany, Hans Hollein of Austria, James Stirling of England or local Frank Gehry, three will be exposed as having been rejected, a position to one likes to be in, especially in the competitive, ego-involved world of design.

Gehry, along with Thomas Beeby of Chicago and Mario Botta of Switzerland, recently had been selected as finalists in a competition to design a new building for the San Francisco Museum of Modern Art. But the museum subsequently canceled the competition that would have involved developing a design concept, and instead, on the basis of interviews, selected Botta. "By not having the finalists produce a design, we saved time and money and probably avoided embarrassment," said a museum official.

The museum's decision raised anew the debate over competitions. These include complaints by architects of convoluted selection processes, predisposed juries and rising costs to produce appropriate submissions.

"Architectural competitions have become a combination marathon and steeplechase," commented New York-based architect Lance Brown, who has served as a professional adviser to competitions.

Yet an increasing number of aarchitects are responding to competitions, spurred on by peer pressure, a chance to display their talent, the need for work and the hope, however faint, for recognition. "They are irrestible, especially if you are young and hungry, or old and competitive, or a combination of the above," Brown added.

Still, for all their warts, competitions are a healthy exercise, especially for major public projects that, in the past, tended to be controlled by political and professional old-boy networks. But because there are no official rules governing competitions—the American Insititute of Architects tends to disdain them—some can get out of hand.

Among the problems have been competitors exceeding requested materials and producing drawings to dazzle juries, juries ignoring programs to peruse their own prejudices or jury members paying debts or scoring points with friends and associates by pressing for their selection, regardless of merit or qualifications. There have been rumors of the latter in the San Fernando Valley competition.

And when the finalists in the West Coast Gateway competitions were recently announced there were complaints from a few participants that the guidelines had been confused. *Disorganized* was one of the kinder words used by competitors Joe Nicholson and Mark Mills of San Diego in suggesting they be reimbursed for their effort.

"Sometimes the role of a competition is to test out a program that just might not be feasible, at least as presented to the competitors," said one of the jurors in the gateway competition. "I think that is the case in this competition. The question is whether the city wants to continue with what certainly will be an empty and embarrassing exercise, or face up to the reality and begin again."

Architectural competitions are now new. One of the first recorded was for a war memorial on the Acropolis sponsored by the Council of Athens in 448 B.C. Other world landmarks conceived in competitions include London's Parliament House, Berlin's Reichstag and Paris' Eiffel Tower. In the United States, it was competitions that generated the designs for the White House, the Washington Monument, the Vietnam Memorial and New York's Central Park.

WHILE EUROPE HAS MAINTAINED A TRADITION OF COMPETITIONS AS THE prime vehicle for selecting architects for public projects, the concept in the United States has waxed and waned. Prompting the most recent resurgence have been generous grants, guidelines and encouragement from the federal National Endowment for the Arts, initiated by Michael John Pittas when he was director of its design program in the early 1980s.

Generally, competitions are viewed by sponsors, be they private developers or public officials, as an excellent vehicle to generate varied solutions to a particular design problem, as well as publicity, public education and support, and, in some cases, financing.

"Frankly they are a marvelous if costly and time-consuming way to launch a project," said Marc Winogrond of the city of West Hollywood, which sponsored an open international design competition for its proposed civic center. "We received nearly 300 entries, the result of which was that we got 300 architects to test out our program instead of one. I'm just glad the jury picked a concept that I think is good and will work."

Said one of the losers: "Competitions give us a chance to show our stuff, and in this respect it is fun. We realize, of course, we are being taken advantage of, but it is our decision, isn't it? And there is always the chance we might win, especially if you have a friend on the jury."

For a critic, competitions also can be fun and instructive, for they offer a snapshot of sorts of current design prejudices. But obviously it is time for some standards, or architects, like turkeys at Thanksgiving, are just going to be increasingly feasted upon by both public and private clients.

—Dec. 4, 1988

In The Spirit of Disney

EVER SINCE THE FOUR FINALISTS IN THE DESIGN COMPETITION FOR THE Walt Disney Concert Hall were selected last March both the local and international architecture communities have been anxiously anticipating the results.

The anticipation was prompted in part by the public nature of the project, the prominent site at 1st Street and Grand Avenue downtown, the Disney name, along with a generous $50-million gift to make it all happen, and the complexity of the program, calling for, among other things, separate concert and chamber music halls, and a recognition of the urban context.

But heightening the anticipation by far was the array of architects selected to compete. In alphabetical order, they were Gottfried Boehm of West Germany, Frank O. Gehry of Los Angeles, Hans Hollein of Austria and James Stirling and Michael Wilford of England. Each is internationally known and respected, and though their respective practices and experiences vary greatly, each has a reputation for innovative designs and singular styles.

While the architects involved have at times contradicted and eschewed the labels that have been pinned on them, they can be generally classified: Boehm as a Neo-Expressionist, Gehry, an Eclectic Constructivist, Hollein, a mannered Post Modernist, and Stirling and Wilford, studied Post Modernists. Over the years, the latter also have passed through various styles, from High Tech to Brutalism and beyond. The fact is all are quite individualistic.

How in a particular time frame these world renowned architects with very different design prejudices responded to the same assignment, in my opinion, makes the Disney competition a yardstick of sorts of contemporary architecture; certainly it has been one of the more coveted competitions in recent years, with the finalists spending about half a year on their submissions. It has made all involved quite anxious.

In preparation for the final judging, the submissions, consisting of various drawings and detailed models, were displayed briefly last week. (One hopes that at a future date they can be put on public exhibition.) As for the winner, the Walt Disney Concert Hall Committee chaired by Frederick Nicholas, is expected to announce its choice within a few days.

No doubt the decision will be a difficult one, for as promised by the personalities involved, each of the submitted schemes is distinctive, each in its unique way seems to meet the complex program requirements of access, acoustics and other such needs, and each appears worthy of selection and construction. However, they do differ dramatically in expressing and accommodating their use, and the city.

Briefly, Boehm's scheme, I feel, is the most idiosyncratic, dominated by a giant glazed, opaque cupola, very much in a modern spirit of a huge Victorian garden folly, ringed in part by raised terraces. The effect at least in model is that of a giant white webbed derby hovering at the end of 1st Street and Grand Avenue. Beneath the derby are the halls, foyers and other such spaces, well detailed, attractively expressed, and welcoming, an impression aided by the architect's exquisite drawings. It is not a derby to be dented.

Gehry's scheme is the most lyrical, featuring a concert hall of simple, sculpted limestone-clad forms gracefully sited and fronted with a foyer in the form of a great glass conservatory, to be filled with native California flora. According to the architect's statement, the conservatory and the plaza it opens up to could be in effect "a living room for the city," a place for promenading, sitting, exhibits and concerts. Edging the plaza is an attractively domed cafe and a bulky chamber music hall begging for a mural or wall sculpture, and to be scaled down. Still, the scheme sings, particularly along Grand Avenue.

110

Hollein's scheme is the most playful, a jumble of colors, forms and materials, including alumnium and gilded surfaces, white marble, green quartzite, red sandstone and gray granite, that from different angles appear like a bright, witty architectural cartoon strip. Yet the variety of landscaped plazas and attractively detailed foyers seem inviting, and the concert hall quite functional, expressing a geometry suggested by the acoustical demands. The total is exhuberant.

THE SCHEME BY STIRLING AND WILFORD IS AN ENGAGING, PROVOCATIVE assemblage, "an ensemble of architectral forms expressing the functional elements of the program . . . a microcosm of the city." It is not what I would have expected from the duo whose recent buildings have been Post Modern exercises with a capital P. There is a very accessible glazed concourse, a variety of active spaces, a jumble of circulation systems, and a striking, flexible concert hall. Also encouraged, as do the other schemes, is a pedestrian oriented Grand Avenue animated by landscaping, street furniture and furnishings, and the hint of sidewalk cafes and vendors.

All also are in sharp and welcomed contrast to the generally bland neighboring buildings, in particular the neo-classical-styled Music Center across the street, which should be energized by the project. As such, all promise in their variety of spaces, forms and styles to be accessible and inviting, very much in the spirit of Walt Disney.

With this spirit in mind, if I was on the concert hall committee and had to make a choice, it clearly would be Gehry's scheme. And not because he is a local, but because his scheme is the most appropriate and the best.

More than his competitors, Gehry's scheme reads Los Angeles, thanks in large part to the proposed conservatory and plaza. He seems in the design to have grasped the promise of the site, dealt honestly with the context, instead of mimicking it, responded conscientiously and with style to the program, and embraced the region's climate and flora. The result is a project that is in sympathy with the user while playing to the potential on Bunker Hill for an appropriate casual, cultural oasis.

—Dec. 11, 1988

Gehry's scheme was chosen.

V

OF STREETS, TREES AND TRAFFIC

THE AGE-OLD CONFLICT IN LOS ANGELES BETWEEN CARS AD COMMUNITIES is escalating, particularly along the Wilshire corridor and west.

Communities there—from the Westlake District to Westwood—are complaining that more and more drivers frustrated by rush-hour traffic are turning to local streets in search of better routes to and from downtown and across the West Side.

"The traffic is like a spike being driven through the neighborhood," says Virginia Kazor of the Ridgewood-Wilton Neighborhood Assn. She adds that the resulting noise, pollution and accidents turn residents away from the street and their neighbors, damaging property values and a sense of community.

The communities want the city to discourage the through traffic by stricter enforcement of speed limits, the installation of more signals and stop signs, changing directions of local streets to create mazes to frustrate drivers or simply by closing streets.

Public officials are sympathetic, but those responsible for dealing with the problems say there is little they can do, given recent budget cuts. They note there are no funds for freeway improvements by the state, increased traffic surveillance by the police and street widenings, signal installations or even just a study by the city.

Even if the city or state could do something, a few concerned planners and administrators contend they should not. In support of their position, or rationalization, is the theory that if nothing is done an intolerable traffic situation will result, prompting the public at long last to demand a reasonable mass transit system.

No major official has come out flatly advocating this theory as policy, yet the city and region might soon find themselves embracing it—by default. Whatever the theories, they offer little comfort to the communities now beset with traffic.

"We have just about abandoned Beverwill Drive to the cars," says Marty Milden of the Beverlywood Homes Assn. He notes that the curving street through the community of 1,400 homes south of Pico Boulevard in effect has become a major highway for commuters to and from Century City.

The traffic really hurts the quality of life here, especially if you live on Beverwill, as I do," adds Milden. "No kids ride bicycles there like they used to. Even getting our cars out of the driveway is a problem because of the traffic past our houses. I just back out and hope for the best."

Milden, Kazor and other spokespersons for affected neighborhoods list traffic just behind crime as the major concerns of their communities. Supporting their perception that an increasing number of drivers are using local streets as alternative routes are various traffic studies.

The last comprehensive traffic study of the West Side was done by the city in 1977. It indicated that traffic then on Olympic Boulevard was averaging about 33,000 vehicles a day, up from 30,000 in 1970. During the same period traffic on 6th Street increased from about 16,000 vehicles a day to 18,000. Other streets showed similar trends.

The increases have probably escalated, particularly since the Santa Monica Freeway, the area's principal artery, reached its capacity in 1979, according to Caltrans. When a freeway is at capacity it is estimated that about 70% of the additional vehicles that would have used the route take to local streets.

According to a planning adage, traffic is like water coursing down a hill. It always finds the quickest and easiest path to flow into. When that path is blocked or reaches capacity, it then searches out another, seemingly oblivious to speed limits, traffic signals and stop signs.

Drivers finding Wilshire and Olympic boulevards or 6th Street too crowded, among others, turn off and wend their way to 3rd or 8th streets or whatever they hope may be clearer at the moment. Other cars follow, creating careering convoys up and down what were once quiet residential streets.

The conflict between the cars and the communities points up a schizoid quality to life in Los Angeles—Angelenos as drivers want the convenience of their cars to go to work and wherever, yet as residents want their communities free from through traffic. It is a contradiction they seem to live with.

"We recognize that people have to use cars to get around the city, but we would like to see a plan that diverts the through traffic and speeders from local streets to commercial streets," says Gary J. Herman of the Hancock Park Homeowners Assn.

One of the many problem streets in Hancock Park is Highland Avenue, where Herman has lived for 17 years. "It once was a lovely residential street, but it's now a semi-freeway," he says. Herman and the association have urged the city to divert the traffic from Highland to nearby La Brea Avenue.

In the Country Club Park area off Olympic Boulevard and Arlington Avenue, the neighborhood association there is circulating a petition to close five streets to through traffic. "The traffic is increasing and really hurting the neighborhood character," says Claudette Mack of the association.

The agency with the prime responsibility for traffic conditions in the city is the Transportation Department. While expressing sympathy for the communities plagued with traffic, the department says there actually is little it can do to relieve the problem.

"TO TRY TO DO SOMETHING ABOUT A PARTICULAR PROBLEM IN ONE AREA BY diverting it to another would create a domino effect," says Alice

113

Lepis, the department's principal transportation engineer. "Such solutions are only temporary, at best."

The department in the past has initiated some limited studies to see if the situation on local streets would be eased by making nearby major commercial streets one way, as has been recommended by neighborhood groups. When merchants on the streets complained to their local councilperson, however, the studies were dropped.

There also were complaints in the department that little consideration was given to traffic planning when the city approved such major developments as Century City, Warner Center and, more recently, Beverly Center. "No one really addresses the traffic impact until it is too late," says an official. "The city really has no transportation strategy."

Actually, the city does have a transportation plan. It was established in 1946 when a city zoning plan was approved designating what roads would be local and connector streets and secondary and major highways. On the West Side, most followed pre-World War II routes laid out when the area was just a collection of scattered settlements, farms, oil and bean fields and the dreams of realtors.

The only major revision to the plan on the West Side was the routing of the Santa Monica Freeway, which was completed in 1966. Its relief was temporary. As building has boomed downtown and west, traffic jams on the freeway have lengthened in size and time, prompting more and more drivers to turn to local streets.

The increase of through traffic and its problems on local streets across the West Side is seen as a harbinger of what in time will be occurring in communities farther out of the central city as the freeway system becomes more clogged.

"When freeways jam, drivers implement what we call an arterial strategy, which means thaty take to local streets," observes Mark Pisano of the Southern California Association of Governments, the region's principal planning agency.

"The situation on the West Side is just the tip of the iceberg," adds Pisano. He notes that there are signs that sections of the Harbor, Hollywood, San Diego and Ventura freeways also are beginning to leak traffic, just like the Santa Monica. "The situation will just get worse until there is a reasonable mass transit system as an alternative to the private car."

THE POSSIBILITY OF A MASS TRANSIT SYSTEM IN THE DISTANT FUTURE OFFERS little comfort to the neighborhood groups concerned with traffic now. What they say offers the best and most immediate relief is increased traffic surveillance of local streets by the Police Department. "More than anything else the presence of police controls traffic," says Kazor.

However, there are only 12 officers assigned to traffic duty on the entire West Side, according to Capt. Bayan Lewis of the area's division. "I sympathize with the residents, but we just don't have the personnel to do the job that should be done," he adds. "We're just operating on a hit-or-miss basis."

"It's really a shame," comments Kazor, whose group has been in a 10-year battle to preserve Wilton Place from 1st to 3rd streets as one of the city's three districts on the National Register of Historic Places.

"Here the city is now, finally, talking about the importance of preserving communities, yet it lets streets become community dividers, moats no one dares to cross, instead of common spaces where people can meet and mingle," says Kazor.

"Streets are critical to developing a sense of community," adds Edmond Ezra of the city Planning Department. "They should bind a community together, not divide it." With this in mind, Ezra has been urging the drafting of community plans that streets not be widened.

"From my experiences as a planner in San Francisco, when you widen streets you harm the local neighborhood character," he says. "And, anyway, no matter how much you widen to ease the traffic situation, the street inevitably fills up again and, in essence, you end up with the same problem you had before."

—Feb. 17, 1982

Downtown Debacle

GROUND WILL BE BROKEN ON BUNKER HILL TODAY FOR CALIFORNIA Plaza, a $1.2-billion commercial, residential and cultural complex that city officials have announced with fanfare will attract pedestrians and upgrade the quality of life downtown. So much for announcements.

Meanwhile, several blocks away, the city is blithely moving ahead on a project to narrow sidewalks and cut down mature shade trees along a portion of Flower Street that is heavily traveled by pedestrians. So much for the city's commitment to the concept of quality of life.

And this despite reams of recent studies concerning the future of downtown declaring how critical it is to enhance street life and encourage pedestrian use. It makes one wonder if those who conduct and write the studies paid for by public funds, and the officials up the municipal ladder to Mayor Tom Bradley who approve and praise them, ever bother to follow up on the policies recommended, or even simply walk the streets in question.

Recommended by the city's Department of Transportation and already routinely approved by the Department of Public Works and the City Council, the estimated $300,000 project calls for resurfacing and widening Flower Street between 6th Street and Wilshire Boulevard. Work is scheduled to begin within the next few weeks.

The widening will involve taking two feet off the sidewalk on the west side of the street and cutting down four mature ficus trees of girths up to about a foot standing gallantly 25 feet tall in front of 615 Flower St. The trees now lend shade for those waiting at the bus stops there and grace to a street that otherwise belittles its name.

The Department of Public Works says the two feet from the west sidewalk along with two more feet from the east sidewalk are needed to widen the street's traffic lanes to better accommodate buses and a left turn pocket from Flower Street south to Wilshire Boulevard east. It adds that the reduction will cut the width of the west sidewalk down to the city's minimum standard of 10 feet, contending that "it is adequate enough."

As for the trees, Marty Rashoff of the department said they would be replaced by three Hollywood Junipers of approximately 3-inch girths in 15-gallon planters. On the east sidewalk, where there are now no trees, five Canary Island pines of approximately the same size will be planted in tree wells.

In addition to destroying the trees already there for want of two feet, hurt also will be the sidewalk. It is now one of the busiest in the city, serving as a passenger stop for the downtown shuttle and other buses as well as a conduit for pedestrians scurrying back and forth between the office towers to the north and the retail shops and restaurants to the south.

Those two feet can make the difference from the sidewalk now being a tight walkway to a bottleneck that will push people out into the street. If anything, the sidewalk should be widened so it can accommodate more pedestrian traffic and even leave a little room for that distinctly urban ritual of meeting a friend at a street corner and standing there and talking while watching the world go by.

For all its grandiose plans to make downtown more accessible and attractive and for which it spends hundreds of thousands of dollars in studies, the city just does not yet seem to understand that walking also is a form of transportation. And a non-polluting one at that.

If the city feels it must have more space for vehicular traffic, instead of spending money to widen the roadway it should simply consider enforcing the no-parking laws in the area—and for which it no doubt would generate income while easing traffic. Despite signs prohibiting it, no less than six cars and two trucks were seen parked illegally between Wilshire Boulevard and 6th Street for at least one hour at noontime last week.

In fact, cars at times were double parked waiting for an illegal space to become vacant, causing buses, as is their practice, to stop in the middle of the street to let off and pick up passengers. As a result, there was a traffic jam.

IF A MAJOR GOAL OF THE CITY IS TO MOVE VEHICULAR TRAFFIC AS QUICKLY AS possible through downtown, as the transportation department states, a better solution might be to simply ban left turns or make all streets one way. But that would take some initiative and coordination that the department and other city agencies, including planning, public works and the Community Redevelopment Agency, have yet to demonstrate.

Of course, the easier it is for traffic to move through downtown or, for that matter, anyplace, the more vehicles the routes will attract. According to a planning adage, traffic is like water coursing downhill. It always finds the quickest and easiest path to flow into. When that path is blocked or reaches capacity, it then searches out another.

Pedestrians don't have it as easy in the city's ongoing conflict between people and cars. Street widenings downtown and along Melrose Avenue—to name just another area—and insensitive developments that discourage pedestrian traffic already have done irreparable harm to the city's burgeoning street life. And at a time when street life is being recognized as a vital element in retail sales, tourism and, generally, the city's ambiance.

The city is reaching a certain point in its development (one would like to say maturity) when it is time to stop talking about quality of life and the new downtown and start becoming more sensitive to those little items that actually shape its cityscape and give it warmth and character. Among such items are the four shade trees and the Flower Street sidewalk.

As a gesture to the city's struggling ambiance and to the thousands of people who work and visit downtown every day and who experience the modest stretch of sidewalk, these items in their modest way are as important to the future of Los Angeles as such major developments as the $1.2-billion California Plaza.

Perhaps after the ground-breaking ceremony on Bunker Hill today the self-congratulating city officials would for once abandon their chauffeured cars (which will probably be illegally parked) and, instead of going to the free luncheon hosted by the developers, take a walk downtown and begin to sense the issue.

—Oct. 12, 1983

The trees were saved.

Pedestrians Wait for the Bus

THE LOS ANGELES STREET SCENE festival was declared a smashing success by the city this year, but the event held a few weeks ago downtown actually had little to do with streets.

And if further examined from an urban design perspective, the festival appeared, if anything, to underscore the city's anti-pedestrian policies and pathetic planning practices.

For the record, an estimated 500,000 persons attended the festival each of the two days it was held in a car-free Civic Center to sample a diverse offering of ethnic foods, arts and crafts and entertainment. From all accounts it was fun.

But the setting created by closing off streets offered a false portrait of the city. Among other things, it is not particularly natural for people to wander off sidewalks, not even in Los Angeles, where many have been narrowed by the city to the width of a path.

The setting for the festival was more like a rambling park than a street. In urban design terms, there was no edge, such as a row of shops where someone might go to buy something. Such an edge defines a street and lends it character.

The festival was a scene, but not a street scene. This is an important distinction for those like myself who feel streets are the rivers of life of a city.

Also, two days a year does not create a pedestrian ambiance for downtown Los Angeles, where an estimated 300,000 persons descend every week day to work, shop and wander—without the benefits of street closings, sidewalk vendors, public toilets and free entertainment that were offered by the festival.

Instead, they must contend with streets flanked by raw sidewalks, forbidding walls, inaccessible plazas, hidden shopping malls and futuristic "pedways." What little character there is downtown, such as along Broadway, in Little Tokyo and in pockets here and there, has persevered despite the city, not because of it.

And seemingly lurking around various corners are bureaucrats who want to keep cutting down mature trees, eliminating viable retail shops and narrowing sidewalks to accommodate the automobile, and discouraging sidewalk cafes and vendors.

Bureaucrats such as Transportation Department manager Donald Howery seem only to worry about vehicular traffic, forgetting that walking also is a form of transportation. The result is that most of our streets are anti-pedestrian.

The attitude is a disservice to the city, for it is not sports arenas, shopping centers, historic landmarks, museums or theaters that charge a city with excitement, though they help. It is the ferment of streets; that is where people really experience a city.

To be sure, the city has talked a lot about wanting to create a healthy pedestrian environment, hinting at stricter design guidelines to prevent blank walls, closing or limiting traffic on select streets and encouraging vendors.

Indeed, three years ago the Los Angeles City Planning Department released a study that called for, among other things, allowing sidewalk cafes, converting a few parking lots to parks, planting more and better trees, actually widening sidewalks and recommending innovative street lighting and street furniture to better serve pedestrians.

The recommendations were drawn in part from the experiences of other cities, such as New York, Boston, Philadelphia and San Francisco, that with varying success had turned their downtowns into places for residents, workers and tourists to go to instead of get away from. In effect, the Los Angeles plan called for what amounted to sort of a permanent street scene festival.

But as usual, nothing was done about the downtown study after the department's director of planning, Calvin Hamilton, milked it for as much publicity as possible. Among the stories was one by me stating that the study was as welcome as a crosswalk signal announcing "WALK."

Asked what had happened to the study, a department official trading candor for anonymity declared that it had gotten lost in the bureaucratic bramble. "The fact is that when it became a little controversial, Hamilton just filed it away," he added. "That is the way things are done here, or, rather, not done."

Also apparently forgetting about a commitment to the pedestrian life of the city beyond the superficial level of holding a street festival once a year was Mayor Bradley. He supposedly blessed the study a few years ago, for whatever that is worth when civil servants are involved.

Lots of words and no action seem to sum up City Hall when planning issues are involved.

The situation is really a crime. Blessed with sunshine and moderate temperatures most of the year, a diverse ethnic population, imaginative merchants, talented designers and the experiences of other cities upon which to draw, Los Angeles should be able to generate a vibrant street scene downtown to match any in the world everyday of the year.

And even where there are some streets in the Los Angeles area that have an active pedestrian life, such as Ocean Front Walk in Venice, Main Street in Santa Monica, Melrose Avenue in West Hollywood and Fairfax and Westwood boulevards, it is a struggle to maintain because of short-sighted officials.

You would think that at long last they would understand that the life of a city is not measured by the height of its skyline, its traffic count, attendance at sporting events or the amount of campaign contributions, but by the quality of its streets.

—Oct. 14, 1984

Threats to Library Open Space

THERE WAS ANOTHER SCENE A FEW WEEKS AGO IN THE LONG-RUNNING TRAGI-comedy of downtown urban design.

The script for this episode involved another rueful attempt to hack away at the promised urbanity of the propsosed Library Square project.

The *femme fatale* of the tragicomedy is the $1-billion project. Imaginatively pieced together by the city's Community Redevelopment Agency (CRA), it consists of two distinctive office towers, a monumental stairway, a renovated and expanded central library and a reshaping of its parking lot and lawns into an attractive park.

The plot is involved. The rejuvenated landmark library no doubt will better serve the public, and the 65- and 73-story towers should lend verve to the city's spartan skyline.

But it is the park, with its sitting areas and scenes inviting pedestrian activity, the stairway and sidewalks that most people will experience. It is also these elements that are being threatened.

The latest scene was staged at a meeting of the City Council, where after some embarrassing buffonery by Chairman Gilbert Lindsay, the attempt to hack away at the project's Flower Street frontage was tabled, but the assault on the 5th Street and Grand Avenue frontage was not.

As for the actors, there was the city's Transportation Department, in its usual role as the villian. With a view of the city as straight and narrow as a concrete drain pipe, the department under the direction of Donald (Hackaway) Howery, wants as much sidewalk and park area it can sink its pneumatic drills into to turn into more traffic lanes that usually become illegal parking zones.

It asked the committee to "dedicate" 10 feet of the Flower Street frontage for a second left-hand turn lane, and up to 10 feet of the Grand Avenue and 5th Street frontages, for more lanes.

119

The takings would come off the space allocated for the sidewalks and park.

But with Flower Street earmarked for one-way traffic, negating the need for left-turn lanes, the department did not press its request for the dedication there.

That was the "compromise" Lindsay indicated was worked out in his office before the meeting and before the eloquent, rational appeals by the library board, Los Angeles Conservancy, committee member Michael Woo and others to reject the dedications.

Wanting all the frontage hacked away was Councilwoman Joan Milke Flores, who complained about how bad it was driving in and out of downtown these days. Though Flores professed to enjoy cities, noting she had just come back from a trip to Europe and "loved" walking there, her contradictory remarks were those of a parochial suburbanite.

Critical to the "compromise" was the CRA, which prior to the meeting had agreed to let the frontage be hacked away in return for the Transportation Department allowing a crosswalk on 5th Street and other concessions.

It was a tragic performance by the CRA. Here was the agency that had conceived and nurtured the project, one of the more ambitious and impressive undertakings in the nation, allowing it to be compromised just like a pathetic, desperate parent in a Third World country maiming a child so it can beg more effectively.

Unfortunately, just a minor actor was Mayor Tom Bradley, who sent a message to the committee through aide Fran Savitch, urging the dedication be rejected and the land reserved for pedestrians. But obviously his own department heads were more persuasive in their quiet appeals. If the meeting had had a campaign fund-raiser or a ribbon-cutting, perhaps the mayor would have attended and been more effective. Perhaps.

While articulate in his statements concerning a "new" and vibrant downtown Los Angeles, taking great pride and credit for such projects as Library Square, the mayor seems quite reluctant to get involved in the critical decisions that actually shape the projects. Just as the park is being nibbled away, so is Bradley's credibility as mayor.

And there, at the end of the meeting, as the curtain came down on the scene, was one of Howery's henchmen proclaiming that the Transportation Department had "won," as if the event had been some sort of athletic contest. What was clear was that the public had "lost."

But the tragicomedy is far from over. The committee's decision to dedicate the frontage now goes to the full council, where there has been a rising design consciousness and concern for the pedestrian.

The hope is that Woo can be joined there by others who realize that downtown is not Lindsay's district, but everyone's district, and that if Los Angeles is ever going to fulfill its magnificent potential as a vibrant city, it is going to have to better encourage and accommodate pedestrians.

A good way to start would be by saving a few more feet of sidewalk and park in the center of downtown.

—Dec. 1, 1985

THE DREAM OF A VITAL DOWNTOWN STREETSCAPE PERSEVERES, THANKS IN part to Councilman Michael Woo. He recently prevailed upon the City Council and its Public Works Committee to stop the Traffic Department from getting its teeth into 10 feet of Flower Street and Grand Avenue for a possible street widening bordering the Library Square. The extra footage would have come out of the proposed park there.

This is the street widening (and park whittling) that had been protested strongly by, among others, the Friends of the Library, the Los Angeles Conservancy, the local chapter of the AIA and in this column. The transportation department had said the widening was needed to facilitate downtown traffic, including a possible left turn lane from northbound Flower to westbound 5th Street.

As we know, the department has made a deity of left-hand turns and has let the resulting religion interfere with the secular administration of its responsibilities. And, as for that administration, the department still can't seem to get out of its 1950s mind-set that downtown exists simply for motorists, that pedestrians are some sort of alien form and pleasant sidewalks somehow are un-American because they generate crowds.

But Woo knows better, declaring in his minority report that "the benefits to motorists do not justify the disadvantage to pedestrians, which would be caused by the street widening." Happily, Woo's minority report overcame the arguments of the Traffic Department, the concessions of the Community Redevelopment Agency and the confusion of the Planning Department to became a majority report.

—Sept. 21, 1986

Improvements Up His Alleys

WITH OUR SIDEWALKS UNDER CONSTANT ATTACK, IT IS TIME FOR THIS column to retreat to the back alleys this week and look at their potential to improve the city's scarred landscape and engender some needed neighborhood pride.

Yes, alleys, those often refuse-strewn, pot-holed, badly lit, dog- and oil-stained linear garbage dumps that were planned generations ago to channel services away from the front of homes to their rear so that streets can maintain their genteel residential ambiance. So much for planning.

"With some improvements, they could be delightful mews," suggested Terry Mitchell, a native of England, as he and his wife, Kathy, ambled along an alley in Santa Monica recently, their boxer, Walter, in tow.

Because Walter needs two long walks a day, Terry, a graphic artist, and·Kathy, a children's book illustrator, have taken to touring the alleys in the Wilshire district of Santa Monica. It is there I often meet them while carrying out the garbage can or being taken for a walk by Max, a bull terrier.

"Alleys are much more interesting, more alive, than the

streets, and with some flower boxes, maintenance and restricted traffic, can become a very attractive, sociable area, just like the mews I experienced when I lived in the Pimlico district in London," added Terry.

Indeed, in the many neighborhoods of two- and three-story apartment complexes scattered across the Los Angeles region, back alleys have replaced front sidewalks as the place where neighbors meet and exchange pleasantries.

Whether it is just carrying out the garbage, walking the dog, jogging, parking or washing the car, doing some work in the garage, or simply taking a short cut to and from the corner market, many alleys have become a social scene.

And they are becoming busier, too, as more and more people use them instead of sidewalks and streets. Reasons include the abysmally poor condition of many sidewalks, which, over the years, have been abused by mindless street widenings and by cities allowing parking on what should have been landscaped front lawns. And watch out for those curb cuts.

If the rears of cars jammed under *dingbat* apartment houses are not blocking the sidewalks, then its their slippery oil stains that have to be avoided. The apartment buildings look as if they are mooning the streets, making walking along sidewalks depressing as well as dangerous.

Alleys also can be dangerous and depressing for pedestrians. Some, connecting to major streets, are increasingly being used by drivers as short cuts, especially during rush hours. Few police patrol cars are ever seen in alleys, certainly not to give out tickets to speeders and to illegally parked cars.

And while most municipalities regularly sweep the streets, alleys have to wait for the Santa Ana winds or the beneficence of apartment owners to be cleaned. And if it wasn't for scavengers cruising for paper and other trash that might have some value, and which the sanitation workers in their rush leave behind, alleys could easily become garbage dumps. Some already are.

But with just a little imagination, a few improvements and some nurturing, alleys instead could become a very attractive and pleasant "people place."

In San Francisco, for example, a group known as the Chinatown Neighborhood Improvement Resource Center, formed something called the Alley Assn. to improve 41 alleyways. Areas along the alleys were created for sitting and art displays, plantings were provided and maintenance was improved, including restricting through-traffic.

As for the problem of blocking of one end of the alleys to stop illegal and annoying through-traffic, but not garbage pickup and truck deliveries, a hydraulic bollard that can be raised and lowered is being used in Europe.

Chains, speed bumps, special paving and gates also have been used to impress upon drivers that in select alleys they have the responsibility to enter and leave with caution, and it is the pedestrian that has the right of way.

In Los Angeles, a start would be to encourage more apartment dwellers facing the alley to put out window planters, insisting sanitation workers be more careful when picking up the garbage, asking dog lovers to clean up after their pets and having the various municipalities sweep the alleys on a regular basis.

Lending alleys charm is just the down-to-earth, here-and-now type of project that could challenge the imagination of some select students in one of the many fine architectural and planning schools in the Los Angeles area. Anything they might do certainly would be more interesting than some abstract design solution to some abstract problem on some Italian hillside 7,000 miles away, a perennial favorite among professors.

An alleyways project also would be a challenge to the planning and development agencies of various cities in the Los Angeles area. Here is an opportunity for them to stop talking about improving the quality of life in their communities, put aside their vague grand plans that never seem to be implemented, and on a very practical level, doing something about it, beginning, literally, in their own backyard.

—May 26, 1985

Woodsman, Spare That Billboard!

ONE OF THE MANY WONDERFUL THINGS ABOUT LANDSCAPING IS THAT IT has the potential of mitigating the visual pollution of an encroaching, man-made world of concrete and steel.

Cultivated and protected, it can in time, block from view architectural and planning outrages, while also lending our cityscapes and freeways texture, tone and color.

The landscaping along freeways is particularly critical. In addition to being pleasant to look at, the growth tends to have a cooling effect, reduces air pollution and tempers noise pollution.

All this apparently was overlooked a few weeks ago, when the state Assembly quietly approved a bill (AB 1279) requiring Caltrans "to trim or replace vegetation on a landscaped freeway for a distance of 500 feet from an advertising display"—if the vegetation obstructs the view of the billboard from the freeway.

The next stop for the bill, introduced by Assemblyman Louis Papan, is the Senate Transportation Committee, headed by John Foran. Both legislators, who are Democrats, hail from Daly City, a sprawling, raw suburban tract south of San Francisco. Perhaps it is no coincidence that their community is not exactly in the forefront of the "City Beautiful" movement.

The Senate committee is scheduled to vote on the bill July 2, just before the long Fourth of July recess and a favorite time for special interests, such as the billboard industry, to lobby for their favored legislation.

"The billboard lobby is at work again," observed local graphic designer Ted Wu who has monitored the industry's "nefarious" efforts here and across the country.

"Similar bills have been passed in other states with disastrous effects," added Wu. He noted that in Florida, according to a spot checked by the federal Department of Transportation, the bill resulted in the destruction of thousands of trees.

Los Angeles Beautiful, a local environmental group, added that if the legislation is approved, "the result would be a proliferation of billboards along our freeways and the destruction of trees, shrubs and other vegetation that have made our freeways much needed greenbelts in communities and the countryside throughout our state."

It called on other beautification and conservation groups to defeat the legislation. We assume that this also includes landscape architect and architect institutes and associations, and all others concerned with the shape and look of our city and landscapes.

—June 23, 1985

HOPE SPRINGS ETERNAL . . . IN THE BREASTS OF THE MEMBERS OF LOS Angeles Beautiful that the city soon will come up with a stronger sign ordinance.

In this not best of all possible worlds, all things are relative. The controls now have about as many holes in them as a "No Shooting" sign across the road from a gun club.

Led by Ted Wu, and up against one of the stronger lobby groups in the state, the environmental group has gotten the city to consider establishing some limited restrictions on on-site billboards.

Some billboards in select commercial zones, in particular along Sunset Boulevard, have a pop appeal that lend a special ambiance to the area. These tend to be in the jurisdiction of West Hollywood, and is that new city's heritage.

But most are in Los Angeles, marching lock step down retail strips adjoining residential neighborhoods, or sitting on, or pasted against, office towers that stand like poorly bandaged sore thumbs. The billboards and signs are, in a word, tacky, making the city look cheap and transient.

Of course, whatever ordinance the city comes up with will only affect future proposals. Existing signs and billboards in the city and across the state are protected under a law signed by Edmund G. Brown Jr. in his waning days as governor.

Brown did save some trees in his environmental crusades, but sometimes it is hard seeing them behind the billboards he has left us as a token of his administration. Then again Gov. George Deukmejian is not doing anything about them to better expose our wonderful California scenery.

—May 11, 1986

SLIPPED BY ALMOST UNNOTICED WAS THE NEWS RECENTLY THAT A BROAD coalition of business and homeowner groups has drafted a new sign ordinance that, with just a few exceptions, bans all new billboards and places strict limits on on-site signs. The package now goes to the City Council.

The rare joint effort orchestrated by Los Angeles Beautiful was prompted by the raw fact that the increasing visual pollution of the city serves no one, except perhaps a few billboard companies and their lobbyists.

Now, if the same groups can begin talking about environmental and developmental pollution, there may be hope for the city yet.

—March 6, 1988

The "rare joint effort" collapsed at the last moment in the face of a concerted push by the billboard lobbyists, and the ordinance was defeated.

A Wider View of Westside Traffic

S OME REFRESHING NEW VIEWS HAVE EMERGED IN THE CONTINUING DEBATE on what to do about the increasing traffic congestion on the Westside.

It appears that no longer are communities there accepting the usual knee-jerk reaction to the traffic by Caltrans and other agencies of street widenings and more street widenings.

Out of obvious frustration with parochial bureaucracies, the communities are beginning to question the widenings in terms of whether they are consistent with proper land-use planning, if not common sense, and the effect they might have on the local quality of life.

In short, they are asking whether there is more to living in Los Angeles than just being able to drive with relative ease to and from work, shopping and the beaches; whether such communities as Westwood, Brentwood, Pacific Palisades and the cities of West Hollywood and Beverly Hills are more than backlot facades mounted along boulevards to serve as decorated sound walls?

These concerns emerged in recent weeks as communities reacted to the release of a two-year Caltrans study of what could be done to improve the traffic flow along an impacted Santa Monica Boulevard, particularly between the San Diego Freeway and Fairfax Avenue.

The study leans very much toward widenings, declaring that they would not significantly affect neighborhoods or community cohesion." If a tunnel Beverly Hills has urged within its boundaries is included, the project's estimated price tag would be an immodest $254 million.

While Beverly Hills has disputed the estimates—it says the cost with the tunnel would be about $100 million less—the thought of spending that amount of funds so cars might traverse the Westside a few miles faster than at present makes one gasp. The way it throws around tax revenues, you would think Caltrans was the defense department.

As Alex Man commented at a public hearing on the study last week, those funds, or just a portion of them, could be much better spent on mass transit projects. Representing the local chapter of the Sierra Club, Man called for improved bus service and better traffic management, including establishing bus lanes and enforcing no-parking regulations.

A member also of the Pacific Palisades Residents Assn. and the Sunset Scenic Safety Committee, the indefatigable Man also has been protesting proposed road widenings in the Brentwood and Pacific Palisades areas. He has argued with proper passion that widenings do not relieve traffic, but rather attract more cars, while irreparably damaging the environment and further disrupting communities.

Others at the hearing expressed concern that the widening along Santa Monica Boulevard also would encourage more heedless office development. And they pointed out that if the boulevard is just widened to Fairfax Avenue, it would most likely create a bottleneck there, with traffic spilling over onto local streets and prompting proposals for more widenings.

"When does the widening stop?" asked West Hollywood Mayor John Heilman.

It was a question that even if they tried, the representatives of Caltrans, and similarly focused agencies as the city's Transportation Department, could not really answer, for such projects are their bread and butter. Perhaps if there was an equally weighted and powerful pedestrian, or neighborhood preservation department, our communities would have a better chance in the bureaucratic battles.

Heilman also raised the issue of the effect of the widening on his community's quality of life, adding that it was time to worry less about the boulevard's role as a thoroughfare and the convenience of drivers and more about its role as West Hollywood's main street and the people, like himself, who "work, live, shop and play" there.

Continuing the theme that the street should be a community resource, Laura Lake of the Friends of Westwood suggested that the unsightly section of abandoned railroad tracks bordering Santa Monica Boulevard between Sepulveda Boulevard and Century park West be developed as a strip park, replete with a bikeway, a jogging path, sitting areas, "tot lots" and landscaping.

The Park Plan, drafted for the volunteer group by the architectural firm of Appleton & Associates, was a refreshing demonstration that communities need not always be defensive, and could with imagination put things in their proper perspective and propose something positive.

Considering the controversy any widening on the Westside provokes and that Caltrans has other "needy" projects elsewhere, it is apparent that the proposed widening of Santa Monica Boulevard will be filed deep in some cabinet downtown. So much for all the sound and fury of the recent public hearings, as well as the work that went into the study.

However, the study did prompt communities to think about how they might protect and actually improve their local landscapes. The strip park is an idea that deserves to be seeded and cultivated, to serve the immediate community and as a demonstration for other communities.

Perhaps the "traffic mitigation" funds sought from developers in the Westwood area would be better spent on such a park than on yet more street widenings. Certainly, it would ease the visual pollution that employees working in all the new office buildings there msut endure when stuck in traffic on Santa Monica Boulevard.

Given the mood of communities these days, drivers may just have to begin to change their commuting habits, consider car pooling, staggered hours and mass transit. Maybe some might even use the bike or jogging paths proposed by the Friends of Westwood.

—Dec. 8, 1985

I NSENSITIVITY, CONTINUED: JUST DOING ITS JOB, SAYS CALTRANS. IN A FUM-bling effort to justify its bureaucracy and budget, the agency is moving ahead with a $1.3 million sidewalk-narrowing project along Santa Monica Boulevard in Westwood.

Being ignored are the current planning efforts of the community calling for increased pedestrian amenities, an imaginative strip park scheme designed gratis by the architectural firm of Appleton & Associates, and a recent $150,000 landscaping of a portion of the street's median by Century City.

If the community's plan is approved in time, and eventually moves into the implementation stage, the sidewalks will probably have to be widened, no doubt by Caltrans, at a substantially higher cost.

—May 10, 1987

T HE IDEA OF REDUCING OR ELIMINATING THE HOME-TO-WORK AUTO TRIPS, and auto trips in general, be it for shopping, dining or whatever, is attractive.

With this in mind, Ken Jewett suggests in a letter that more, not less, condos be built on Wilshire Boulevard in Westwood, but at affordable prices to attract members of the UCLA faculty and administration. He adds they then could walk or take a shuttle bus to work.

"This could be a major step toward a minor start to reduce traffic in Westwood Village," he states. Though Jewett's proposal has flaws, the concept is a good one.

In the same spirit, why should Crown Hill, west of the Harbor Freeway, be viewed as a parking area for downtown workers, as suggested by the myopic Central City Assn., or for marginal offices, and not as site for housing for the workers and others?

If ever there was an area ripe for an intensive, imaginative mixed-use development it is Crown Hill, a fact we trust will dominate the urban design to be drafted for the area by a consortium of local interests.

Imagine if the office workers didn't have to drive in from the Valley, or wherever, to park there, but simply could walk to work and to the increasing attractions of downtown, including Little Tokyo. No doubt, both the freeways and downtown would benefit.

Maybe walking in Los Angeles is an idea whose time is ripe.

—March 6, 1988

Hope (Street) for Walkers

T HE HOPE OF A MORE PLEASANT, ATTRACTIVE AND MEMORABLE CITY BEGINS this year, appropriately enough, on Hope Street downtown.

To be considered within the next month by the city Planning Commission is an inventive urban design scheme to turn a stretch of the forlorn street into a vital link in a downtown pedestrian network.

The first phase of the project—labeled the Hope Street Promenade—would connect the proposed west lawn of the Central

Library to a proposed park at Olympic Boulevard by widening and landscaping the sidewalk along Hope Street.

The promenade is part of a larger scheme proposed by the city's Community Redevelopment Agency to connect the emerging California Plaza complex on Bunker Hill, down the proposed grand stairway of the imaginatively conceived Library Square project to the ambitious South Park redevelopment project.

THE PEDESTRIAN NETWORK IS THE STUFF OF DREAMS THAT HAS THE POTENTIAL to turn the auto-oriented, fragmented and not particularly distinguished downtown into a more cohesive and engaging district—prompting people to walk, shop and enjoy.

But it is not a pipe dream or something that would take billions of dollars and decades to accomplish.

As conceived by the CRA's dedicated planning staff, given form by renown urban designer Lawrence Halprin, aided by Campbell & Campbell, and enthusiastically supported by the central business district's Open Space Task Force, the network is quite achievable and relatively inexpensive.

What the Planning Commission is being asked at this stage is to simply initiate a so-called community plan amendment limiting future roadway widths on Hope Street between 6th Street and Venice Boulevard to 44 feet and requiring minimum sidewalk widths of 18 feet.

AT PRESENT, THE ROADWAY WIDTHS ARE SET AT 56 FEET, OR SIX LANES, FOUR for traffic and two for parking, with the sidewalk varying from about nine feet to 12. Landscaping consists of a few sad trees.

Under the proposed plan, the roadway would be four lanes, most likely all for traffic and none for parking. The balance of the street width would be heavily landscaped and devoted to the pedestrian, with the sidewalk meandering through a sort of linear park.

The hope is that under the guidance of an inspired Halprin (who also is the landscape architect for the Library Square and Olympic Park projects) Hope Street will become an enticing stretch of cityscape in the spirit of, say, Barcelona's Ramblas, Paris's Champs Elysees or Rome's Via Condotti, encouraging window shopping, sidewalk cafes, flower stalls and promenading.

Given the climate and growing cosmopolitan population of Los Angeles, the potential is certainly there.

PUTTING THE HOPE STREET PROPOSAL IN PERSPECTIVE, IT WAS NEARLY FOUR years ago that this column railed against the city "improving" Flower Street downtown by cutting down trees and widening it. Instead, it was suggested then that the city narrow the roadway and widen and improve the sidewalk with more trees.

And though three trees were spared (on the west side of Flower just north of Wilshire), the city went ahead with the widening, arguing at the time that if it wasn't done it would lose federal aid.

Subsequent inquiries reported here revealed that the aid was not dependent on widening the street, but simply improving it. And tht such improvements could include narrowing roadways, creating more space for sidewalks and increasing so-called pedestrian amenities.

It is with this history mind that the Hope Street proposal is welcomed.

THE PROPOSAL ALSO IS WELCOMED AS AN ILLUSTRATION OF THE TYPE OF planning the city desperately needs—practical planning applied on a street-by-street basis with tender loving care.

This is the type of imaginative planning that has marked many CRA projects and given the city, among other things, the sparkling new Museum of Contemporary Art, a revived and expanding Little Tokyo, an increasing inventory of well-designed, subsidized housing complexes and the promise of the South Park and Library Square redevelopment projects.

This is also the type of planning that cannot be shifted to the city's Planning Department, as now being talked about by the current cast of would-be downtown power brokers operating in the vacuum of Mayor Tom Bradley's leadership. The current polemics concerning downtown's future is no substitute for solid planning.

And while the ultimate responsibility for comprehensive planning should rest in the Planning Department, the nuts and bolts of it, at least downtown, should remain with CRA. As if no one has noticed, the Planning Department at present has its hands full with a host of major land-use issues and actions.

If the management consultant operating in the dense woods of CRA needs grist for his mill before grinding up planning, he should look at the increasing interference in agency operations by its current stewards.

In the meantime, the hope is that the Hope Street proposal can move forward.

—Jan. 4, 1987

It has, but slowly.

'Wrong Way' Signs Spare Neighborhood

THE SIGNS AT THE STREET CORNERS ON THE WEST SIDE OF FAIRFAX AVENUE between Wilshire and Olympic, declaring "Do Not Enter" and "Wrong Way," are ugly and loud—and just what the community of Carthay Circle ordered.

To residents there the signs are victory banners in a battle they waged for two years to seal off their historic mid-Westside community from through traffic.

They'll be celebrating their victory Sunday at 2 p.m. with a symbolic planting at the base of the signs, to be followed with a block party on De Valle Drive, west of Fairfax.

MY FAMILY WILL BE CELEBRATING WITH THEM, FOR LINDSEY ROSIN, A PLAY-mate of my son, Josef, lives in that neighborhood. It was through Lindsey's father, Charles, that I first heard of the campaign to close the Carthay Circle neighborhood to at least some of the workday traffic from Fairfax and Wilshire boulevards.

Previously I had known the area simply as a well-scaled subdivision of mostly subdued stucco and redtiled Spanish Colonial Revival houses, a style that swept across the city in the 1920s and in a variety of forms is still quite popular.

Carthay Circle has one of the best collections of the style, and viewing it on occasion has become a pleasant diversion when I'm in the neighborhood, catching an exhibit at the nearby County Museum of Art, or doing research at the California Historical Society at 6300 Wilshire Blvd.

Lending Carthay Circle further distinction is the fact that it was the first subdivision in Los Angeles to bury its utility lines, no small gesture in the early 1920s—nor now.

In addition, the tree-lined streets were laid out at angles and with mid-block pedestrian paths focusing on a neighborhood commercial center. Dominating that center was a first-run movie house, the Carthay Circle Theater. ("Gone With the Wind" had its Hollywood premier there.)

The result was a pleasant, family-oriented community of about 200 homes, desirable for its comfortable houses, tree-shaded streets, congenial elementary school and convenient location midway between the ocean and downtown and just a few minutes from Beverly Hills and the mid-Wilshire District.

But it was this location that also in time began to undermine what residents saw as the integrity of the community. The center and the landmark theater were demolished in 1968 for an office complex. Other offices went up along an increasingly congested Wilshire Boulevard to the north, dumping traffic onto local streets.

Nevertheless, Carthay Circle continued to attract young couples, such as the Rosins. And with the couples came children, and concern over the traffic.

"The streets no longer were our own," recalls Barbara Caplan, a mother of three children, ages 4 to 10. "You wouldn't dare let them ride a bicycle, even along the sidewalk. Our street just was a constant stream of transient traffic, which at rush hour backed up at least half a block."

So when residents learned that a 16-story office building, scheduled to rise at the southwest corner of Fairfax and Wilshire, would dump even more traffic on the local streets, it was a call to arms.

"An environmental report indicated that the traffic on our streets might triple," comments Rosin, who heads the Carthay Circle Homeowners Assn.

After some debate, the community decided to appeal to the city for barriers to prevent traffic from Fairfax Avenue from entering three local streets, Del Valle, Warner and Barrows drives.

Petitions by the community to the city's Department of Transportation were at first ignored, says Rosin.

Eventually the department, prodded by local Councilman Zev Yaroslavsky, agreed to the barriers. But it added that the city would not pay for them, which because of the need to resolve drainage problems would cost an estimated $60,000.

While the community tried to get the office building developer to pick up some of the costs as a gesture of good will, George Snelling, a city engineer, came forward on his own initiative to show how the drainage problem could be handled simply and inexpensively.

Snelling's solution prompted the developer to do the street work as part of a package of required site improvements, with the result that a few weeks ago the community had its barriers, replete with city-donated signs.

THE EFFECT WAS IMMEDIATE. THE STREETS ARE QUIETER, SAFER AND FRIEND-lier, say residents. "You can now hear the birds instead of the traffic," adds Caplan.

Of course there has been a price. Drivers who used the streets as through routes must now stick to the main boulevards, aggravating congestion there. Also inconvenienced have been Carthay Circle residents, who cannot make left turns onto Fairfax, or enter their community with ease from the east.

"It is a little enough price for us to pay for having created what amounts to a small town, right in the middle of Los Angeles," Rosin comments.

If you want to visit Carthay Circle, I suggest you park on the adjoining boulevards and walk. You'll enjoy it more, and the residents will appreciate it.

—Oct. 23, 1986

Taking Narrow View of Sidewalks

BURIED IN A RECENT MAGAZINE ARTICLE DESCRIBING A DAY IN THE LIFE OF Los Angeles City Council President Pat Russell was a revealing few paragraphs devoted to a meeting she had held at City Hall with three traffic engineers.

Discussing how traffic congestion in her west Los Angeles district might be relieved, one of the engineers suggested widening Lincoln Boulevard by reducing its sidewalks to seven-foot widths.

"Seven feet?" Russell is quoted asking the engineer.

"That's what there is on Melrose," replied the engineer. "We know because we went out and measured it. It works. People don't have a problem with it there. . . ."

Yes, sections of the sidewalk on Melrose Avenue are just seven feet wide, narrower if you consider the obstructions in the form of lampposts, parking meters and newspaper vending machines.

AND, YES, SERENDIPITOUS MELROSE WORKS. PEOPLE ON THE SIDEWALK SEEM to squeeze by one another, though it is hard when couples walking hand-in-hand are confronted by couples walking in an opposite direction. Stopping to look at a window display also can be hazardous.

Yes, Melrose works, but not because of the narrowing of the sidewalk; rather despite of it. And certainly it does not work as well as it could have if the sidewalk had been left alone, or indeed improved.

Just consider how much more attractive and successful Melrose could have been with wide sidewalks; if there were room for engaging sidewalk cafes, a canopy of trees to shade the strollers from the harsh midday sun, flower displays to brighten the street and benches on which to sit and rest weary feet and watch the crowds pass by.

In the narrowing of Melrose's sidewalks, Los Angeles lost another opportunity to create a very special pedestrian environment, a street for promenading.

MEANWHILE, TRAFFIC ON MELROSE IS NOT MOVING MUCH FASTER THESE days, despite a few new left-hand turn lanes. The little vacuum that was created by the widening has quickly filled up.

And what if the trendy stores of Melrose pull the plugs on their neon signs and move on, as such stores tend to do?

Then Melrose with its sidewalk forever sacrificed will be just another ugly street, with no canopy of trees, no sidewalk cafes and no landscaping. That is what happens when the planning of a city is usurped by the short-range projects of traffic engineers.

As for Lincoln Boulevard with its profusion of mini-malls, tacky signage, used car lots and random commercial development, it is hard to imagine how narrowing the sidewalk would make the strip through Venice and into adjoining Santa Monica any uglier. But it will.

And after the narrowing and other such street "improvements," merchants there, no doubt, will still be blaming the poor business on the lack of parking and the traffic congestion. And the city, no doubt, will once again turn to the traffic engineers for a solution.

While traffic engineers should not be faulted for doing their job, which is to analyze and facilitate traffic, one would hope that before the city starts chopping up streets, the broader implications should be considered.

Even assuming that a street widening does facilitate traffic, at least for a while, is it worth the cost in terms of neighborhood disruption and permanent damage to the streetscape?

There is more to a city than just being able to get from one place to another easily. After all, what does one do when he or she gets to wherever they are going? It is nice to be able to drive to Melrose, but really nicer still to be able to park and walk and window shop along the street.

Perhaps it is time to hire some pedestrian engineers to form a bureaucratic lobby to counter the knee-jerk recommendations of street widenings by the traffic engineers. And if not pedestrian engineers, what about planners? Aren't they the professionals who are supposed to be responsible for the shaping of the city's land and streetscapes, not traffic engineers?

OF COURSE, WE ALSO CAN HAVE AN ENLIGHTENED TRANSPORTATION DEPARTment that understands the nature of a changing city and tries to adjust policies and projects to serve both traffic and pedestrians.

This hope was prompted recently by the visit here of New York City's Deputy commissioner of transportation, David Gurin. Though on vacation, visiting friends, Gurin, a respected planner, could not help but make some observations.

Concerning street widenings, Gurin declared that in most cases they are "utterly counterproductive." He called them an ancient solution that has proven wrong wherever tried in established urban area.

"It is axiomatic that any street widening will fill up with cars," Gurin said. "What you want to do is discourage traffic in residential and select commercial districts, not encourage it. In New York, wherever we are now reconstructing streets, we are exploring how they can be redesigned to better serve pedestrians and the neighborhoods."

He declared that streets should not just be viewed as conduits for vehicles. "Streets also are used for parking, walking, bicycling, deliveries, for neighbors to meet, for exploring" Gurin said. "They are the life of a city, more important than its buildings, and should be protected.

—April 19, 1987

Design Debate on Sunset Strip

THOUGH SUNSET BOULEVARD IN WEST HOLLYWOOD IS SUCH A SPECIAL street, I thought there might be some lessons to be learned from the urban design issues raised by a controversial project there.

The project is a combined office and residential complex at No. 8981. When, two years ago, I first glanced at its plans and renderings in an issue of Progressive Architecture magazine, they looked quite promising.

Designed by the Architectural Collective of Venice, Charles Lagreco, principal, the project had won a coveted citation from the magazine for its intention of providing a more intense use and edge to the famous Strip.

The project subsequently also won a citation from the local chapter of the American Institute of Architects, with the jury stating, among other things, that it "comes to grips with complex constraints and mixed uses."

However, as the 6-plus-story complex on the sloping site neared completion, I felt its promise had waned. Stating in a column last summer that while I liked the mixed-use nature of the project, thought the scale appropriate and didn't mind the arbitrary coloring, its street-level facade was anti-pedestrian and disappointing. I labeled the building "a bully."

Lagreco took exception to the description, contending in a letter that I had not taken into consideration the "restless crowds" generated by the neighboring nightclubs that each evening overwhelm the sidewalks.

"What the solution is trying to do is both clearly to define a positive relationship to the street and allow the building to survive in a sometimes hostile environment," the architect explained.

"If Sunset Boulevard is to achieve a successful transition from its current dynamic, if deficient, condition to a more stable, balanced pattern of use while preserving what makes the Strip unique, Lagreco

133

concluded, "it needs carefully considered alternatives that are respectful of all users."

It was a good point, but one I didn't think the project demonstrated. In being possibly respectful of the project's tenants who enter through the basement, the blank walls and yawning garage at the street level were quite disrespectful of pedestrians. I felt the project's design reflected an anti-urban, bunker mentality.

What it seemed to me Lagreco had done was to follow a basic principle in the unprincipled world of advertising: That when you find out something wrong with your product, deny it. (A classic example of this was a lemonade concocted of chemicals, being promoted a few years ago with the slogan, "Tastes Like Real Lemonade.") to me 8981 was a flawed conction.

WANTING ANOTHER PERSPECTIVE BEFORE I PERHAPS WOULD WRITE MORE on the subject, I went a copy of the Lagreco's letter to Mark Winogrond, the city's chief planner. His subsequently reply to Lagreco, with a copy to me, was an urban-design primer.

Stating that the building "has little positive relationship to the street," Winogrond observed that "it does nothing to draw the pedestrian into the project; it does nothing to invite the passenger driving by in an automobile. In fact, it presents barriers to the street." He added:

"My strong belief is that the building's primary design responsibility is contextual; in an already developed urban environment, it must succeed within and add to the established urban fabric and context," which Winogrond said 8981 does not.

With this in mind, the planning official said under present laws in West Hollywood, the building would not be approved.

It was Winogrond's contention that "such a lack of urban design perspective" the building displayed "is what has led communities and planners across the country to impose more restrictive, often more arbitrary regulations.

The architect and the architectural profession pay a price for such limited, project-oriented approaches. In the end, everyone loses: The community is stuck with the inappropriate building, the street has its context injured and the architect is stuck with reactionary rules that may not actually address the problem which his or her building created.

"What we have learned firmly from our work in West Hollywood," concluded Winogrond, "is that pedestrian life, healthy urban life, succeeds through linkages: one building linked to another linked to another. To the degree that individual buildings present obstacles to that linkage, our success is hampered."

Lagreco replied in a letter that the urban design issues involved were indeed complex. Noting also that West Hollywood was evaluating a requirement that in commercial zones, the ground floor of all developments contain retail, the architect went on to make a number of points he hoped would be considered.

While stating that "the concept of sustaining and intensifying activity along the street is, in my opinion, critical to the life of the city," Lagreco contended that a multi-use facility such as 8981 "has requirements for privacy and security as well as a responsibility to the street." He also cited problems with parking requirements, among other items.

THERE WAS A FURTHER EXCHANGE OF LETTERS, WITH LAGRECO TAKING EXCEPtion to some of Winogrond's statements. "The irony is that 8981 Sunset is exactly about linkages and your (arguably) one-sided interpretation of that attempt is testimony to the difficulties involved."

In turn, Winogrond reiterated his objections to the design of the ground floor while stating his appreciation of the architect's "willingness to enter into this dialogue, especially in the light of the harshness of some of my comments."

In one of his replies, Lagreco enclosed a copy of an excerpt from the architect treatise, "A Pattern Language," in which author Christopher Alexander discusses the idea of fronting a street with a private terrace. This "was what we were trying to do," added Lagreco.

For the record, architectural guru Alexander recently came out with a new treatise entitled, "A New Theory of Urban Design" (Oxford U. Press: $39.95), in which he declares that the single overriding rule is that, "Every increment of construction must be made in such a way as to heal the city."

Now to me, that statement had the tartness of real lemons with which to make a tasty jug of lemonade.

—March 27, 1988

Cars, Neighbors and Convenience

A s Los Angeles inexorably grows, our love/hate relationship with the car is becoming more intense.

While we embrace our own car and the freedom it affords us, we tend to resent the cars of others for increasing traffic on the streets, polluting the air, clogging the freeways and snapping up parking spaces.

The car, in effect, has become the ultimate self-interest machine, distorting the relationships of individuals to their neighbors, neighborhoods, city and region. As such, it also has become the major determinant in the planning and design process.

In the proposed siting and shaping of buildings and their convoluted reviews by local authorities, architectural style is quite secondary to such issues as how many parking spaces are provided and whether the surrounding street system can handle the increase in traffic. It is the stuff of conflict.

Almost everywhere, it seems, communities are at war with themselves, local businesses and government and, most of all, real estate developers, over traffic and the related issue of development. Appeals to bear witness and write commentaries on specific skirmishes dominates the mail I receive.

As readers of this column know, I tend to sympathize and side with the residential communities, prompted by the belief that neighborhoods are the bedrock of a city, the basis for its sense of place and identity, and the measure of its quality of life.

At the same time, there is recognition that neighborhoods and conflicts vary, and what may, on the surface appear similar, on closer examination sometimes differs considerably. And there also has to be concern about the selfishness, hypocrisy and demagoguery that the conflicts seem to stir, even in the warmest of homeowner hearts.

A CASE IN POINT, SADLY, IS THE DEBATE IN MY OWN NEIGHBORHOOD IN SANTA Monica over the future of Montana Avenue, which in recent years has been losing neighborhood stores to trendy restaurants and boutiques with a regional appeal. Among the results have been sharply escalating commercial rents, increasing traffic and parking problems.

Most residents in the area, including myself, are concerned. We would like to see the neighborhood-oriented services, such as supermarkets, drugstores, shoe repair, flower and barber shops remain, the traffic better controlled, and parking less of a hassle.

Some changes are welcome. I, for one, am glad to see the gas stations there being replaced by stores. The stations were not pedestrian-friendly, generating more traffic than a mini-mall over their raw asphalt curb cuts while belching noxious fumes. Much more engaging, and safer, are sidewalks lined with stores.

In response to concerns over traffic and the need for more parking, in particular to serve the older establishments that have no off-street spaces, the city, to its credit, initiated a study to see whether the avenue could be reduced from 4 to 2 lanes, made safer, and be landscaped to accommodate diagonal parking.

And though the avenue may not be wide enough for diagonal parking on both sides, I felt the study was very much in order, as well as a look at other traffic-mitigating measures, including cul-de-sacs for select streets and alleys, installing more traffic lights and, generally making it more attractive for pedestrians. Also mentioned was permit parking.

At the same time, a local developer proposed a plan to relocate on the avenue the Sweet 16 Grill, a modest coffee shop that, after 46 years in the neighborhood, had been forced to close because of escalating rents. All that was required was a variance to allow 8 parking spaces below the minimum, at most a possibly mild inconvenience to nearby residents.

The plan seemed reasonable to me, as well as nearly 4,000 persons who signed a petition in support of it, and I mentioned the item in a column last month. The response was some angry letters and phone calls.

Despite the persons bemoaning the loss of neighborhood services on Montana, such as the Grill, they were opposed to the variance because they felt it would exacerbate the local parking problem.

In a letter to the editor, one woman wrote that "while, as he (Kaplan) says, some tables at the Grill may be filled by people who walk, bicycle or skateboard to the restaurant, many also are filled by construction workers with a truck parked outside for each."

IN SUBSEQUENT LETTERS AND CALLS, AND AT A MEETING LAST WEEK IN A local school called by a self-appointed, so-called Montana Avenue Task Force, it became evident that a vocal group of homeowners was opposed to the variance, to diagonal parking and just about anything that might cause them an inconvenience.

Their opposition displayed a lack of sympathy for the merchants they say they want to help and a lack of understanding of traffic management that bordered on petulance.

Shouting from the audience, a few residents suggested that certain services, such as gas stations, be forced to remain on the street; that commercial rent control be instituted, and that development on the avenue be severely limited. And this from persons who live in a neighborhood where "tear-downs" are going for $350,000, and the second topic of conversation usually revolves around what they bought their house for and what it is now worth.

There was no talk of freezing the cost of merchandise or service offered by the stores, controlling the escalating prices of homes in the area, or of recalculating apartment leases at market rate to reduce the discretionary income of local renters who frequent the boutiques on the street.

Braving the crowd, Santa Monica City Council member Chris Reed noted that gas stations were leaving because they would not upgrade their underground storage tanks to protect the local water supply, that the city could not force anyone to stay in business and that perhaps some of the traffic problem was being caused not by the stores, but by residents and their help living in the "6,000-square-foot houses, with four-car garages" being built north of Montana, and by occupants of "bootleg" rental rooms and apartments there.

For this Reed was booed. It was apparent that the mostly well-coiffured crowd was of the type that doees not like to be confronted, nor does it like being inconvenienced by having to drive a few extra yards for a parking space or a few blocks south to Santa Monica Boulevard in search of a full-service gas station.

Said Gina Tognetti, a neighbor sitting next to me who supported the parking variance for the Grill: "These people certainly want to have their cake and eat it too. They won't compromise, but they want everyone else to."

For the city of Santa Monica and those seeking some solutions to our increasing traffic problems it appears the road ahead is going to be very bumpy.

—April 17, 1988

VI

PRESERVING
THE PAST

A s Los Angeles inexorably stumbles forward into the future, it becomes more important than ever to preserve the fragments of its past.

Be the fragments landmark houses, such as the Gamble in Pasadena, or the Ennis Brown in Los Feliz; the Rococo Los Angeles theater downtown or the Moderne Alex in Glendale; streetscapes such as Boulder Road in Altadena or Alvarado Terrace in the Pico Union neighborhood; singular structures asthe Watts Towers or the Tail o' the Pup hot dog stand; or simply the giant Moreton Bay Fig tree on National boulevard, they offer a sense of time, place and pride vital to our civic identity.

Contrary to popular cliches perpetuated by aspiring taste-makers catering to east coast publications and prejudices, Los Angeles is not just some thin cartoon concoction of glitz and gossamer; a cauldron of "hot properties"; an asphalt-covered, chainlink-wrapped playground for aging adolescent and self-promoting architects, or a maxed-out mini mall.

To be sure, these little vanities and crass commercialism do exist here, thanks in part to a growing public appetite for gossip and gaucheries, fed by a starry-eyed local tradition of hucksterism and buffoonery. But as more and more persons are discovering, beyond these shallow worlds is a Los Angeles with a rich and diverse architectural and cultural history.

Celebrating that history this fall as it marks its 10th anniversary is the Los Angeles Conservancy. Beginning as a small band of persons to fight the threatened demolition of the Central Library, the conservancy has grown in a decade to nearly 5,000 members to become one of the city's major and more responsible civic groups.

Its efforts combined with other public and private interests over the last decade helped save the landmark library, which after a disastrous fire more than two years ago is scheduled to undergo a major renovation and expansion as the centerpiece of a major downtown redevelopment plan.

The conservancy also has been in the forefront of the continuing battle to preserve a number of the city's marvelous movie palaces, most notably to date the Art Deco Wiltern Theater. In addition, it has lent invaluable support in the host of efforts to save a variety of notably designed residences, public buildings, and commercial structures, and to have distinctive neighborhoods declared historic districts.

In a fractured metropolis of scattered neighborhoods aggravated by an insensitive bureaucracy and an arcane political structure that encourages duplicity, the conservancy has provided a network and a resource for an awakening community consciousness, and dozens of other historic societies asserting themselves across Southern California. (These groups also deserve to be celebrated.)

Though frail and thin, the network and resources have proved valuable in the recurring, and increasing, battles to save Los Angeles from itself.

Less dramatic but no less important has been the quiet involvement of the conservancy in the struggle within city government by a few conscientious civic servants to develop a reasonable approach to seismic compliance, and a responsible environmental review process, one that takes into account historic structures and neighborhoods.

And, of course, there is the conservancy's engaging educational programs, including its popular architectural house and historic neighborhood tours and special events. These have included lectures, issues forums, socials, and film programs. No local educational institution has done a more effective job reaching out to the public, and at such reasonable prices, too, thanks to the conservancy's dedicated docents.

THE CONSERVANCY DESERVES TO PAUSE, LOOK BACK AT ITS ACHIEVEMENTS OF the last decade, take pride in them, and accept the thanks, of those concerned with improving the quality of life in Los Angeles.

But not for too long. While congratulating itself the conservancy also would do well to rededicate itself to the task of protecting, and improving, Los Angeles. To paraphrase a quotation of 18th century philosopher John Philpot Curran, that is also attributed to Thomas Jefferson, the price for a livable city is eternal vigilance.

The battles continue. "Awareness and support for preservation has grown enormously, but at the same time development pressures are threatening more historic buildings and districts than ever before," commented conservancy executive director Jay Rounds in the organization's current newsletter. "This is a critical period for determining what Los Angeles will look in the future."

WHAT WON'T BE IN LOS ANGELES' FUTURE IS THE BEVERLY THEATER. AS IF an example was needed of the continuing asault on our landmarks, the Art Deco-styled theater on Wilshire Boulevard in Beverly Hills is being demolished after what seems a half-hearted attempted to save it by the city and the owner, the Columbia Development Partners, a joint venture involving Columbia Savings & Loan.

There was a great deal of discussion in a limited study of the costs in terms of dollars of rehabilitating the structure, transferring air rights, and what-have-you, but little discussion of the architectural and historical value to the city. The apparent tone of the study and debate was not how to save the building, but how to soft sell its destruction. And then to have an apologist for Columbia praise the institution for its patience. The chutzpah!

So much from Beverly Hills, a city celebrating its 75th anniversary by allowing one of its few landmarks to be knocked down, and Columbia Savings, a government-chartered institution supposedly founded as a financial vehicle for community betterment. If there was a will, I am convinced, there would have been way to save the Beverly.

While the Beverly, alas, soon will be dust, still perservering across Los Angeles are other architecturally and culturally significant buildings, places and districts entwined with our history. But many of them are endangered, so many in fact, that I have to postpone listing them until next week and more space.

—Oct. 9, 1988

Landmarks In Need of Help

E NOUGH ALREADY WITH THE OPPOSITION BY THE LA BREA AND FAIRFAX neighborhoods to the proposed plans to recycle the landmark Pan Pacific building.

As the residents there know, and are quick to tell this *boychik* at the drop of a teabag into a glass of hot water, we live in an imperfect, sweet and sour world, where on occasion we have to take a little lemon with our sugar.

So it is with the Pan Pacific, where the price of saving what is left of the evocative Streamline Moderne styled structured is its adaptive reuse as an ice rink, a gymnastic center, two restaurants and five movie theaters.

Residents contend the uses will attract "traffic" and "criminals." While no doubt traffic will increase somewhat, the facilities should generate a healthy use that, if anything, will make the area safer. We look forward to such a finding from the environmental impact report the community has requested.

Certainly the uses are better than letting the Pan Pacific continue to deteriorate to where, if it doesn't collapse first, it will have to be demolished. Then who knows what will be proposed for the site if it is sold on the basis of highest and worst use, as is the tradition in government.

To lose the Pan Pacific, a local, state and national landmark that has the potential of once again becoming a focal point of pride for the area, would be a *shanda*, Yiddish for a shame. There are too few landmarks int he Fairfax district to squander.

To be sure, crime and traffic are problems in the neighborhood, and the park there at times can get rowdy. But the Pan Pacific should not be punished for it. Instead, residents would do well to stop complaining and push for a positive plan to make the area safer, such as cul de sacing local streets, widening sidewalks, improving lighting, increasing police patrols, and generally encouraging pedestrian use.

You don't have to love the firms of Kornwasser & Friedman, and partners Goldrich & Kest, who made the proposal, or the county and Supervisor Ed Edelman, who embraced it, to recognize that the proposal has merit.

Los Angeles may not have turned out to be the *goldeneh medina*, the golden country as promised in Yiddish lore. But I think an ice rink and a gymnastic center, and a policy of early bird specials at the restaurants and movies proposed for the Pan Pacific, along with more of a police presence, might help.

THE PAN PACIFIC IS JUST ONE OF THE REGION'S MANY LANDMARKS FACING extinction unless some bold actions are taken.

Heading the endangered architecture list in Los Angeles are our marvelous movie palaces. These include the Los Angeles, Tower, Mayan, Million Dollar, Palace, Orpheum and Globe Theaters, a free-for-all of exuberant architectural styles that form a national historic district along downtown's Broadway. And let us not forget the California Theater a few blocks away on South Main.

While the theaters are still operating, they are the worse for wear and on shaky financial grounds that could bring their curtains down in the too near future. Other palaces being threatened are the Alex in Glendale and the Golden Gate in Whittier.

The Brockman Building, which includes the Brooks Bros. store, lends a sense of history and place, as well an urban scale, to the 500 block of West 7th Street downtown but it is the target of a proposed mega development being considered by a Japanese investment firm. The dropping of this bomb is being held up by an environmental impact report now being drafted and the slight hope that the architects involved might find a way to save the buildings and their local reputation.

Up for sale, the Ambassador Hotel has been eyed by the Los Angeles Unified School District as a high school site. There are ways the hotel could be recycled and the balance of the land used for educational facilities, but one has learned when dealing with the district not to expect any imaginative planning or sympathy for historic landmarks, as evidenced by its failed land grab of last year.

Also up for sale is the Beaux Arts styled Canfield-Moreno estate atop Micheltorena hill in the Silver Lake area. The hope is that someone will buy and save the villa, and develop on the remaining land a complex of compatible residences. The fear is that the entire estate will be leveled so that as many as possible of the usual overpriced, ticky-tacky units can be accommodated.

Unless a benefactor is found, that most likely will be the fate of the faded Italian Renaissance-styled McKinley Mansion, at the southeast corner of Lafayette Park Place and 3rd Street, and the Rivington Place apartment court complex on Ocean Avenue in Santa Monica. Both appear to be victims of greed, aggravated in the case of the mansion by time, and in the apartment court by Santa Monica's self-defeating rent control laws that precluded a fair rate of return and discouraged maintenance.

Also showing the effects of time, and speculation, is the Market Place block of Colorado Avenue in Old Pasadena. Purchased and scheduled to be rehabilitated in the early '80s with the blessing of the city, the block today is derelict, an eye sore inviting a disaster. In a similar state is the Huntington Sheraton, which had been the subject of a heated referendum last spring. There has been much talk about both projects, with lots of paper being shuffled, but so far no construction.

The Breed Street synagogue in Boyle Heights, the oldest remnant of Jewish roots in Los Angeles, is facing demolition if it is not renovated up to seismic standards. There is a slight hope the Jewish Historical Society might come to the rescue if somehow it can tap some of the funds now going to the more fashionable museum projects on the Westside.

Other endangered landmarks include the concrete block houses designed by Frank Lloyd Wright that are slowly decaying; an array of public facilities, in particular many branch libraries; and various streetscapes and neighborhoods threatened by insensitive overdevelopment.

Unfortunately, the list can go on and on. While we can take heart in the growing awareness and appreciation of the city's rich historic and creative legacy, what obviously also is needed is a renewed dedication to preserving it.

—Oct. 16, 1988

Recycling The Throwaway City

AT THE CEREMONIES LAST WEEK ANNOUNCING THE RECYCLING OF THE landmark Pan Pacific Auditorium, the comment was made that "Los Angeles is a throwaway city" that for years has discarded some its most interesting buildings.

The implication was that the planned restoration of the Stream-line Moderne-styled structure as a film and video center combined with a hotel and commercial complex was an exception and should be celebrated.

Celebrated the announcement should be, for the 50-year-old auditorium with its distinctive facade accented by four curved towers in the form of fins has over the last decade suffered from fire, vandalism and neglect to totter on collapse.

To lose the landmark—considered by architectural historians to be one of the outstanding examples of the streamline style that expressed America's love affair with machines and speed in the 1930s—would have been a tragedy.

But the auditorium's planned recycling is not an exception. Indeed, inspired by preservationists, there is a growing trend in the Los Angeles region and elsewhere across the country to save historic structures by having them adapted to new and updated uses.

Spurring the trend are such considerations as significant tax incentives, pride for communities that preserve their heritage, and, for politicians who support preservation, an aura of enlightenment.

The substantial list of local buildings of historical interest that have been or are being recycled include a former stock trading center into a threater complex, a bakery into an antique showroom, a funeral parlor into an office center, a jail into a community center, and a firehouse, jewelry store and haberdashery into restaurants.

With the help of the city's community Redevelopment Agency,

a variety of downtown office buildings on the National Register of Historic Places have been converted into, among other things, a design center and senior citizen housing. And just recently the agency announced that it is soliciting proposals to recycle three more office buildings.

"THE CONCEPT OF RECYCLING AN HISTORIC BUILDING IS BECOMING MORE AND more popular," observed Wayne Ratkovich, who, as a partner in the development firm of Ratkovich, Bowers Inc., rehabilitated the Oviatt and Fine Arts office towers downtown and the Wiltern Theatre and Pellissier Building in the mid-Wilshire district. "Their advantages in marketing and costs are catching on."

In Monrovia, an 80-year-old deteriorated hotel is being recycled as low- and moderate-income senior citizen housing by the nonprofit Los Angeles Community Design Center. "The project contributes to our historical efforts downtown, while promoting needed housing and commercial space," commented city official Steve Cervantes.

And what was once a landmark Whittier College dormitory, then an office building, has been converted into a retail and commercial complex. In West Hollywood, a plant store became a bank, and a furniture store that was once a gas station became a pricey, attractive restaurant, Trumps.

Actually, one of the most distinguished landmarks in Los Angeles, the Bradbury Building at 304 S. Broadway, was constructed in 1893 as a garment factory and only converted years later to an office building.

One of the more successful recycling efforts in recent years was the updating of a variety of athletic facilities for the 1984 Olympiad. Playing a major role in the retrofitting was the architectural firm of the Jerde Partnership, the offices of which, perhaps not incidentally, are located in a converted Pacific Electric Railway substation.

Ambitious as well as unique was a project completed this month in Pasadena. It involved the relocation across the city of a six-unit, 75-year-old Craftsman-styled bungalow complex, known as Gartz Court, and its sympathetic rehabilitation directed by the architectural firm of De Bretteville and Polyzoides as affordable housing.

The project was a joint effort of the City of Pasadena and Pasadena Heritage, the local preservation organization, which joined forces a few years ago when the court had been threatened with demolition to make way for an office complex.

Noting the construction details of the bungalows that include Arroyo stone chimneys, hardwood floors and beamed ceilings, Claire Bogaard of Pasadena Heritage commented that it would be impossible to reproduce the structures today, especially at the $70,000 to $90,000 price for which they were sold at a lottery last year.

The executive director of the Los Angeles Conservancy, Ruthann Lehrer, added: "People are beginning to recognize that historic rehabilitation makes economic sense, is marketable and is important in creating in communities a needed identity and sense of place."

—Jan. 25, 1985

Playing Politics With a Landmark

If you ever wonder why certain stretches of Los Angeles look so alien—why sympathetic landmarks are demolished and why tacky developments are allowed—consider the saga of a historic Hollywood bungalow complex.

It was just a few months ago that the City Council, at the request of then-Councilwoman Peggy Stevenson, declared the 13-unit complex at Highland and Camrose avenues a historic-cultural monument. And it followed that action up with a no-nonsense, one-year building moratorium, specifically focused on the Highland and Cahuenga area.

A question was raised at the time whether the complex was of sufficient historic interest to warrant the designation. I agreed with an impressive list of architectural historians and felt it did. (Because the demolition of landmarks is irreversible, and the city's architectural heritage so frail, if one errs it should be on the side of preservation.)

There also was a question whether the designation and the subsequent moratorium were approved, not because of their merits, but simply to help Stevenson win neighborhood support in her unsuccessful reelection campaign against Michael Woo.

Whatever the motivation, the fact is that the council voted for the designation and the moratorium. The council, in effect, gave its word to support the preservation effort, if only for six months, and the building moratorium there for one year.

However, the situation changed when Woo defeated Stevenson. With the lame-duck Stevenson absenting herself (so much for her abiding commitment to neighborhoods), the council on her last day in office reversed itself and granted an exemption to the moratorium to the owner of the bungalow complex.

The action was a clear message to the owner, the Jan Development Co., to ignore the landmark designation and the moratorium and to move ahead on plans for a 180-unit apartment house on the site. Within weeks the company was seeking approval of demolition permits.

From a broader perspective, the council's action also was so blatantly political, and handled in such a questionable manner, that it raises issues that go far beyond the fate of the threatened landmark.

These issues include the integrity of the city's cultural heritage ordinance and the character of the City Council. They have been sullied by the affair, prompting a harder look at how the council reviews planning and preservation issues.

The council seems to have forgotten very quickly that the idea behind the designation—and the cultural heritage ordinance itself—was to give the tenants, the owner, the city and, perhaps other interested groups, time to explore the possibility of preserving the fragile housing complex.

Critical to the process is the element of good faith, which, in this case, seems to have been missing. At least that is the way the situation appears judging from the subsequent actions of Jan Development, which ignores calls, tenants claim, to meet and discuss how the complex might be saved, if not simply maintained in compliance with basic health, safety and building codes.

Instead, the Beverly-Hills-based company headed by Jan Czuker apparently was making other phone calls as it lined up support for its request for an exemption.

And who else should Jan Development turn to but Councilman Arthur K. Snyder. Holywood may be far from Snyder's district, but if there is a developer who needs help, Snyder has been known to extend his concerns beyond council lines, as he has in the past to call developers for campaign contributions.

Snyder has announced that he will resign from the council. However, he now says he is reconsidering his decision to resign and just may run again. If so, he will need a well-funded campaign chest.

Exactly how Snyder came out of the woodwork to be appointed a substitute for the absent Robert Farrell as a member of the influential Planning and Environmental Committee on the day the exemption was heard is not clear, thanks in part to Council President Pat Russell. She did not return phone inquiries, though her staff did note that she was absent the day of the vote. How convenient.

Acting that day as council president, Joan Milke Flores, in a rare legislative move, appointed Snyder to the committee. The other members of the committee are Howard Finn, chairman, and John Ferraro. But before the exemption could be heard—it was the last item on a long agenda—Finn had to hurry off to a previous commitment. With Ferraro ducking in and out of the hearing, Snyder assumed the position of acting chairman.

According to persons who were there, Snyder was very sympathetic to the representative of Jan Development Co. while all but ignoring the opposition. A subsequent reading of the committee report submitted to the council by Snyder, and the letter to the council by the company requesting the exemption, indicates a number of similar discrepancies.

These include statements that the moratorium was never intended to include the landmark property, when in fact it was the centerpiece of the action. Also misrepresented to the council was the cost of the property. According to the committee report, the developer said in a plea of hardship that the property was purchased for about $2 million. The figure on the registered trust deed is $1,040,000.

The Highland-Camrose affair has to be one of the more ignominious in the council's history, going beyond a simple question of whether a particular bungalow court is worthy of landmark status or whether indeed it can be saved.

But of course, what the council has done it can undo. At stake is the council's integrity, or what is left of it.

—July 21, 1985

A HAPPY ENDING JUST MIGHT BE IN STORE FOR THE HISTORIC HIGHLAND-Camrose bungalow court that had been threatened for nearly a year with demolition to make way for a large apartment complex.

Failing to negotiate its purchase from the Jan Development Co., the county Board of Supervisors has voted to condemn the property, with a view to recycling the bungalows as classrooms for the Los Angeles Philharmonic Institute for Young Musicians and Conductors. Some of the land also would be used for picnic grounds and parks, serving both the nearby Hollywood Bowl and the community.

There are still problems to overcome, but so far the community has demonstrated a remarkable acumen in getting its way. Helping has been a responsive councilman, Michael Woo, and Supervisor Ed Edelman.

—April 20, 1986

They were saved, and are scheduled to be rehabilitated.

ONE LANDMARK STILL INTACT, THANKFULLY, IS THE BLACKER HILL HOUSE at 1177 Hillcrest Ave., Pasadena, a magnificently detailed California bungalow designed in 1907 by Charles and Henry Greene. It has been proposed for the Nationald Register so that it cannot be altered without a lot of aggravation for the owners.

However, the house recently has been listed for sale with Coldwell Banker. The asking price for the dark-shingled, sprawling 12,000-square-foot house is $1.95 million. Let us hope someone or some organization out there with resources appreciates the fact that it isn't every day a piece of living art goes on the market.

—Sept. 2, 1984

ALERT. . .THE HISTORIC BLACKER HOUSE IN PASADENA, DESIGNED AND built by Greene & Greene in 1907 and considered by some to be more impressive than their Gamble House, has been sold. That is fine, but Pasadena Heritage reports that many of the exquisite interior craftsman fixtures have been removed for sale.

The preservationist group is concerned because the fixtures had been designed by Green & Greene specifically for the house, and their removal lessens the value of the fixtures, the house and its historical integrity. They are urging the new owner, who lives in Texas, to return the fixtures. Keep turned for further details.

—May 19, 1985

UPDATE ON THE TEXAS CHAIN-SAW MASSACRE OF THE HISTORIC BLACKER house, considered one of the finest examples of the California craftsman bungalow style.

For those who might have forgotten, the melodrama involves the purchase of the house last spring for $1.2 million by Texas cattleman Barton English. It seems that English then stripped the house of an estimated 40 to 50 light fixtures and other furnishings of Tiffany glass and crafted wood and leather that had been designed expressly for the house by the Greenes and is valued at up to an estimated $25,000 a piece.

Outraged, preservationists across the country protested, with their echo being heard in Texas, where English said he would consider returning the fixtures and selling the house, presumably to a preservationist group for safekeeping.

This quieted things down as preservationists scurried about trying to line up support, some funding and perhaps a "fat cat" or an institution that would like to make the Blacker their home.

But no sooner had the media stopped calling and marched off, so did English. Negotiations have stalled, with the fixtures being said to be in Texas at English's ranch, or in New York City with an art dealer, or with some at both. Wherever, they are not in the Blacker house where they belong.

—Sept. 22, 1985

Pasadena's Threatened Heritage

PASADENA IS A COMMUNITY WITH ONE OF THE NATION'S RICHER ARCHITEC-tural heritages, and thanks to local preservationists, a relatively sophisticated recognition of how well that heritage serves the city's pride and real estate values.

The heritage includes a wealth of distinctive California Bungalows, gracious Spanish Colonial mansions, a smattering of dainty Queen Anne Revivals, a delicious wedding cake of a city hall centering an exuberant civic center, and a few remnants of the era when Pasadena was one of America's posh resorts.

Among the more revered remnants are the gilded Hotel Green, a Moorish concoction that perserveres as an apartment complex, and the palatial, rambling Huntington Sheraton Hotel, the fate of which now lies in the hands of the city it so graciously served for 80 years.

The Pasadena Planning Commission is scheduled to make a decision Wednesday on a request for a zoning change that would permit the demolition of the landmark structure designed by Charles Whittlesey and Myron Hunt. The request comes from a fledgling group of local investors currently in escrow to purchase the property from Keikyu USA Inc., a Japanese conglomerate

LAST YEAR, IN THE WAKE OF THE MEXICO CITY EARTHQUAKE, KEIKYU CLOSED down the main structure of the hotel, claiming it was seismically unsafe. But while stating loudly that the structure would have to be demolished, Keikyu quietly retained a land-use consultant to see how the 23-acre site might be redeveloped.

Now we have the local group, headed by Lary Mielke, claiming the same thing Keikyu did, and adding, for good measure, that it is also economically infeasible to renovate the landmark—as if—just because they are local—their plea should have any more merit than Keikyu's. And in the shadows, as before, is the Sheraton as the potential operator.

The time has come for the city to become a little more responsible in this melodrama and order for itself, impartial, thorough engineering and economic studies.

The city should not have to depend on the obviously prejudiced good will of the potential developers, who in footing most of the bill

147

for the studies, also have interpreted them to their obvious benefit, and not necessarily in the interest of the preservation-minded community.

The city also should not be swayed by the promise that if the developers are allowed to demolish the hotel, they will replace it with a replica. At this point in the debate, that is like saying let the patient die so we can use a few limbs and organs to build a better model.

No thank you, Dr. Frankenstein.

There is no question that the Huntington desperately needs help; indeed that sections of it might have to be demolished. Certainly, the tacky renovations it suffered over the last few decades at the hands of the Sheraton should be excised.

But before whatever major surgery is allowed to be undertaken, let us be sure that it is necessary, and that the hotel cannot be treated more kindly and restored.

The Huntington is just too entwined with Pasadena's heritage to be abandoned on the basis of partial studies and the good will and slick public relations efforts of neophyte developers.

ALSO BEING DEBATED THESE DAYS IN PASADENA IS THE FATE OF A PROPOSAL to declare a select neighborhood studded with some classic bungalow-styled houses in the city's first official Landmark District.

Known as Bungalow Heaven, the neighborhood bounded by Lake and Hill avenues and Washington and Orange Grove boulevards, still retains much of the flavor of when it was developed in the 1910s and '20s.

However, in recent years in response to maintenance problems and bad advice, a few owners not knowing the historic value of the bungalows, have stripped the exteriors of detailing and covered the outside walls with stucco.

The result has been a loss of charm and, ultimately, a loss of value for not only the individual house, but for the whole neighborhood. In addition, a rare enclave of architectural interest and character has been diminished.

As a district, design guidelines most likely would be established, restricting what an owner might do to the exterior of his or her house facing the street. Along with the restrictions will come city advice and possible aid.

While obviously an infringement on the prerogatives of ownership, such guidelines certainly are in the best interest of neighborhood pride and value and preserving and protecting a piece of Pasadena's history.

ONE OF THE EVENTS THAT RAISED THE CITY'S CONSCIOUSNESS OF ITS RICH architectural heritage was the strippping of the valuable fixtures of the Blacker House by an out-of-town collector who had purchased the Greene & Greene-designed and crafted landmark.

Since that sad time, there have been various successful attempts to discourage the cynical sale of the fixtures and unsuccesssful attempts to both buy back the house and to have the fixtures returned.

One of the more notable attempts was a proposal by the Los Angeles Museum of Science and Industry to get a donor to buy the house and dedicate it to the public for use as a residence for visiting dignitaries and scholars. Even the intransigent owner-collector liked the idea.

But the donor the museum was counting on is said to have lost interest, and the proposal faltered. While it has the enthusiasm, the museum just does not have the money to pursue the idea.

—Aug. 24, 1986

Struggling West Adams Shows Its Stuff

A DOZEN HISTORIC HOUSES AND A RECYCLED FIRE STATION ARE ON DISPLAY today and tomorrow in the fourth annual home tour in the struggling West Adams community southwest of downtown.

The mix of stately, well-detailed Victorian, Craftsman and Mission Revival-style buildings to be shown are engaging, as are the scattered pockets of the community in which they are nestled.

Also on display, and worthy of admiration and praise, is the human spirit motivating the renovations and the attempt to restore the once (and future?) fashionable area.

The effort in racially mixed West Adams has been slowly gaining momentum over the last decade, prompted by relatively reasonable prices for some well-appointed, spacious houses, increasing interest in historic restoration and the encouragement of preservationist groups.

Each time I have visited the area, most recently last weekend with my family, there is cause for celebration: another landmark renovated, a cluster of houses preserved and the sometimes controversial resolve of residents stronger, if not wiser.

Roughly paralleling the Santa Monica Freeway from about Vermont Avenue west to Crenshaw Boulevard, the area contains some notable remnants from the time when it was—for nearly half a century—*the* desired neighborhood of the rich and famous.

However, more prevalent at present is the deterioration and insensitive development of the last few decades. The scars of discrimination, joblessness, crime, neglect and poor planning are depressingly visible in West Adams.

It is no wonder that some long-time and long-suffering residents have viewed the restoration movement with suspicion, wondering if it too is just another gimmick by hustling outsiders to spend a few years in the community, extract a profit and move on.

I frankly doubt that that is the motive of the vast majority of preservationists in West Adams, given the commitment on display there, knowing the blood, sweat, tears, frustration and money that restoration efforts exact, and sympathizing with the anxieties of those who move into so-called changing neighborhoods.

But even if profit is the motive of a few, it is not the preservationists who subdivide once proud mansions and comfortable houses

149

into clusters of bootleg units, strip historic buildings of ornaments and value, abandon cars on streets and lawns, strew garbage in vacant lots or bulldoze landmarks to put up raw, insensitively designed and cheaply constructed apartments.

And if some preservationists do move on, they certainly leave the community improved, its property values higher and its heritage as an attractive, convenient residential area enhanced.

Communities are constantly in a state of change. It is nice that on occasion it is for the better.

—Nov. 9, 1986

ALERT: AN OMINOUS CLOUD HAS GATHERED OVER ONE OF THE CITY'S MORE lovely spots, the rose garden in Exposition Park.

It seems the garden, with about 16,000 bushes representing 190 varieties, would be the site of a parking garage being proposed by the Los Angeles Coliseum Commission.

Of course, to find out, you had to read between the lines of a report disclosing that the commission is seeking authority from the state to issue $75 million in bonds to build parking structures.

No doubt the commission will argue the below-grade-level facility it is proposing between the museums of Natural History and Science and Industry will be built in such a way that garden could be replicated on the garage roof.

But don't bet on it.

Even if the commission kept its word, the critical access and scale of the now sunken garden would be ruined, bushes would be damaged and killed, and the rhythm of the garden irreparably harmed. Such efforts hardly ever work.

To be sure, more parking is needed to serve the Coliseum and Exposition Park and its museums, though it should not be at the price of the rose garden.

Other potential sites exist, and those are what the commission should concentrate on.

As for the rose garden, the commission should not even be thinking about it as a site for anything other than a stroll.

—Nov. 10, 1986

The garden was spared.

Craftsman Period: a Time of Glory

OUR APPRECIATION OF THE ARTS AND CRAFTS MOVEMENT THAT FLOUR-ished in Southern California at the turn of the century continues to grow.

The movement called for an idealized, simple life, respectful and reflective of the local environment, history and culture, dedication to the revival of handicraft and an all-encompassing architectural style.

This style of so-called "sweetness and light" was based on the proposition that good design involved good craftsmanship; and in serving the user, that it envelop him or her as a total experience, and not be simply applied as ornamentation to catch the eye and be a conversation piece.

(The proposition is a particularly refreshing one for those interested in architecture to consider, especially in these days of self-indulgent designs that all but ignore the user in vain attempts of self-promotion disguised as art.)

Leading the pursuit of the movement's admirable goals with uncommon fervor were the brothers Charles and Henry Greene, who as architects and artisans designed, built and furnished a number of exquisite Craftsman-styled houses in the early 1900s, most of them in and around Pasadena.

It was a glorious time for Southern California architecture; a time perhaps best expressed in the lovingly preserved and presented Greene & Greene designed and furnished Gamble House in Pasadena.

And now, thanks to a group of anonymous donors and an agreement announced last week between the USC School of Architecture, the Gamble House and the Huntington Library, a variety of additional furnishings designed by the Greene brothers will go on public display in the Virginia Steele Scott Gallery on the Huntington's grounds in San Marino.

The center promises to provide a needed resource to serve the growing interest among scholars and the public in the Arts and Crafts movement and the works of Greene & Greene. It is an interest that has been nurtured over the last 20 years by a dedicated Gamble House staff and docents council, orchestrated by director Randell Makinson under a joint agreement between USC and the City of Pasadena.

Their continued efforts to preserve the fruits of a singular period in Southern California's marvelous architectural heritage deserve the thanks of present and future generations.

More good news for Greene & Greene fans: The vultures that had been circling the historic Pratt House in Ojai—as it wallowed in an involved inheritance hassle—at last have been driven away.

Unfortunately, as the dispute dragged on, the vulture collectors were able to snatch up some valuable Greene & Greene furnishings, thanks to ill-advised auctions prompted by Security Pacific National Bank trustees.

But there will be no more auctions now that the house and its 52 acres have been sold to Pasadena preservationist Ken McCormick, replete with deed restrictions and protective easements that, hopefully, will preserve the Craftsman landmark. As for the bank, perhaps as penance it can aid in the effort to have some of the furnishings returned.

Not so good is the news that the ambitious plans announced a few years ago with much fanfare to recycle the historic Pan Pacific Auditorium in the Fairfax district as a hotel and film center have fallen through.

With its flagpole pylons shaped like giant fins, the sculpted facade—hinting of speed and energy even in its deteriorated state

151

today—is still a marvelous example of the Streamline Moderne style. It was designed in 1935 by William Wurdeman and Welton Becket and is listed on the National Register of Historic Places.

Since the major design element is just a facade, more or less tacked on a barn of a building, the landmark could lend itself to a variety of reuses on the site, or moved elsewhere. Certainly, it should not be demolished, as Los Angeles County Supervisor Ed Edelman has hinted it might be.

It is unfortunate that the plans for the hotel and film center collapsed; that graffiti has been sprayed on portions of the building, and that there have been some unfortunate incidents involving things in the adjacent park. But one should not blame the Pan Pacific for these problems and punish it with demolition.

Indeed, a viable reuse of the building and site, generating activities and crowds, would be a much more positive influence on the park than a vacant lot patrolled now and then by wary police officers.

The park needs a recycled Pan Pacific, and so does the Fairfax district, to lend it a distinctive focal point, and the city, to remind it of rich design history. Demolition of the Pan Pacific would be a tragedy.

ALSO DESERVING A REASONABLE TIME FOR A VIABLE USE TO BE FOUND FOR IT before being sacrificed to the wrecker's ball is the venerable Ambassador Hotel on Wilshire Boulevard.

Though it would be hard to classify the 66-year-old hotel as an architectural landmark, it is certainly a cultural one, with a history entwined with that of the city's.

In addition, given its 23.5-acre site, other uses could be developed on it to help subsidize the operations of the hotel, or to recycle and include it in a possible residential and commercial mixed-use project. What is needed is some imagination and resolve.

What also is needed is time. Following a request earlier this month by the owners for a demolition permit, the city has from today six weeks to declare the hotel a landmark. This would delay demolition from six to 12 months and allow the owners and preservationists to explore ways the landmark might be saved.

There is really no need for the hotel to become a fading memory and its site another vacant lot on Wilshire. If we keep allowing our landmarks to be demolished, Los Angeles could become just another lobotomized sprawl, an anonymous city north of Orange County.

In destroying our history, we also destroy our future.

—June 21, 1987

MAKING SENSE. IN THE PLEASANT ENCLAVE OF MELROSE HILL IN SOUTHEAST Hollywood, residents are debating a proposal to designate the neighborhood a Historic Preservation Overlay Zone. For anyone concerned with the area's sense of place, and future, there really should be no debate.

As a historic district, residents would be able to review proposed local construction projects to determine whether they are consistent with the architectural style and spirit of the neighborhood, at present a well-scaled eclectic mix of houses built during the first 20 years or so of this century.

While only advisory, these powers would insure the neighborhood some protection against slapdash housing additions and overscaled apartment slabs. The latter dingbats seem to be rising in pockets of the city these days like toadstools in a lawn after a rain, to replace mini-malls as the current bane of neighborhoods.

Being a historic district also should help bind the residents to rally for more positive actions, such as tree plantings, street maintenance, neighborhood watch, while at the same time lending the area a sense of pride. This inevitably translates into higher property values, which one would think would appeal to the Philistines at present opposing the designation.

—Aug. 2, 1987

VERY LATE IS THE HOUR FOR THE LOS FELIZ THEATRE ON NORTH VERMONT Avenue, at least under the management of the Laemmle organization. The theater is scheduled to close to the public tonight after more than 50 years of serving movie lovers and, more importantly, as the anchor of one of the few urbane neighborhood retail streets in Los Angeles.

For me, for years, a big night out on the town was a dinner at one of the ethnic restaurants in the area, a movie at the Los Feliz, and later browsing and inevitably buying a book at Chatterton's, at 1881 N. Vermont Ave.

I fear, as does the community, that without the theater there the vital character of the street would begin to unravel. That is why the effort to somehow keep the theater functioning, if not under the Laemmles then someone else, is so critical, and has rallied local merchants and residents to form Friends of the Los Feliz Theatre.

The theater is vital to the social and economic well-being of the surrounding community and should be considered, if not a historical landmark, then certainly a cultural one, with every effort made to save it.

—Oct. 11, 1987

The Los Feliz Theatre, and the Melrose Hill neighborhood, perseveres.

A Renewed Boyance About Piers

THERE IS SOMETHING REFRESHINGLY REAL YET MAGICAL ABOUT PIERS. They can take you out to sea to enjoy in relative safety its expanse, scents, surf and mesmerizing sunsets.

From piers, also, you can glimpse from a vantage point the delights of the beach, or look back for a rare synoptic view of the sprawling beach towns and the city and mountains beyond.

And in this increasingly avaricious, pay-as-you-go or one-admission-price-covers-all city, the piers are free.

To enduring fishermen, the piers occasionally even reward the old-fashioned virtues of patience, fortitude and hope with a day's catch.

Or, as on the Santa Monica Pier with its captivating carrousel, bumper car ride and funky food stands and shops, they can evoke the spirit of a festive, if frayed, past when seaside promenading was a popular activity.

INDEED, IN THE 1920s SANTA MONICA BAY WAS A PROMENADER'S PARADISE, studded with so-called pleasure piers replete with careening roller coasters, opulent restaurants and all sorts of honky-tonk attractions, fanciful sights and enticing smells.

Then came the Depression, World War II, the liberating car, Disneyland, Knott's Berry Farm and Magic Mountain, among other distractions, along with fires and bruising surfs to reduce the piers to a frail few.

These thoughts came to mind last weekend when, at the Manhattan Beach Old Hometown Fair, I was asked to sign a petition to save the 66-year-old Manhattan Beach Pier. Circulating the petition was the local historical society, which declared in a mimeographed handout that the pier, a vital element in the community's identity and character was threatened.

It seems that the county, not wanting to foot a steep repair bill and worried about liability, on Oct. 1, had turned the pier over to the state. According to the organization appropriately labeled Pier Pressure, the state is now considering whether to repair, replace or possibly tear down the structure, and has asked for public opinion. Hence the petition.

In Manhattan Beach, emotions concerning the pier are running as deep as summer tans there, and that's deep.

Residents are worried that if the pier is replaced—at an estimated cost of $4 million—the state will insist it be encrusted with food stands and shops to generate funds to pay for the structure and its continued maintenance. From the state's point of view, this is not an entirely unreasonable request in these days of tightening budget strings.

Most Manhattan Beach residents want the crumbling concrete pier simply repaired—at an estimated cost of $2 million—and the marine study laboratory, bathrooms and hamburger stand at its ocean end kept at their present modest size. And, of course, they want the state to foot the bill.

But Manhattan Beach is a bottom-line community that understands finances, and on the pier itself, along with the odors of hot dogs, hamburgers, tanning lotion, fresh-caught fish and the sea itself, I smelled a compromise brewing.

Nevertheless, I took a stand. Being sentimental in general about piers and specifically about Manhattan Beach, where I was married some years ago in a house overlooking the ocean, I signed the petition and also purchased a T-shirt declaring "THE MANHATTAN BEACH PIER, AN IRREPLACEABLE LANDMARK."

THOUGHTS OF PIERS ALSO PROMPTED ME TO PAY A VISIT TO SANTA MONICA Pier and see how its restoration was progressing. One of the last amusement piers on the California coast, it has been battered in recent years by fierce winter storns, unsavory crowds and convoluted local politics.

Happily, the one constant in the Santa Monica stew has been a commitment from all quarters to save and upgrade the pier, and there are signs that it is at last happening.

An inviting children's play sculpture and new stairways and ramps—designed with characteristic style by the firms of Moore Ruble Yudell and Campbell & Campbell—mark the southern entrance to the pier. There are also new pergolas, palm trees and lighting, as well as a tastefully restored carrousel building.

This, plus some freshly painted facades and the echo of a popular summer concert series there, all hinted of a more family-oriented, relaxed pier reaching out to the ocean, and to a broader community.

To be sure, much more needs to be done to restore the pier and its spirit. Like people over time, piers change and need care.

—Oct. 11, 1986

The Manhattan Beach pier was saved.

Historic Houses Need Getty Help

THE GETTY TRUST SEEMS DETERMINED TO CREATE AN ARCHITECTURAL landmark in the hills of West Los Angeles, having spent years and hundreds of thousands of dollars selecting an architect and earmarking at least $100 million for construction.

We wish it well and hope that architect Richard Meier will rise to the occasion, as we are sure he will to the budget, and create something beyond his usually predictable pristine, well-composed but ultimately unsympathetic structures.

With an endowment of an estimated $2.3 billion, making it the richest institution of its kind in the world, the trust envisions a complex in large part dedicated to the conservation of art and to art education. It is a noble cause.

Meanwhile, as the Getty goes about planning for the complex and gathering in art, three of the world's masterpieces are under siege right here in Southern California. It is a situation that begs the involvement of the trust, if not for the conservation of the art, then simply as a politic gesture to its host community.

The internationally acclaimed art pieces are the Ennis-Brown House in Los Feliz designed by Frank Lloyd Wright, the Blacker house in Pasadena and the Pratt House in Ojai, both designed by Charles and Henry Greene.

It is not that any one person, corporation, community or agency is acting out of maliciousness, as would a vandal, but the effects are the same. Despite the good will and intensions from almost all quarters, the design integrity of two of the houses is being savaged and the third is deteriorating.

While the situations involving the responsibility for the restoration and preservation of each of the properties are quite different, the bottom line for all is the harsh economics of owning and maintaining a historic house.

Historic they are, with the Ennis-Brown house considered the best example of Wright's Mayan-styled, concrete-block design; and the Blacker and Pratt houses superb renditions of the quest of the Greene brothers for the ultimate California bungalow, replete with exquisite furnishings and finishes.

The result is that not only are the houses works of art, they also are civic treasurers, nourishing the public's pride and sense of history, and Southern California's cultural aspirations.

As works of art, the houses therefore should be treated as such, just as if they were in a private collection or a public museum. Certainly they are as valuable as, say, a rare vase. It also seems they are as fragile.

In the case of the Ennis-Brown house, an estimated $500,000 is needed to preserve the concrete blocks that distinguish the design and another $100,000 a year to simply maintain the structure. To raise the money, the present owner, the nonprofit Trust for the Preservation of Cultural Heritage, has had to resort to renting the house for receptions and parties, which nobody likes, particularly and understandably, the neighbors.

If the neighbors' recent protests have done anything, they have exposed the present tenuous state of the maintenance and management of the house.

As for the Blacker house, it was sold last spring for $1.2 million to a Texas cattleman, who, on the questionable advice of a New York art dealer, proceeded to strip the house of its integral furnishings and fixtures. The resulting protests prompted the Texan to offer to sell back the house and fixtures, if a responsible preservationist group can be found with the money.

The situation surrounding the Pratt house is a little more complicated, with the house and its 52 acres in Ojai being controlled by bank trustees while the Pratt family tries to resolve inheritance problems. And, of course, there are lawsuits and the usual gathering of vultures. Meanwhile, a few furnishings are said to have been sold, and the house and grounds deteriorate.

IN REVIEWING ITS GOALS, THE GETTY HAS SAID IT DOES NOT WANT TO USE ITS enviable financial resources in unfair competition with other institutions to obtain art objects. But there is no real competition for historic houses, with enlightened patrons very much in demand. Here is an area ripe for the trust, and in keeping with the preservationist interests of its founder, the late J. Paul Getty.

The trust also has said it did not want to get involved with 20th-Century art. Presumably, it meant the fine arts, where the competition is fierce and fickle. But if it meant architecture as well, we hope exceptions can be made, bearing in mind that flexibility is the hallmark of all great institutions.

As for the often sticky aspects of restoration, preservation and operations, the Getty could work through other institutions or set up a new one. A fine example is how the USC School of Architecture joined with the city of Pasadena, and how together with a support group, they operate the Greene & Greene Gamble House.

A similar association could serve the Brown, Blacker and Pratt houses, but first they must be saved. Asking local agencies and schools to step in at this point would only waste time. None has the resources of the Getty.

The trust already has demonstrated its commitment to create a new architectural landmark in Los Angeles. By becoming involved in conserving the Wright and Greene & Greene houses, it could also demonstrate its commitment to existing landmarks, as well as Southern California's rare and rich architectural heritage.

Considering what is at stake, it is a modest proposal.

—Oct. 6, 1985

NEEDED, THE GETTY TRUST, OR SOMEONE COMMITTED TO THE PRESERVATION of art coming to the rescue of the Ennis-Brown house in Los Feliz designed by Frank Lloyd Wright, the Blacker house in Pasadena and the Pratt house in Ojai, both designed by Charles and Henry Greene—three world masterpieces under seige. Of course, the Getty is a logical choice, given its endowment of an estimated $2.3 billion dedicated to the conservation of art, as opposed to, say, Michael's restaurant near the Trust's offices in Santa Monica, where the Trust often wines and dines visitors at no modest cost. Perhaps a fraction of this expense can be used instead to maintain local architectural landmarks.

—Dec. 15, 1985

This was an idea I would not let go of, and kept pushing the Getty.

Waiting for The Getty to Step Forward

MANY OF THE CITY'S LANDMARKS ARE IN NEED OF HELP. The decorated concrete blocks that compose Frank Lloyd Wright's magnificent Ennis-Brown house in Los Feliz are slowly crumbling. Hurting also are Wright's Freeman and Hollyhock houses in Hollywood.

Other landmarks needing help, ranging from minor rehabilitation to major structural repairs, include the Garnier Building, Fire Station No. 30, the Eagle Rock Library, the Landfair Apartments, the Wattles Mansion, Little Tokyo's Union Church and the old Venice city hall and police station, to name just a few.

And then there is an aging Los Angeles City Hall. It has been selected as the prime target in an ambitious effort, labeled Project Restore, which is trying to rally public and private institutions and citizens to aid in the preservation and conservation of historic municipal facilities.

Project Restore has the enthusiasm, but, unfortunately, not the money. Though it has received some help from the city's Community

Redevelopment Agency and a smattering of private pledges, the total of nearly $500,000 is just a fraction of what is needed to do a proper restoration of the 60-year-old landmark.

THE SAME PROBLEM PERPLEXES THE VARIOUS PUBLIC AGENCIES AND PRIVATE nonprofit groups that oversee most of the other landmarks in the city. Funds for minimum maintenance are scraped together out of sparse budgets and by holding endless benefits, conducting tours and renting out facilities for film locations or weddings, or anything. Little is ever left over for any substantial rehabilitation.

Meanwhile, the rich, diverse architectural landmarks of Los Angeles continue to deteriorate.

Most of the deterioration may not be as vivid as the growing pile of crumbled concrete blocks lying on the slope beneath the proud Ennis-Brown House, but it is happening. Any person or institution with an appreciation of art history must be moved.

With this in mind, it is time for yet another appeal to the Getty Trust.

Though the trust in the past has deflected such appeals, using arbitrary guidelines as an inflexible shield, the logic for its involvement remains.

Certainly the landmarks present a wonderful opportunity for the Getty to make a magnanimous gesture to its host city while also reaffirming its incorporated commitment to the preservation of art.

The timing also could be auspicious for the Getty. Recently, the trust has been the subject of some strong criticism of a few of its administrative policies and priorities and personnel, and could use such a challenging program as historic preservation to demonstrate its institutional mettle.

IN ADDITION, THE GETTY IS SCHEDULED WITHIN THE NEXT FEW MONTHS TO request from the city needed zoning approvals for its ambitious art center proposal for the hills above Brentwood. An extra dose of local good will, generated by aiding the needy landmarks, might help to overcome some of the criticism that the siting of the center consciously isolates an imperious Getty from the city at large, while impacting a particular area.

Aside from the planning issues, I am hopeful that the design of the center by noted architect Richard Meier be both sympathetic and singular. With its 52-acre setting and a projected $100-million-plus budget, the center does promise to be an imposing edifice for the Getty and an architectural landmark for the city.

Such philanthropic organizations do like their edifices, as demonstrated, for instance, by the luxurious landmark that Kevin Roche and the late John Dinkeloo designed for the Ford Foundation in New York City.

But while the foundation did expend a considerable amount on the building and, in particular, the interior design, it also established a generous fund for its host city.

Known appropriately as The Fund for The City of New York, it was set up to receive in lieu of tax payments from the Ford Foundation to be used for social sciences and services on the local level consistent with the Ford's commitment on the national level.

Whether its creation was motivated by guilt or good will, the fund has served New York City well and could serve as a precedent for the Getty's relationship with Los Angeles.

SPECIFICALLY FOCUSED ON THE PRESERVATION OF ARCHITECTURAL LANDmarks, such a "fund for the city of Los Angeles" certainly would be consistent with the Getty's local prominence and international purpose.

As for the fund's budget, a modest 10% of the Getty's mandated annual expenditures of an estimated $156 million seems a reasonable beginning. That would be about $15 million, which also is just about 15% of what the Getty is projecting it will spend in attempting, with the help of Meier, to create its own architectural landmark.

(For comparisons to the projected $100-million-plus cost of the Getty fine arts center, it will take perhaps $1 million to restore the landmark Ennis Brown and Freeman houses, $5 million to spruce up City Hall, and $10 million to recycle the Terminal Annex building downtown for an expanded and desperately needed Children's Museum.)

There is no reason why a commitment to "art" must be confined to museums or the vaults of study centers with limited hours and access, serving limited, generally privileged users.

If the Getty can accept the concept that architectural landmarks are indeed art, then it should think of Los Angeles as a museum without walls, and be prepared to aid it accordingly.

—April 26, 1987

The Getty announced an architectural preservation program in the fall of 1987. The first grants were issued a year later.

Preservation: the People's Choice

IN KEEPING WITH THE SPIRIT OF AN ELECTION YEAR, THE THEME FOR NAtional Preservation Week that begins today and runs through Saturday is "the people's choice."

Judging from what I see and hear in neighborhoods in Los Angeles and elsewhere, it is no contest. Preservation as a planning and design movement with political, economic and social implications has grown to be a major force in the shaping of our cities in recent years.

Very much on the increase has been the adaptation of dated buildings, historic or otherwise, to new uses, the restoration, conservation and preservation of others, and generally, a sensitive attempt to create a more varied and rich urban fabric.

The result has been new life and value to old neighborhoods and the laying to rest of the criticisms in real estate circles that preservation is a self-indulgent movement prompted by fear of progress. (Though, to be sure, there is no preventing some residents from using preservation as a banner to cloak their greed and prejudice.)

But overwhelmingly, the preservation movement has been a heartening response to an emerging awareness and appreciation of our rich architectural legacy and its potential to lend a city a sense of time, place and pride.

Nowhere is this more evident than in the rise of neighborhood activism. As noted by Daniel Hoye in the Los Angeles Conservancy's current newsletter, "community and homeowner groups are using the tools of preservation to instill pride of ownership, improved neighborhood image and a better quality of life." Hoye continues:

"By organizing to create a voice, neighborhood groups can better address civic issues, such as traffic, parking, crime, graffiti, improved city services, adjacent developments and incompatible land use. At the same time, they can protect architectural integrity through designation processes, which often provide economic benefits for homeowners."

These, of course, are not just preservation issues, but quality-of-life issues that apply to all neighborhoods, be they architecturally or historically distinctive, or not. It is a linkage that our politicians, planners and bureaucrats would be wise to recognize, given the drift of Los Angeles in the present and foreseeable future from a collection of first-growth suburbs into a logjam of a second-growth city.

—May 8, 1988

VII

SPECIAL
PLACES

Los Angeles' diverse and diverting design seems to glisten and glimmer, beckon and beguile, and fascinate and infuriate just a little bit more on weekends.

With most people putting work aside for the two days and the traffic easing, it is a time when one can explore with relative ease the shifting shape of the cityscape and its architecture, the persevering historic landmarks and the purposeful new ones, and generally the scenes that lend Los Angeles its verve.

Of course, for me as a design critic, it is work, albeit engrossing work—for one of the wonderful things about Los Angeles is its propensity for change. A problem is trying to keep up with it.

Sometimes it appears to me as I wander across the landscape that every day a new Los Angeles is born; a city of constant surprises and paradoxes, a brash, energetic, eccentric conglomeration.

Though historians may take exception, I am convinced it was not accidental that the automobile culture, the movie and aerospace industries, and Disneyland took root in and around Los Angeles, and that almost every conceivable, and a few inconceivable, fads and fashions have at some time or other sprouted in its consenting climate and spirit.

Certainly its architecture reflects this spirit. On select blocks in the Los Angeles region one can see everything from simple adobes, overwrought bungalows and stylized ranch houses to florid Victorians, sprawling Spanish Colonials, contentious French chateaux, curious Georgians, sleek moderns, and all sorts of eclectic and neo-eclectic experiments.

Such an encyclopedic range of structures can be found, among other places, north of Montana Avenue in Santa Monica, where on weekend mornings I usually take my 1 ½-year-old son, Josef, and my faithful English bull terrier, Max, for long walks.

While I try to decipher the architectural styles, Max tends to be more interested in the landscaping, and Josef the battered toys in the scattered garage sales.

Another area good for sales and architecture on weekends is West Hollywood, in particular Haverhurst Drive between Sunset and Santa Monica boulevards. Among the varying apartment buildings, there are the striking courtyard complexes designed in a flambouyant Spanish Colonial Revival style by Arthur Zwebell in the 1920s, and still attractive today.

And then a few blocks south is Melrose Avenue and its marvelous mix of punk, modern and Moderne-styled stores and shops, pulsating.

But walking along the serendipitous street, one wonders how much nicer it would be if the city and county did not narrow the sidewalk as was done a few years ago, and there was more room to stroll, for sidewalk cafes, and for landscaping. It certainly would have made it easier to push a stroller there.

We left the stroller outside and had to carry Josef into the landmark Storer House a few weekends ago for a reception there to benefit the Los Angeles Conservancy. Though it was obvious that when Frank Lloyd Wright designed the textile block structure in 1923 he did not have children in mind, the tour of the house tucked away in the Hollywood Hills was fascinating. Wright's rich Los Angeles legacy perseveres.

BUT THIS SATURDAY MORNING WE WILL BE WALKING SOUTH OF MONTANA Avenue in Santa Monica, where we live, collecting signatures on a petition for the 20th Street Alley Safety Committee to get the city to do something about the cars that use the alley as a through street.

The alley also is used by children for skateboarding and by adults to wash cars, walk dogs and exchange greetings and gossip. Indeed, it is the alley and not the traditional sidewalk that has become a focus of the neighborhood, and is now threatened by careening cars.

Once the ink dries on the petition, it is off to another spirited neighborhood, this one in Manhattan Beach for the annual arts and crafts fair there, to eat lunch, browse and perhaps take a peek at some of the new beach houses.

Maybe there also will be time to drive a few miles south to Torrance to tour a new Tower Records store there designed by a New York-based architectural firm, Buttrick White & Burtis. From the photographs of the plans of the building sent to me it looks as if the flashy, freestyle structure might be fun.

I want to get there soon, before the store and the style fades, as some designs do when basking in the sun too long. One must move quickly in Los Angeles to keep up with change, if not perhaps stay ahead of it.

Having a child in a stroller, and having a weekend to push it, helps.

—Oct. 4, 1986

On The Plaza

LIKE WELL-TRAINED PIGEONS, THE MORNING RUNNERS HOME IN ON MALaga Cove Plaza, wending their way with gritty determination along tree-shaded, lushly landscaped residential streets and lanes that gently dip, rise and curve through Palos Verdes Estates, finally to descend, panting, on the pleasantly faded, red-tile-topped plaza.

There, they tend to downshift with a sigh into the Sidewalk Cafe and Bakery, which everybody seems to call "Jack's" after a former owner, and in a rush of rationalization ("I must have burned up 3,000 calories getting here") reward their morning tribulation with a heavily sweetened pastry ("it goes right into the bloodstream and to the muscles") and a cup of coffee ("it helps jump-start my heart for the run home").

The runners are only the first of successive waves of local residents and occasional visitors that each day roll into Malaga Cove Plaza, tucked into the northwest slope of the hilly, verdant peninsula, just off of circuitous North Palos Verdes Drive. Replete with a slightly smaller, 1930s marble replica of Nettuno—a famed 16th-Century Bolognese bronze fountain—in the central piazza-cum-parking lot, the collection of arcaded, flower-bedecked commercial buildings is one of the more engaging people places in Southern California. "It's our hangout," says Janet Connolly-Berens as she somehow, with the aid of friend Donna York-Ames, bottle-feeds her two infants in separate strollers and takes intermittent bites of her luncheon salad at a cafe table.

She adds that "BC"—before the children—she used to jog with her husband, Jerry, almost every morning from their home to the plaza, 3.5 miles, have a pastry and a cup of coffee, say hello to friends and acquaintances and jog back. "That's the sort of place this is—more of a meeting place than a food place," she says. "My husband still runs, while for my exercise I push strollers. But we both still come here, he in the morning—he likes his pastry and coffee—and me at lunch, when I can. It's casual, relaxed, peaceful. You wouldn't think you were in LA."

"What makes it so friendly is that we get a lot of regulars here," says Mike Corcoran, who grew up in P.V.—as locals tend to call Palos Verdes. Among the more notable regulars, he whispers, is actor Ray Milland.

"Almost everyone knows one another here," interjects Dana Lemesh as she purchases a pastry to go. Also raised in the area and now working for a doctor in the plaza, Lemesh adds that the arcades, brick paving and plantings greatly aid the ambiance. "It makes for a very pretty little village," she declares.

Creating that effect was a very conscious decision made more than 60 years ago when New York banker Frank Vanderlip, the developer of what was to become Palos Verdes Estates, directed the prestigious design firms of the Olmsted Brothers and Charles Cheney to draft a master plan for 3,200 of the 16,000 acres that he had bought sight unseen in 1913. The brothers were strong advocates of the so-called City Beautiful tradition, a movement founded in part by their father, Frederick Law Olmsted, one of the foremost American planners of the late 19th Century.

Vanderlip wanted a plan that would take advantage of the peninsula's rolling terrain and views, detailing extensive landscaping and parks while creating a series of model villages surrounded by exclusive residential areas. And to make sure that the architecture to follow would be sympathetic with those plans, he formed an art jury to review design proposals and appointed as its head Myron Hunt, Los Angeles' leading architect of the period. The jury soon afterward established the Mediterranean look of thick stucco walls and terra-cotta tile roofs as the area's guiding architectural style.

Although the Olmsted-Cheney plan called for four commercial centers, Malaga Cove Plaza, designed by the firm of Webber, Staunton and Spaulding, was the only one built, with the first building completed in 1925. Other buildings designed by other architects followed, keeping in the spirit of the Mediterranean style but adding a little more personality. The Palos Verdes General Store, crafted by Walter Swindell Davis, is particularly charming. The store's nooks and crannies crammed with knickknacks, toys and silver, the low beamed ceiling and the smell of potpourri combine to create a down-home atmosphere. The quaint tower above the store completes the scene. Davis also designed the unpretentious, cluttered, convenient Moore's Market, a grocery popular in the plaza for more than 50 years.

"The plaza, with its modest scale and styling, certainly lends the area its personality—laid-back and easy-going but with taste," says architect Donald Hendrickson, whose office overlooks the Sidewalk Cafe. "It really is a wonderful place to work, especially if most of your work is in the area, as is mine." Rolando Julio, of Hendrickson's office, agrees but notes that the cost of a cup of coffee at the cafe recently rose from 50 to 75 cents.

Rising costs in the plaza are a problem, particularly in rents. Hendrickson—along with Connolly-Berens, Jill Yalch of the General Store and others—observes that recent increases forced out a number of businesses, including a bookstore and a designer tile shop that had lent the plaza diversity. In their place have come boring banks and ubiquitous real estate offices, a trend that could undermine the area's charm.

Still, the plaza perseveres as a distinctive gathering place, a sharp and welcome contrast—indeed, a relief—to the spread of deadeningly homogenous mini- and maxi-malls now mauling other communities. It deserves to be toasted, preferably with a cup of coffee at the Sidewalk Cafe.

—Oct. 20, 1985

Halcyon Days

IT IS A TRIP BACK IN TIME, PAST THE ERRATIC COLLECTION OF MIRRORED monoliths and taut towers that line the 134 Freeway from Burbank, through Glendale, to Pasadena, announcing for all who care to look that they are "now." Then north on sedate and settled Orange Grove Boulevard and into a neighborhood known as the Upper Arroyo Seco, marked by large houses and lush landscaping hinting of a simpler era.

A turn onto Westmoreland Place, down half a block or so, and there on a crest is the august Gamble House, a rambling, dark, woodshingled structure with broad, overhanging eaves, a haunting mix of Alpine and Occidental styles. Through the welcoming, finely detailed stained-glass front door and into an interior of exquisitely joined, hand-sculpted wood, Tiffany lamps, crafted furnishings, all polished and aglow, and it is 76 years ago.

One of Southern California's most precious period pieces, a local, state and national historic landmark, the Gamble House is a marvelous example of the concern and care that went into the design, construction and furnishing of homes for the gentry in the early 1900s. "I seek till I find what is truly useful; then I try to make it beautiful," said Charles Sumner Greene, who with his brother, Henry Mather Greene, designed this sprawling, sublime residence.

Every detail in the planning of the Gamble House appears to have been carefully considered, from such major decisions as siting, scale and massing to more minor but no less critical decisions like whether to cover the brass screws fastening the interior wood trip with square pegs of ebony, mahogany or oak. The result is that the entire house—floors, walls, windows, moldings, ceilings, cabinets, lighting fixtures and brackets—is a work of art.

That is not exactly what David Gamble (of Procter & Gamble) had in mind when he asked the Greene Brothers to design the house in 1907. Gamble had retired to Pasadena, a favorite watering hole for the wealthy at the turn of the century, and in the spirit of the time and place wanted something comfortable that would take advantage of the region's benign weather. He wanted an unostentatious, rustic house, although one executed with elegance, and with room, of course, for servants, house guests and large parties that could flow with ease between the house and the landscaped gardens—in short, something that would give form to an idealized vision of life in Southern California.

Ever since the Greene Brothers had arrived in Pasadena in 1893, fresh from the Midwest, they had been seeking that form, experimenting with materials and styles in executing increasingly challenging commissions for increasingly affluent clients. "The prime goal (of the Greene brothers) was to design pleasant places for living, loving and working, in a logical and humane way," explains Randell Makinson, author of two definitive studies of the works of Greene and Greene and curator of the Gamble House. "But at the same time they were asking such questions as 'What is California?' and 'What is it like to live here?' "

The result of their search is the Gamble House. It has been described as a cross between a Swiss chalet and a Japanese *minka*, and also as, simply, "the ultimate bungalow." If a bungalow, it is certainly a very privileged rendition of the modest, wood-shingled, porch-encrusted structures that sprouted out of the builders' catalogues of the early 1900s and sprawled across the burgeoning Los Angeles landscape (thanks in part to the cheap lumber that was just beginning to flow into Southern California by ship from the Northwest). The Gamble House also cost about 50 times more to build than the average bungalow, coming in at a price of $50,400. Another $3,500 was spent on the garage, along with $7,000 for the furnishings and fixtures.

If anything, it is an example—some consider it the finest example—of the Arts and Crafts Movement that flourished in the halcyon period around the turn of the century. The movement was dedicated to the proposition that good design involves good craftsmanship and that it should envelop man as a total experience and not simply be applied as ornamentation. Of all the architectural styles that have swept through Southern California over the last 100 years, from florid Victorian and sentimental Spanish Colonial to mannered Modern and high-gloss High Tech, the Arts and Crafts Movement seems to have been most at home here, however fleeting.

It is that brief period that is captured in the Gamble House, especially when lit with a golden haze filtering through the stained glass during the day and from the Tiffany lamps at night. The ambiance prompts reverential whispers from those who visit the house, which is open for guided tours Tuesdays, Thursdays and Sundays.

The tours are conducted by the docents council of the Friends of the Gamble House, which is 300 members strong. It was formed as a support group after the Gamble family made a gift of the house to the City of Pasadena in 1966 in a joint agreement with USC. The school, with the help of the Friends, now operates the house as a national monument.

In discussing the Greene Brothers' concern for details ("the noblest work of art is to make common things beautiful for man," Charles Greene once commented) and the docents' concern for preservation ("Please take your shoes off and put on these soft slippers," the tour guides request), Makinson says that "love created the house, and love maintains it."

—Nov. 3, 1985

Around the Venice Circle

THERE IS, OF COURSE, MORE TO VENICE THAN THE MOTLEY, MOVEABLE carnival that is funky Ocean Front Walk, the city's premier pedestrian promenade for exhibitionists and sightseers.

Venice also is a diverse, patchwork community of some pleasant, modest streets and a few unpleasant, immodest ones, with a smattering of architectural attractions and distractions blessed with a brisk ocean breeze.

Bounded roughly on the south by Marina del Rey, the north by Santa Monica, the east by Lincoln Boulevard and the west by the Pacific, the area is very much a singular urban village, seemingly adrift in a not always friendly sea of change.

These thoughts came to mind recently standing with local architect David Ming-Li Lowe in the middle of a raw traffic circle at the confluence of Windward Avenue, Main Street and three other streets, across from the Venice post office. The circle is marked by a mottled piece of vanity sculpture someone abandoned there a few years ago.

LOWE AND LOCAL HISTORIAN TOM SEWELL ARE TRYING TO DRUM UP SUPPORT for an architectural and design competition to realign and recast the forlorn circle into an attractive and appropriate focal point for Venice.

"What we have here now is an insult to those of us who live and work in the area," Lowe said. "Given its central location, given the need in Venice for public space, a sitting and meeting area— Ocean Front Walk is for the tourists—the circle could be marvelous."

Seventy years ago the traffic circle was the Grand Lagoon, the focal point of a romantic web of canals lacing the seaside community of Venice—then being fashioned with imagination out of an expanse of marshy tidal flats by real estate developer Abbott Kinney.

According to old maps and photographs, on the site of the post office was an ornate viewing pavilion; to the south an amusement park featuring a roller coaster; to the north a bath house; to the west welcoming steps leading to a fairway; and to the east a complex of bungalows. In the middle of the lagoon stood a five-story tower.

By the late 1920s the discovery of oil in Venice, competition from other amusement parks and the incorporation of the city into Los Angeles had taken their toll. The lagoon and most of the canals were filled in and the buildings lost to fire, the banks and wrecking crews.

A glimpse of this early history of Venice—from amusement park to oil fields, and Kinney himself—can be seen in a fine, but fading mural by Edward Biberton on the south interior wall of the post office.

Also within strolling distance of the post office and traffic circle are glimpses of Venice's recent architectural history, including some innovative as well as self-advertising efforts.

A block south at 308 Venice Way is Lowe's steel-framed and metal clad studio, a respectful and sensitive nod to the machine aesthetic.

To the west, at North Venice Boulevard and Pacific Avenue is Rebecca's, an overwrought restaurant designed by Frank Gehry in a vain attempt to marry art and architecture. Happily, the most successful elements of the design—the white onyx frame of the door and the tin-collage door itself, the later crafted by Tony Berlant—can be seen from the street.

More subdued and successful is the Gargosian Art Gallery and apartments above, just north of Windward, at 51 Market St. It was designed by Craig Hodgetts and Robert Mangurian, in a well-composed updated Moderne style.

Across the street is 72 Market Street, a restaurant designed by the firm of Morphosis in the form of a self-conscious architectural happening. A few of the arbitrary details can be seen through the window and by glancing toward the ceiling. Nearby on 19th Avenue west of Pacific Avenue is an earlier, relatively more modest effort by the firm, an addition sheathed in corrugated aluminium.

Despite these structures being "different," they all in an odd way fit relatively comfortably into the chaotic context of Venice, indeed a few even seem to be swallowed up in it. Whether they are comfortable structures is another matter.

—Nov. 15, 1986

Long Beach Comes of Age

First Street paralleling the ocean bluffs in Long Beach is one of those rare, lovely streets that hint of a simpler time.

Set back from the broad, tree-lined boulevard in the Bluff Park area is an appealing mix of rambling houses representing a range of rich architectural styles from Craftsman to Mediterranean Revival.

Most of the houses were built in the 1920s when the area boomed, thanks to the oil gushing in nearby Signal Hill, which turned the seaside resort of Long Beach into a thriving city and Bluff Park into prime residential real estate.

Now bicycles and tricycles on expansive lawns, and late-model, car-seat-cluttered station wagons in driveways indicate a boom of another sort, a baby boom, that has brought new life to the area and made the large houses there more desireable than ever.

I had gone to Bluff Park to meet with a group of local preservationists to review their continuing battle to raise the city's consciousness about its rich history, and also to glimpse some of the area's surviving landmarks.

A favorite of mine is the Raymond House, 2749 E. Ocean Blvd., a lesser-known work of Irving Gill and one of the few that remains relatively intact. Designed in 1918 in Gill's distinctively straightforward Cubist style, it stands as a precursor of the Modern movement.

In the preservationist group, Luann Pryor, a founder of the city's Cultural Heritage Commission, and Richard Gaylord, chairman of the city's Planning Commission, talked of efforts to save select buildings downtown, and to protect Long Beach's diverse neighborhoods. And just this week the City Council joined the effort by curtailing future high-density residential development.

Unfortunately, not much of historic downtown Long Beach has survived the wrecking balls of an aggressive redevelopment agency. Among the more prominent survivors is the Breakers Hotel, a richly restored Spanish Colonial-style relic of the 1920s, and the Villa Riviera Apartments, a towering, Chateauesque-topped cooperative. Both grace Ocean Boulevard.

Also downtown are a few frail fragments of Long Beach's golden age of Art Deco design, and a marvelous mosaic of 30,000 tile pieces crafted in the 1930s by artists employed in a federal work project. It stands at the north end of the pedestrian mall at 3rd Street.

But what interested me most was not downtown, but the neighborhoods. They seemed to exude an enticing small-town spirit, no doubt a remnant from a half-century ago when Long Beach began receiving a steady stream of migrants from the Midwest, predominately from Iowa. It was this same small-town spirit that about 10 years ago stopped the march of high-rise apartment houses that were threatening the scale and ambiance of Bluff Park. The spirit has subsequently spread to other neighborhoods, which are now involved in a variety of preservation efforts.

A few blocks north of Bluff Park just east of Junipero Avenue is Carroll Park, with its curving, well-landscaped streets lined with appealing Queen Anne and Craftsman-style bungalows. The polished condition of most of the houses indicates a pride of ownership and respect for historical value.

The same spirit is on display in a line of unpretentious bungalows along a less affluent stretch of Junipero Avenue, from 7th to 10th streets; and in scattered Craftsman and Queen Anne-styled gems in struggling Willmore City north of downtown along Chestnut and Cedar avenues.

They and singular, stately Victorians and Colonial Revivals a little farther out in the Drake Park area persevere amongst ticky-tacky, trashed stucco and clapboard apartment conplexes, and shabby commercial structures.

"It hasn't been easy saving and restoring these houses," said preservationist Peter Devereaux. But he added that if Long Beach is to retain its sense of history, and also serve its less-privileged residents, it is in such neighborhoods as Willmore City that it will happen.

In contrast, to the east and beyond Bluff Park is comfortable Belmont Heights, trendy Belmont Shore and pricey Naples. A sort of snug Westwood-by-the-water, the Belmonts bob with boats, bicycles and yuppies, while Naples drifts contendly off shore.

"For a small city we have some very diverse neighborhoods," said Pryor, who with Devereaux was consuming a cup of frozen yogurt on 2nd Street, the east end's principal street for shopping promenading and preening.

Having just traversed Long Beach through a variety of poor, moderate and wealthy areas, populated to varying degrees with a mix of Asians, blacks, Latinos and whites, young and old, I had to agree.

The coast of Iowa it is not.

—Nov. 22, 1986

Tail o' the Pup on a Roll

Hot dogs and historic preservation are being served up again with mustard and relish at the Tail o' the Pup.

The enticing fast-food stand in the shape of a giant hot dog coated with mustard in a fluffy bun is steaming at a new location, on the west side of N. San Vicente Boulevard just above Beverly Boulevard.

An architectural and gourmand landmark, the 17-foot-long stucco hot dog and roll sculpted on a chicken-wire frame survived as an outgoing order from its previous site a few blocks away on La Cienega Boulevard.

The stand almost was gobbled up there in a real estate transaction—ironically, to make way for a rich architectural souffle consisting of a new Ma Maison restaurant crowned by a multi-storied luxury hotel.

The stand had teetered on the La Cienega site for nearly 40 years as one of the most successful and attractive cxamples of programmatic architecture—a style that in effect uses a building as a sort of three-dimensional billboard to catch the eye and hopefully whet the appetite of passing motorists.

There was a time when such fanciful structures dotted the Southern California landscape. They included giant chili bowls, tamales, ice cream buckets, milk bottles, doughnuts, a coffee cup, a coffee pot, a pumpkin and a pig, the latter serving barbecue ribs and other porcine delights.

Motivating the design and construction was the theme that if you could see it, you would probably eat it. The style also has been known as "pop" and "eat me" architecture.

In the non-consumable category, there has been a florist shop in the form of a flower pot, a shoe repair shop as a shoe, a music school as an accordion, a piano showroom as a piano and a camera store as a camera. The facade of the latter still exists at 5370 Wilshire Blvd., but now behind the lens of the front window is an Indian restaurant.

Also advertising itself was the Brown Derby restaurant in the form of, of course, a brown derby, Van de Kamp's Bakery as a windmill, the Hoot Hoot ice cream parlor as an owl, the Samson Tyre and Rubber Company with its Babylonian facade, and a hosiery shop topped by a well-turned leg.

OF THE FOOD STANDS, ONLY A FEW HAVE SURVIVED SHIFTING TASTES AND rising land prices. Among them is Randy's Donuts, just west of the San Diego Freeway on Manchester Boulevard in Inglewood, with a huge doughnut delicately balanced on a small shop. Further east on Manchester Boulevard is a restaurant topped by a teapot. A couple of oversized chili bowls also have been sighted, unfortunately in need of a dishwasher.

The Tail o' the Pup has been one of the more venerable, pampered for nearly two decades by operator Eddie Blake with the help of his son, Dennis, and championed as a landmark by preservationists and customers. Its economics also have been aided by its status as a setting for TV commercials. When the stand was first threatened with extinction six years ago, local architect/activist Bernard Zimmerman led an effort to get the city's Cultural Heritage Board to designate it a historic-cultural monument. But because the stand was then existing on a month-to-month lease, the petition was turned down.

The repainted and patched-up stand is now anchored to its new site by a five-year lease, along with steel reinforcing bars and the continuing love and affection of customers and preservationists.

And though the kitschy stand still does not qualify for consideration by the city as an official monument, it is nonetheless a local architectural and social landmark to be cherished, preferably while consuming a hot dog.

—Dec. 13, 1986

L.A. Under The Palms

LIKE THE UNABASHED TOURISTS THEY WERE, THE FAMILY OF FOUR FROM Wyoming gathered for a group photograph to commemorate their vacation in Los Angeles.

If the family had gone to New York they most likely would have posed before Rockefeller Center; if Paris, the Eiffel Tower; or London, Big Ben.

In Los Angeles they posed beside a palm tree with the beach and Santa Monica Bay as background.

The fact is, man-made creations do not dominate Los Angeles, as they do in most other cities. One must think hard before suggesting a particular structure that somehow conveys the image of L.A., such as the White House does for Washington, St. Peter's for Rome, or the Golden Gate Bridge for San Francisco.

CERTAINLY NOT OUR CITY HALL, THE NEO-CLASSICAL MONUMENTAL DESIGN which is said to have been inspired by the state capital building of Nebraska. The flashy Pacific Design Center in West Hollywood is a unique structure, but could very well be in an Orange County office park off the San Diego Freeway.

Perhaps more appropriate would be the craftsman-styled Gamble house in Pasadema designed by the Greene brothers, Frank Lloyd Wright's Ennis House in Hollywood, the futuristic Chemosphere in the Hollywood Hills by John Lautner or one of Cliff May's many rambling ranches?

While any one of these houses may say "L.A." to those with a knowledge of architecture, most persons viewing photographs of them probably would not be able to locate them.

No, the instincts of the family from Wyoming were correct. More prominent, and in many ways more important than the buildings in Los Angeles are the spaces between them and beyond—the open spaces, the lush landscaping, and the beaches. Accentuated by a benign climate, they mark the Southern California outdoor-oriented life style.

The Wyoming family was posing before the beach at Ocean Park in Santa Monica, and the windmill palm they stood beside is one of many recently planted along a promenade there as part of a welcomed public project in the last stages of construction.

I happened on the family while touring the project recently with two of its principal designers, Douglas and Regula Campbell. We were accompanied by my son, Josef, who tested out one of the two new playgrounds there, and Alexander Campbell, who at 6 weeks of age still has a few months to go before becoming a field inspector for his parents' firm.

Stretching from about Bay Street south nearly a mile to the Santa Monica city line and Venice, the project very much recognizes the vital role of open space in the Los Angeles life style, and how it can be better sculpted to serve people as well as cars.

Funded by the city of Santa Monica, the project's goals involved connecting the adjacent Ocean Park neighborhood to the state beach—without the loss of any of the 2,000 spaces in a sprawling parking lot that in effect formed an asphalt barrier between the neighborhood and the beach.

In addition, local residents wanted the promenade above the parking lot renovated in the style of the city's popular Palisades Park north of the Santa Monica Pier. The residents, who participated in a series of pre-project workshops by the Campbells and the allied architectural firm of Moore Ruble Yudell, were asked to contribute their views to the design of the project. The final design was the work of the Campbells and the Moore Ruble Yudell firm.

Also on the neighborhood wish list were a couple of new playgounds and a renovated Crescent Bay Park, then a forlorn, four-acre expanse at Bay Street and Ocean Avenue that over the years had been trashed by derelicts.

Key to the imaginative design solution that evolved was "capturing" land for the promenade and its plantings by narrowing Ocean Avenue from about six lanes to two and four lanes. Where there was a raw sidewalk and street is now a soft, linear park.

"The street had what is called excess capacity and didn't have to be as wide as it was," Doug Campbell explained. "Also by narrowing it, we made it safer and more scenic."

To better link the neighborhood to the beach, tree-lined and landscaped pedestrian paths were laid out in the parking lot, which was imaginatively redesigned so that no parking spaces were lost. The paths also have had the effect of softening and providing shade for the parking lot while discouraging speeding.

Of particular interest is the mix of native and exotic plants, including along the pedestrian paths ground cover of wild strawberries and ice plants, and broad-leafed evergreen trees, for color and shade. And, of course, there are the new, marvelous, ungainly palms marching along the Ocean Avenue promenade, providing tourists such as the family from Wyoming a recognizable prop for their photographs and local residents a sense of place, and pride.

—Jan. 10, 1987

The Heights of Hollywood

HOLLYWOOD HEIGHTS' FORMAL BLOCK PARTY CELBRATING ITS COMMUNITY spirit is held every August; the informal party is every day.

Climbing the hills northwest of Highland and Franklin avenues, the community's cluster of Mediterranean, Moorish and Moderne-style houses and apartments is one of those architectural enclaves in the varied landscape of Los Angeles that manages to be inclusive and welcoming.

Blossoming vines spill over stucco and concrete block walls lining twisting, turning streets; potted plants sit on window sills and terraces, and occasional tile work and individualistic doorways peek out from behind wrought-iron fences.

THEN THERE ARE THE HILLSIDES, LACED WITH MEANDERING PUBLIC PATHS AND stairways tunneling through profusions of wild vegetation and presenting, from raw crests and melanges of balconies, breathtaking views of Hollywood and the city beyond.

The setting and a sprinkling of landmark structures, including singular houses by Frank Lloyd Wright and his son, Lloyd Wright, have lent themselves well to a strong neighborhood identity and spirit.

Hollywood Heights has needed this spirit, for like so many other communities in and around Los Angeles over the last few years it is involved in a continuing effort to keep its quality of life from being nibbled away by avaricious developers and insensitive bureaucrats.

These efforts have included fighting off a proposal for an out-of-scale and out-of-character housing complex on the site of a dated bungalow court by helping to get the court declared a landmark and get the county to assume responsibility for recycling it.

MOST RECENTLY IT WAS JOINING WITH THE NEIGHBORING COMMUNITIES OF Outpost Estates and Whitley Heights to exact an agreement from a developer that more than half of the space of a commercial complex planned for the area would be set aside for a full service market.

Not content with the agreement, the communities then had it translated into a city ordinance that defines the type and number of stores to be included in the complex. The resulting precedent-setting ordiance emphasizing neighborhood services was approved last month by the City Council

"We don't need more one-hour photo service shops, video stores or junk food stands that are included in typical mini-malls," explained Grayce Baldwin, president of the Hollywood Heights Assn., at a luncheon amid a hanging garden on the terrace of her Camrose Avenue house.

"WHAT THE COMMUNITY NEEDS IS A SUPERMARKET, LIKE THE ONE WE HAD that was knocked down for the mall," said Theo Wilson. A former ace reporter for the New York Daily News, Wilson edits a tart, tasty newsletter for the association that has done much to keep the community informed and local politicians alert.

"And that is what the ordinance guarantees, and what we are going to make sure we get," said Bonnie Wolfe, who represents the association in reviewing the architectural plans of the mall's developer.

After the luncheon celebrating the ordinance and not incidentally Baldwin's cooking (she is caterer of note), there was a tour of the tight community of about 750 families.

This included a ride up a private elevator in a mock Bolognese tower at the end of Hightower Drive to emerge amid the hillside cluster of houses and apartments. (Maintained by the 30-member Hightower Elevator Assn., the elevator requires a key. The alternative access is by stairs and pathways.)

Most of the structures in the slick, Moderne style were designed and developed in the 1920s by architect Carl Kay. An exception is 2200 Broadview Terrace, a delightful Expressionist exercise of Lloyd Wright build in 1922.

Wright's father two years later constructed one of his famous concrete "knit-block" houses on an adjoining hill at 1962 Glencoe Way. Known as the Freeman house, it is a national historic landmark.

Nearby on the top of Sycamore Drive is one of Los Angeles' more delightful spots, the Yamashiro restaurant. Set in a garden with a marvelous view of the city, the sprawling structure, a cross between an oversized California bungalow and a Japanese post-and-beam palace, was built in the early 1910s as a private home for Adolph and Eugene Berheimer, two importers of Oriental art.

Also on the commercial edges of Hollywood Heights is the French nouveau Gothic splendor of the Magic Castle, at 7001 Franklin Ave.; the imposing English neo-Gothic First Methodist Church of Hollywood, 6817 Franklin Ave., and the tile-ornamented, modern Classical-styled American Legion Hall at 2035 Highland Ave., which for the last few years has served as an evocative stage set for the hit play "Tamara."

But what distinguishes Hollywood Heights most is the rapport one senses among the buildings, the landscape and the residents.

"This really is a special place," says Wilson.

It indeed is because those who care about the entwined heritage and future of Hollywood Heights have made it so.

—Jan. 24, 1987

The City as a Movie Studio

MY IMAGES OF LOS ANGELES BEFORE MOVING HERE WERE FORMED IN THE dark of New York City's movie theaters, viewing such films as "Double Indemnity," "Sunset Boulevard" and, later, "Chinatown" and "The Long Goodbye."

On the lighter side, there was Charlie Chaplin, Harold Lloyd, Buster Keaton, Laurel and Hardy, and others, careening across the Los Angeles cityscape, sideswiping trolleys, racing over cliffs, hanging from rooftops and bending clock hands high over streets.

To me, through the movies, Los Angeles was not a city, but a sprawling studio with a variety of sets featuring broad beaches, dramatic seaside cliffs, rolling countryside, raw canyons, majestic mountains, deep forests, stereotypical suburbs and gritty downtowns.

Though living here has changed my image of Los Angeles to one of a paradoxical city of suburbs and subcultures containing real people and not actors, the fact that movies are made here still enthralls me.

WHENEVER I COME ACROSS A PRODUCTION ON LOCATION I AM INEVITABLY curious about what is being filmed, so I slow down and stare. And when I pass a movie studio I am reminded of the fanciful worlds that have been created there and wonder what new ones are being shaped on its stages and back lots.

Though I must have driven north on Motor Avenue toward Pico Boulevard at least 100 times, I am still enchanted by the glimpse of the 1890s New York street set built 20 years ago on the 20th Century Fox Studio lot there for the filming of "Hello, Dolly!"

Evocative also is the white mansion at 9336 W. Washington Blvd. in Culver City, a brief view of which opened the credits of those marvelous David O. Selznick films a half century or so ago, including "Gone With the Wind." And though the mansion was not Tara, much of what was behind it were sets for that epic and other films.

There, on a few acres off what is now Culver City's automobile row, was where the city of Atlanta burned, the original King Kong reigned, the King of Kings walked, jet pilot John Wayne flew, Citizen Kane built Xanadu for his illicit love, E.T. spent most of his days on Earth, and William S. Hart rode out into dozens of sunsets.

Further west on Washington Boulevard near Overland Avenue can be seen the classical columned gates of Lorimar-Telepictures Studios. In previous and more colorful years it was the home of MGM and various incarnations.

Actually, the gate itself was constructed in 1916 for Ince/Traingle Studios, with land and financing supplied in part by Harry Culver, who was then looking for a clean and expanding industry for his fledgling city.

The studios indeed did expand under a succession of moguls. There behind the gates was created the Rome of Ben Hur, the Mississippi of "Meet Me in St. Louis," the Pacific on which the crew of the Bounty mutinied, David Copperfield's London, Gene Kelly's Paris and, perhaps most memorable, the land of Oz.

Under contract to the studios golden days of the 1930s and 1940s were such stars as John Gilbert, Greta Garbo, Judy Garland, Mickey Rooney, Jean Harlow, Clark Gable, Katharine Hepburn, Spencer Tracy and Elizabeth Taylor. They were the stuff of legends.

The sets for the classics in which they starred have long since been struck and sold, and the remaining sound stages are now serving the television productions of, among others, "Dallas," "Knots Landing," and "Perfect Strangers."

But as film historian and archivist Marc Wanamaker points out, it is not the current productions or the architecture of the stages that makes them interesting, but their history.

Past the historic gates, and past the Moderne-styled Irving Thalberg Building honoring the legendary studio chief, "the studio is really just a factory," says Wanamaker. "But what a factory."

—March 7, 1987

An Eye for L.A. Images

LOOKING AT LOS ANGELES CAN BE ENGROSSING. FOR ALL THE PERMANENCE of its streets, freeways, bridges and buildings, the city is very evanescent.

To be sure, the engineering and architecture appear solid—each element rooted for the decades, for better or worse, in concrete and steel. But the totality of the elements, the city's so-called urban design, is ever changing, and very much an imperfect art.

That is how it has seemed to me at least, these last few weeks as I searched out select structures to comment on in these columns. Engaging me more and more as I wandered farther and farther across the city sprawl was not the engineering and architecture, but the urban design.

175

WHAT I FOUND MYSELF LOOKING FOR WERE CLUES TO WHAT DISTINGUISHED each area—what was its visual quality, its public image. In short, what was its "imageability," a word the late noted planner Kevin Lynch liked to use to describe how easy it was to "read" and identify a particular community.

But while Boston, where Lynch lived and practiced, may have a high "imageability"—as do, say, sections of San Francisco— what about Tarzana, Playa del Rey, East Los Angeles, Monterey Park, Claremont or Monrovia, to name a few areas I recently visited.

To be sure, this "imageability" I was looking for is based on transitory perceptions. I don't live in these communities—in effect, I'm just a tourist with an interest in design and a love of cities, experiencing for the most part a community's publicly accessible spaces, its streets, beaches, parks, playgrounds, restaurants and stores.

So there I was a few weeks ago in Tarzana, checking out a new mini-mall and a remodeled car wash on Ventura Boulevard and think- ing there must be more to the community than a convenient but crass commercial strip.

What I did find off the boulevard on a succession of curving streets was a tidy residential community of what seemed to be com- fortable, well-maintained and well-landscaped houses. Behind those houses I presumed there were swimming pools, barbecue pits and jungle gyms, where the community's true spirit is displayed.

But for me the public image of Tarzana that unfortunately re- mains is the baleful blur of Ventura Boulevard.

MY IMAGE OF PLAYA DEL REY, PERCHED AT THE WATER'S END OF CULVER Boulevard, always had been of a comfortable melange of modest stores and restaurants, nondescript condos, a few funky houses, a pleasant park and a marvelous broad beach. It is a nice place to bike to.

But recently, while looking for a singular design there by an architect of note, I drove up a relatively new 81st Street and thought I was in the far reaches of a Conejo Valley tract development. Looking moderately bloated, most of the recently constructed houses just do not capture the spirit of this vest-pocket beach town.

Still, there is the beach, which for me remains the com- munity's dominant image. Happily, when in Playa del Rey I tend to look out at the water and not back at the structures abusing the bluffs.

On the way to Monrovia the other day I turned off the freeway and cruised through East Los Angeles and Monterey Park. The El Mercado at 3425 East 1st St. seemed a little worse for wear. More spirited was Whittier Boulevard, where a landscaping and reha- bilitation program is struggling to take root. But a pervasive image escaped me.

To the northeast, Monterey Park with its sprawl and signage is beginning to look more and more like a suburb of Hong Kong, and appears very much in the process of change. The Saturday traffic was a test of nerves.

Some old images of the community do remain, like Cascades Park off Atlantic Boulevard at El Portal Place. Its fountain still serves as a backdrop for photographs of wedding parties, frequently Asian and Latino.

As for Monterey Park's most interesting "community" space, to me it was not the streets or parks, but select restaurants. Each time we have eaten there, be it a quick lunch or a weekend dinner, the restaurants have taken on the congeniality of small public plazas.

—April 18, 1987

Covering the Waterfront

S UMMER IS A MARVELOUS TIME FOR STROLLING ALONG THE BEACH, A TIME while dodging volleyballs to watch the waves roll in and swimmers drift out.

And for those like myself who are interested in architectural styles somewhat more stable than sand castles, a stroll these days along the Manhattan Beach oceanfront can be particularly diverting.

With a broad beach overlooked by a compact cluster of houses marching inland up narrow streets and alleys, and a low-scaled, low-keyed business district, Manhattan Beach exudes a seaside spirit that makes every day seem a vacation day.

It is no wonder that the town long has been a favorite of families who like to walk from hearth to surf barefooted, as well as the more conspicuous singles in search of deep tans and shallow relationships.

These diverse, beach-oriented life styles are reflected in the architecture along The Strand, which in effect is the town's main street and a pedestrian delight stretching from 45th Street and the enclave of El Porto south to First Street and Redondo Beach.

Always looking for an excuse to go to Manhattan Beach, where I have family and was married, I recently took a walk along The Strand to view the more recently constructed, modern-styled houses there.

The nicely weathered, clean-lined, cedar-sided, purple-detailed house at 4300 was designed by Barton Choy.

A similarly scaled and wrapped house two blocks south at 4100 was designed by John Blanton, who has been practicing in Manhattan Beach with distinction for more than 20 years. Note the rhythm the pattern of windows lend the facade. This is a trademark of Blanton's, who began his career working under modernist master Richard Neutra.

Less apparent is the care that obviously went into the selection of materials and the careful cladding of 4100. Because of the constant battering of the houses by salt air and windblown sand, Blanton prefers the more resistant cedar shingling and specially treated window frame.

At 3318-20 is a modern-styled post-and-beam delight designed by Edward Fickett. The house is an excellent example of the popular 1960s style, sited and constructed with sensitivity.

A few steps south at 3300 is a polished example by Tim Smith of the currently popular updated rendition of the Mediterranean villa

177

style, replete with arches and toned in a subtle white and pinks. Less subtle is the window detailing.

There had been a well-scaled graceful Spanish modern-styled house 2920, but it is gone now in the current "rip-em-down and overbuild-em" craze along The Strand, a disease that recently drifted down to Manhattan Beach from Santa Monica. One looks at what is being framed at 2920 with some apprehension.

Up 17th Street, at 209, is another Blanton-designed structure. Once again his placement and detailing of windows lend the building grace.

Certainly the most dramatic structure rising on The Strand these days is at 1600. Designed with a futuristic flair by Ray Kappe and Dean Nota, the building is marked by a sweeping, curved balcony and curved walls, presenting an interesting fusing of forms. When completed I would not be surprised if it somehow broke away from its granite steps and floated away on a cloud.

There also is along and just off The Strand a varied display of other Modern-styled houses, along with some strange structural and stylistic hybrids a few cute, and a few overly cute Victorians, and a half dozen or so misplaced weathered ranch and fraternity houses. Comment on these will just have to await another column.

Also along The Strand are a selection of Cape Cod and Colonial styled structures that seem to have somehow drifted off of the New England coast, down the Atlantic Ocean and up the Pacific, to settle in Manhattan Beach.

Given the ambiance of this beach town, you can hardly blame them, or anyone, for making the trip.

—July 25, 1987

Schindler's Spirit Survives

MODERN ARCHITECTURE DID NOT COME TO LOS ANGELES IN THE FORM OF a sleek 1950s office tower, as in most other cities, but in 1922 with a fragile one-story complex tucked away in West Hollywood.

Designed by R. M. Schindler as a double house and studio for himself and a colleague, the striking horizontal structure at 835 N. Kings Road was sited to embrace as much of the grounds as possible, so that rooms flowed out into common courtyards.

The design also featured a communal kitchen for the two resident families and open, covered porches (Schindler called them "sleeping baskets") on the roof. The resulting informality and flexibility of the structure lent it an air of modernity.

But what really distinguished the complex as a modern architectural landmark was the innovative materials and construction methods. These included a concrete pad foundation, poured-in-place tilted concrete slab walls, the extensive use of glass as infill between the slabs and as clerestories, and generally leaving the structure and materials unfinished.

"What you see is what you got, which gives the house a refreshing moral simplicity," observed Robert Sweeney, who, as president of the Friends of the Schindler House, oversees the operation and maintenance of the landmark structure.

Sweeney made his remarks while reviewing with architectural historian Kathryn Smith the first phase of an ambitious restoration of the house and grounds timed to coincide with celebration of the 100th anniversary of Schindler's birth.

Born in Vienna on Sept. 10, 1887, Rudolf Michael Schindler came to Los Angeles in 1920 to supervise construction of Frank Lloyd Wright's design of the Hollyhock House, in what is now Barnsdall Park in Hollywood.

A year later Schindler established his own practice here, designing in time numerous houses marked by a melding of the severe style of the modern movement with a rare sensitivity to the varied sites and climates of Los Angeles. He died in 1953.

Many of the houses Schindler produced are noteworthy, among them the Lovell House in Newport Beach, the Buck House in the mid-Wilshire District, the How House in Silver Lake and the Elliot House in Franklin Hills. But it is the complex in West Hollywood that is considered the most exceptional.

Schindler seemed to have known that. When the structure was near completion in May, 1922, he declared in a letter to a friend: "Architecturally I am satisfied—it is a thoroughbred—and will either attract people—or repulse them— my fate is settled—one way or other."

Attract people it has since being declared a historical landmark in 1971 and opened to the public in 1980, due in large part to the efforts of the Friends of the Schindler House and a grant from the California Office of Historic Preservation.

—Sept. 12, 1987

L.A.'s Mean Streets

THIS IS THE SEASON WHEN THE HIGH-DESERT AIR, BAKED BY THE SUN, BE comes the Santa Ana winds that lash out across the city to the west, fanning fires, creating havoc and generally getting on everyone's nerves.

For me, it is a time to stay out of harm's way, avoid the freeways, Dodger games, cocktail parties and conversations with the ex-wife; give in to the whims of the children and the present wife; have an extra beer, water the lawn and reread Raymond Chandler.

His detective-hero, martyr, design critic, alter ego Philip Marlowe summed up the city he experienced, and the season, in "The Long Goodbye":

"When I got home I mixed a stiff one and stood by the open window in the living room and sipped it and listened to the groundswell of the traffic on Laurel Canyon Boulevard and looked at the glare of the big angry city hanging over the shoulders of the hills through which the boulevard had been cut. Far off the banshee wail of police or fire sirens rose and fell, never for very long completely silent. . . Out there in the night of a thousand crimes people were dying, being maimed, cut by flying glass, crushed against steering wheels or under heavy tires. . . . People were hungry, sick, bored, desperate with loneliness or remorse or fear, angry, cruel, feverish, shaken by sobs. A city no worse than others, a city rich and vigorous and full of pride, a city lost and beaten and full of emptiness."

Exactly where Marlowe is standing and the locations of other buildings and places from Chandler's rich legacy have challenged readers with curiosity, writers without much else to do and editors looking for a gimmick since his novels and short stories began appearing in the '30s.

As a result, various articles have been written, maps published and tours offered purporting to locate the scenes and settings of Marlowe's doings and undoings in Los Angeles.

But as someone who has dog-eared Chandler's novels, and scoured the Los Angeles cityscape, I don't trust the gumshoeing of others. And there is no way to check with the prime suspect: Chandler died—nonviolently—in 1959 in La Jolla at the age of 70.

And even if Chandler were alive today I don't think I would trust the addresses he might offer. Certainly Marlowe wouldn't trust him, for the Los Angeles that Chandler created was a conscious construct of allusions and lies.

Still, there are enough clues in the novels, and in publications such as "The Raymond Chandler Mystery Map of Los Angeles" (Aaron Blake Publishers.), to aid the curious in search of Marlowe's Los Angeles. If not exact locations, then similar moods and scenes.

The house from which Marlowe viewed the city in "The Long Goodbye" is off Lookout Mountain Avenue, above Laurel Canyon.

The avenue still exists, off Laurel Canyon Boulevard, but we don't know where the house is.

More evocative is his house in "The High Window"—clinging to a cliff above High Tower Drive in Hollywood Heights, marked and reached by a fanciful elevator tower.

That is where he also lived in the movie version of "The Long Goodbye," starring Elliott Gould, and that in my mind is where Marlowe belongs, drink in hand. You can find the tower at the end of High Tower Drive, a short street that runs north from Camrose Drive, which is west of Highland Avenue. Apartments, duplexes and single-family houses still cling to the cliffs above the drive. The elevator, however, is not open to the public; you need a key to get in.

The detective's office was two small rooms on the sixth floor, in the rear, of the Cahuenga Building (It might be 615 Cahuenga Blvd., but then again, it might not), with a pebbled glass door panel lettered "Philip Marlowe. . . . Investigations" in flaked black paint. It is described by Marlowe, in detail, in "The High Window":

"I looked into the reception room. It was empty of everything but the smell of dust. I threw up another window, unlocked the communicating door and went into the room beyond. Three hard chairs and a swivel chair, flat desk with a glass top, five green filing cases, three of them full of nothing, a calendar and a framed license bond on the wall, a phone, a washbowl in a stained wood cupboard, a hatrack, a carpet that was just something on the floor, and two open windows with net curtains that puckered in and out. . . ."

MARLOWE DOES NOT LIKE OFFICE BUILDINGS. THE BELFONT DOWNTOWN ON 9th Street, as described in "The High Window," "was eight stories of nothing in particular that had got itself pinched off between a large green and chromium cut-rate suite emporium and a three-story and basement garage that made a noise like lion cages at feeding time. The small dark narrow lobby was as dirty as a chicken yard."

There is no Belfont there, but there are other buildings nearby fitting the description. Walking east on 9th at dusk, then north on Spring, one can get a feel of the hard-edged city of the 1930s and '40s and now.

Marlowe also does not paint a pretty picture of what goes on in these buildings. In the Fulwider at Santa Monica Boulevard and Western Avenue, described in "The Big Sleep," there were "plenty of vacancies or plenty of tenants who wished to remain anonymous. Painless dentists, shyster detective agencies, small sick businesses that crawled there to die, mail order schools that would teach you how to become a railroad clerk or a radio technician or a screen writer—if the postal inspectors didn't catch up with them first."

Government buildings do not fare particularly well either. Bay City, a thinly disguised Santa Monica, is the site of numerous Marlowe adventures. Marlowe describes Bay City's City Hall in "Farewell, My Lovely":

"It was a cheap-looking building for so prosperous a town. It looked more like something out of the Bible Belt. Bums sat unmolested in a long row on the retaining wall that kept the front lawn—now mostly Bermuda grass—from falling into the street. . . . The cracked wak and the front steps led to open double doors in which a knot of obvious City Hall fixers hung around waiting for something to happen so they could make something else out of it. They all had well-fed stomachs, the careful eyes, the nice clothes and the reach-me-down manners. They gave me about four inches to get by."

The scene at City Hall at 1685 Main St. is more polished now, but the Santa Monica Pier at the foot of Colorado Boulevard still can have a raucous quality, and, in the evening when the fog rolls in, a hint of mystery. As described in "The Big Sleep," it is the Bay City Pier, from which Marlowe and others catch a launch to an off-shore gambling ship.

Chandler also played with addresses. "You could know Bay City a long time without knowing Idaho Street. And you could know a lot of Idaho Street without knowing Number 449," he writes in "The Little Sister." And he is correct, for the scene described certainly is not Idaho Avenue in Santa Monica—not with a lumber yard, broken paving, and "rusted rails of a spur track [that] turned in to a pair of high, chained wooden gates that seem not to have been opened for 20 years."

That sounds more like something off of Colorado Avenue, in Santa Monica's industrial area.

But Chandler adds that "Number 449 had a shallow, paintless front porch on which five wood and cane rockers loafed dissolutely, held together with wire and the moisture of the beach air. The green

181

shades over the lower windows of the house were two-thirds down and full of cracks. Beside the front door there was a large printed sign 'No Vacancies.'" The latter description clearly places the house in Santa Monica's Ocean Park neighborhood. For a hint of that mood, look at some of the fading beach houses, many divided into apartments, in the area bordered by Pico, Lincoln and Ocean Park boulevards.

There is no mistaking Malibu in the description of Montemar Vista in "Farewell, My Lovely":

"I got down to Montemar Vista as the light began to fade, but there was still a fine sparkle on the water and the surf was breaking far out in long smooth curves. . . . Beyond it the huge emptiness of the Pacific was purple gray. Montemar Vista was a few dozen houses of various sizes and shapes hanging by their teeth and eyebrows to a spur of mountain and looking as if a good sneeze would drop them down among the box lunches on the beach."

In "The Big Sleep," Marlowe is at the palatial home of Gen. Sternwood where "faint and far off" he can see some of the old wooden derricks from which the Sternwoods had made their money. Says Marlowe, the narrator:

"Most of the field was public now, cleaned up and donated to the city by Gen. Sternwood. But a little of it was still producing in groups of wells pumping five or six barrels a day. The Sternwoods, having moved up the hill, could no longer smell the stale sump water or the oil, but they could still look out of their front windows and see what made them rich."

But Marlowe adds "I don't suppose they would want to."

As for the house, the model for it is said to have stood on the 7000 block of Franklin Avenue in Hollywood, where one can see on a clear day the Baldwin Hills oil fields on South La Brea Avenue.

A portrait of Beverly Hills between Santa Monica and Sunset boulevards is painted in one line in the short story "Mandarin Jade": "The Philip Courtney Prendergasts lived on one of those wide, curving streets where the houses seem to be too close together for their size and the amount of money they represent." That is not a bad sketch of the area today.

A house in the Oak Knoll section of Pasadena is described in "The High Window" as "a big solid cool-looking house with Burgundy brick walls, a terra cotta tile roof, and a white stone trim. . . ."

It could be one of a number of houses there. The Chandler Mystery Map puts it on the 1200 block of Wentworth Avenue. You take your pick.

The mood and directions are quite clear in "The Little Sister"—as Marlowe drives east on Sunset Boulevard, but doesn't go home.

"At La Brea I turned north and swung over to Highland, out over the Cahuenga Pass and down on to Ventura Boulevard, past Studio City and Sherman Oaks and Encino. There was nothing lonely about the trip. There never is on that road. Fast boys in stripped-down Fords shot in and out of the traffic streams, missing fenders by a sixteenth of an inch, but somehow always missing them. Tired men in dusty coupes and sedans winced and tightened their grip on the wheel and ploughed north and west towards home and dinner. . . . I drove on past the gaudy neons and the false fronts behind them, the sleazy hamburger joints that look like palaces under the colors, the circular drive-ins as gay as circuses with the chipper, hard-eyed carhops, the brilliant counters, and the sweaty greasy kitchens that would have poisoned a toad. Great double trucks rumbled down over Sepulveda from Wilmington and San Pedro and crossed the Ridge Route, starting up in low-low from the traffic lights with a growl of lions in the zoo."

WE HAVE FREEWAYS NOW, BUT STRIPPED-DOWN CARS STILL SHOOT IN AND OUT of the traffic, drivers wince and grimace and the trucks growl.

Gone is Bunker Hill, which Marlowe described in "The High Window" as "old town, lost town, shabby town, crook town," with "women who should be young but have faces like stale beer; men with pulled-down hats and quick eyes that look over the street behind the cupped hand that shields the match flame; worn intellectuals with cigarette coughs and no money in the bank. . . cokies and coke peddlers; people who look like nothing in particular and know it. . . ."

Now these lost souls can be seen on Skid Row, in the doorways on 6th and 7th streets east of Alvarado Street, in the alleys off of Hollywood Boulevard, along the Venice and Santa Monica beachfronts, and even on Rodeo Drive, if only for a few minutes before they are hustled off by the police.

Marlowe's mean city is a little more hidden today, but it is there.

—Oct. 3, 1987

MacArthur Park Alive

ONE OF THE MORE DESIRABLE NEIGHBORHOODS IN LOS ANGELES A CENtury ago was the area surrounding MacArthur Park at Wilshire Boulevard and Alvarado Street, then known as Westlake Park.

The tone was genteel suburban and the streets were studded with comfortable houses in the latest Victorian styles. Glimpses of these still can be seen along the faded 800, 900 and 1000 blocks of South Bonnie Brae Avenue.

That gentility continued into the 1920s and took the form of some ornate apartment hotels, a few of which persevere on West 6th Street, north of the park. A particularly rich example, replete with larger-than-life statues adorning the facade, is the Park Plaza Hotel at the southwest corner of 6th and Park View streets

However, a neighborhood is distinguished not only by its buildings but by its public spaces, and Westlake Park was for half a century the city's most gracious; a place to promenade with the family on weekends, to see and be seen. It anchored the neighborhood, giving it a focal point and lending it value.

WHETHER IT WAS THE PARK OR THE NEIGHBORHOOD THAT STARTED TO DETEriorate first in the 1950s is debatable. The reality is that by the 1980s the park was being overrun by undesirables, seemingly abandoned by the city and left to rot.

But happily it was not abandoned, at least not on weekends and holidays, by the families from Central America who live in the area or by the Otis Art Institute of Parsons School of Design, located across from the western edge of the park and whose students use it as a campus.

With Otis/Parsons taking the lead, a MacArthur Park Community Council was formed a few years ago and an ambitious public art and park maintenance program launched. The program was frankly geared to involve some of the youths who had been trashing the area, and to lend the park, its users and the surrounding neighborhood a new pride.

There was recognition—long understood by urban designers—of the critical position of parks in the city fabric, particularly in lower-income neighborhoods crowded with immigrant populations in need of a place beyond their small apartments in which to socialize and let their children play. In 1848, prominent social reformer and landscaper Andrew Jackson Downing said:

"You may take my word for it, [parks] will be better preachers of temperance than temperance societies, better refiners of the national morals than dancing schools and better promoters of general good-feeling than any lectures on the philosophy of happiness."

With the help of increased police patrols, the combination of art and maintenance seems to be working in MacArthur Park. More families and the elderly are using the park, while the unsavory elements appear to have dwindled and moved to the fringes along a raw Alvarado Street.

CERTAINLY THE PARK HAS BECOME MORE ENGAGING. ON A RECENT WEEKEND there with my family, the lawns were mowed and free of litter, the refurbished playground bustled with children and the art beckoned.

Happily, most of the art is not of the so-called *plop* variety, those large awkward pieces seemingly dropped down from a great height to confront viewers and consume valuable park space.

"We like to think of the public art here as art with a small *a*, art tailored to the needs and concerns of the people who use the park," says Al Nodal of Otis/Parsons and the park council.

Inviting my 2-year-old son, Josef, and a few other children to climb up and over them were two ceramic-tiled pyramids, designed by Judith Simonian. The pyramids, about 30 yards apart, also have an additional attraction of being connected by an underground tube through which childdren, and adults, can speak. Josef loved it.

On a shaded slope on the north side of the park is a modestly sculpted poetry garden fashioned by Doug Hollis and Richard Turner. And if you don't hear anything—the plan calls for speakers in the benches there to broadcast poems—you might consider bringing a book and reading aloud.

The murals on the band shell, a utility building and the entries to the pedestrian tunnels underneath Wilshire Boulevard are strong stuff, with a color selection that appears to discourage graffiti artists.

They were produced by neighborhood youths under the direction of Patssi Valdez.

My favorites are three pieces created by artist Alexis Smith, bordering the northwest section of the lake. Two are terrazzo-and-bronze installations embedded in the pedestrian path, the third a small bronzed suitcase next to a bench.

One installation shows a prizefighter knocking down another, with an inscription declaring: "Mine was the better punch, but it didn't win the wristwatch." The other installation is of a formally clad couple dancing; the inscription reads, "Crazy as a pair of waltzing mice."

The quote on the bronze piece: "She sat in front of her princess dresser trying to paint the suitcases out from under her eyes." According to Nodal, who will be leaving soon to take a cultural post in New Orleans, the suitcase serves as a reference to the apartment hotels in the area, the neon signs of which can be seen in the evening from the park.

I like them because the quotes are from three evocative stories of Los Angeles by Raymond Chandler, and because they are unobtrusive, so-called personal discovery art pieces and do not compete with the park for attention. Now that it's emerging again as a valued public space, MacArthur Park deserves all the attention it can get.

—Nov. 14, 1987

Courting a Neighborly Style

OF THE VARIOUS RESIDENTIAL DESIGNS THAT HAVE SPROUTED IN LOS ANgeles, courtyard housing has to be one of the more appealing, taking advantage of the region's benign climate and reflecting the relaxed life style.

The basic idea of the courtyard design is the sensitively scaled clustering—on one or two building lots—of small attached or detached houses, town homes or apartments around a well-landscaped, common open space.

Such courts were first developed nearly 100 years ago in the form of modest bungalows to provide inexpensive housing for both the waves of newcomers then settling in Southern California and others who vacationed here.

With front porches and common areas encouraging mingling among the residents, bungalow courts became, in effects, neighborhoods with a sense of identity and place, providing for the newcomers pleasant enclaves in an increasingly anonymous city. For the vacationers, the courts were like a camp.

One of the oldest and best examples of this housing type is Bowen Court. Tucked onto a lushly landscaped site behind an Arroyo stone wall at 539 E. Villa St., about 1½ blocks east of Los Robles Avenue in Pasadena, it exudes a rustic charm.

The court was designed by Arthur Heineman in 1911 in the then-popular Craftsman style as a cluster of about two dozen distinctive vacation cottages, featuring, among other things, stone porches and chimneys. In time, the court was converted into a 34-unit apartment complex, happily not at the cost of its architectural integrity.

Also of note nearby is Reinway Court, a cluster of 11 Craftsman-style bungalows containing 24 apartments facing a central garden and walkway on an L-shaped site at 380 E. Parke St. It was designed in 1916 by architects Charles Buchanan and Leon Brockway.

Another, more modern-styled variation of the courtyard housing concept can be seen on Hollister Avenue, about a half block east of Ocean Avenue in Santa Monica. There, at No. 140 on a 60-foot-wide lot, architect Irving Gill sculpted his Horatio West complex, a two-story composition of plain walls, arched openings and corner windows that belie the court's 1919 construction.

But it was not the modest, neo-Modernist style demonstrated by Gill in the Horatio West project that replaced the bungalow style in the design of courtyard housing in the 1920s. Rather it was a fanciful Spanish Colonial Revival style. Red-tile roofed, rambling, rough-textured, stucco complexes encrusted with arches, terraces, French doors, deep-cut windows, ornate ironwork and hand-painted tiles focused on a formal garden, replete with tropical plantings and, usually, a gurgling fountain.

Among the more opulent of these courts was a series concocted by Arthur and Nina Zwebell, builders with no formal architectural education who went on to become movie set designers. Perhaps their best-known project is the aptly named Andalusia at 1471-75 Havenhurst Drive, just below Sunset Boulevard in West Hollywood.

Beyond the tiled automobile courtyard, under a broad archway and beneath a second-story balcony, is a lush courtyard, in the center of which is a tiled fountain fashioned after one found in Seville. As for the corner tower and the cantilevered balconies, they match the dreams of Mediterranean paradises.

Other courtyard complexes worth a glimpse in the West Hollywood area include the Patio del Moro at 8225 Fountain Ave., and the Villa Primavera at 1300 N. Harper Ave., both designed by the Zwebells. Nearby at 1355 N. Laurel Ave. is the Villa d'Este, where in addition to an evocative common court, each unit has a private, walled patio. It was designed by Walter and Pierpoint Davis very much in an Italian Renaissance mode, right down to the detailing of the eaves and the quoined grand archway.

—April 9, 1988

Semi-Secret Places

There are scattered throughout Los Angeles what I would describe as semi-secret public places; mostly out-of-the-way settings, accessible to all, that evoke a simpler, more gracious time and an appreciation of the city's unusual landscape and benign climate.

It was these settings decades ago that lent Los Angeles a pastoral, genteel image, generating such descriptions as the New Eden or the American Riviera and attracting waves of settlers seeking a more relaxed and healthful life style. California dreamin'.

These pastoral public places seem more important now than ever, given the increasing problems in Los Angeles of insensitive development and gridlock. In addition to reminding us of the unique, semitropical setting of the city, they also, frankly, offer an escape from the present.

My list of these places is, happily, fairly extensive. Included is Will Rogers State Historic Park, north of Sunset Boulevard and west of Brentwood, particularly on the weekends when polo matches are held there; Palisades Park in Santa Monica, especially north of California Avenue about sunset; the Huntington Library and Art Gallery in San Marino; and a certain plot of sand edging the ocean at Manhattan Beach.

A recent addition to my list is the Virginia Robinson Gardens, tucked away behind a wall at the end of Elden Way in Beverly Hills. The house, pavilion, terraces and in particular the lush gardens that make up the 6.2-acre estate offer a marvelous view of the opulent early years of Beverly Hills.

THE GRACEFULLY DETAILED ONE-STORY HOUSE WAS BUILT IN THE SPIRIT OF A Mediterranean villa in 1911 for Harry and Virginia Robinson, of Robinson's department store fame. A neoclassical pool pavilion, styled after the Le Petit Trianon at Versaille, was added in 1924 to provide a formal setting for the couple's extensive social gatherings. The house is listed on the national Register of Historic Places.

But for me, the major attraction of the estate are the gardens that Virginia Robinson shaped and cultivated during her 66-year residency. She died in 1977, a few days shy of her 100th birthday, leaving the estate to Los Angeles County for use as a public botanic garden. It is maintained and operated by the county Department of Arboreta and Botanic Gardens, with loving assistance from the volunteer Friends of Robinson Gardens.

To wander along the garden's footpaths, up and down its brick stairways and pause by its many fountains is to experience a botanical lexicon. Among the delights are clusters of camellias, a spectacular palm grove, stately cypresses, towering erythrinas and a rose garden. After the rains of last week the gardens should be particularly stunning, offering a rich display of colors and filling the air with fragrances.

At the request of neighbors, the gardens are only open Tuesdays through Fridays for one-hour guided tours, beginning at 10 a.m. and 1 p.m. Reservations are a must.

It is hoped that some day soon, in keeping with Virginia Robinson's wishes, the agreement with the county and Beverly Hills will be amended to have the gardens open on weekends.

—April 30, 1988

Rodia's Watts Towers

NEW YORK CITY HAS ITS EMPIRE STATE BUILDING, SYDNEY ITS OPERA house, Moscow has the Kremlin, London its Big Ben, and Los Angeles has Watts Towers.

In a city not world renowned for any particular architectural or engineering extravaganza (after all, we have our beaches and benign weather), most guidebooks to Los Angeles declare the towers "worth a detour" or a "must see."

Indeed, when I viewed the hand-sculpted towers recently with a gaggle of architecture students from Cal Poly Pomona, the group we were in was mostly tourists.

They did not seem fazed, as some Angelenos are, that the towers are in an out-of-the-way and not particularly attractive neighborhood, at 1765 E. 107th St. near the convergence of Willowbrook Avenue and Santa Ana Boulevard, about two miles east of Interstate 110 in South-Central Los Angeles.

The towers consist of nine sculptures, ranging in height from about 13 feet to 100 feet and dominating the frayed surroundings. The towers are of steel rods and pipes, wrapped with iron mesh, tied with wire, coated with mortar and decorated with about 70,000 sea shells and salvaged pieces of glass, pottery, porcelain and tiles.

THE GLASS INCLUDES QUITE A BIT OF GREEN FROM 7-UP BOTTLES AND A smattering of brilliant blue from Milk of Magnesia bottles. Adding to the color and glisten of the structure are a bright palette of pieces of flower pots, vases, dishes and tiles. The result is a folk-art masterpiece that engages and enthralls.

It was fashioned over from 1921 to 1954—without the aid of scaffolds, a welding torch or power tools—by Sabatino Rodia, an Italian immigrant. The towers have become a cultural-heritage monument of the city, listed on the national register of historic places, and a world-recognized curiosity.

Rodia, also known variously as Sam, Simon and Don Simon, was a construction laborer who worked on the towers evenings and weekends. He built with materials he brought home from his different jobs and with what was scavenged by him and the neighborhood children, whom he paid. As a result, the towers are studded with a fractured treasury of dated houshold items.

When Rodia felt the structure was complete in 1954, he deeded it and his adjoining house to a neighbor—and walked away. The house burned down a few years later and the towers were vandalized and threatened by the city with demolition. Happily, they were saved by citizen efforts, principally by Bud Goldstone, an engineer who proved to the city that the structure was sound.

Asked years later why he had sculpted the towers, Rodia replied: "I had in mind to do something big, and I did." He died in 1965.

—June 18, 1988

Celebrating Spaces

THIS BEING THE FOURTH OF JULY WEEKEND, ONE WONDERS WHERE, IN CASE of another revolution, or better yet a celebration of universal peace, Angelenos would gather to bear witness to the event.

Unlike most other cities, Los Angeles does not have a major

public welcoming space in which crowds can gather for scheduled or spontaneous celebrations; no Champs Elysees as in Paris, no Times Square as in New York, Grant Park in Chicago, the Mall in the District of Columbia, Red Square in Moscow, Trafalgar Square in London or Piazza Venezia in Rome.

THE PROBLEM WAS ILLUSTRATED RECENTLY BY THE RELATIVELY MODEST crowd, estimated at 100,000 people, that turned out to cheer the Lakers for winning the National Basketball Assn. championship. Similar events in other, smaller cities have attracted as many as 1 million people or more.

The lack of a large crowd here could be attributed to the fact that there simply was no single open, attractive space downtown to accommodate the fans. All that could squeeze into the stretch of Spring Street between 1st and Temple streets, facing City Hall where the team gathered on the steps, was a liberally estimated 40,000 persons, with perhaps another 60,000 having viewed the motorcade on its way there.

The city once had an attractive and popular Central Park. However, after being renamed Pershing square in 1918, the park suffered a series of some very ill-conceived redesigns to become a frayed, isolated space.

The best free, open space in and around Los Angeles is its sprawling, sun-bleached beaches. They are sand-covered piazzas, with different stretches catering to varied groups and activities, as piazzas do. All the beaches are linked together in a marvelous welcoming expanse. That is where we tend to migrate on July 4.

But the beaches are linear and have no real focus other than the ocean. Perhaps to celebrate their championship, the Lakers should have been put on a grandstand atop an open barge and towed just beyond the breakers as their fans lined the beaches to cheer.

Griffith Park and Elysian Park are well-located open spaces relatively near downtown, but their topography, landscaping and scattered facilities preclude large, clustering crowds. Nevertheless, their varied picnic areas make them attractive public places for celebrating holidays.

THE CITY'S MOST HISTORIC PUBLIC SPACE IS THE PLAZA IN EL PUEBLO DE LOS Angeles State Historic Park, at the southeastern end of Olvera Street downtown. Though it has been whittled away over the years and cannot accommodate large crowds, the plaza still functions as a gathering place for select events, such as the Cinco de Mayo celebration, the blessing of the animals at Eastertime and Las Posadas at Christmastime.

I expect also if there was a major public event to spontaneously celebrate, crowds might gather in Pasadena at the broad intersection of Garfield Avenue and Holly Street in front of City Hall; outside the Coliseum in Exposition Park off Figueroa Street; in Westwood Village, especially when traffic is banned, and along select stretches of Melrose Avenue and Hollywood, Sunset, Pico, Wilshire, Ventura and Whittier boulevards.

As for just wanting to be in a crowd to watch or be watched, especially on a holiday weekend, there are the lines outside a host of popular eateries, particularly for brunch: the tables at the Farmers Market in the Fairfax district, and the Brentwood Country Mart, 26th Street and San Vicente Boulevard. Or you can just meander along Ocean Front Walk in Venice.

There is also Palisades Park in Santa Monica where with my family (usually after waiting in line to get ice cream), I like to watch the sunset. It might not be the Lakers passing in review, but to us the sunset is a great, free public event.

—July 2, 1988

VIII

SPECIAL
PEOPLE

Julius Shulman, Photographer

WHEN JULIUS SHULMAN BEGAN TAKING HIS EXQUISITELY COMPOSED PHO-tographs of man-made structures about 50 years ago, there was no such vocational description as architectural photographer.

If an architect or a builder wanted a "professional" photograph of a particular project for a portfolio or a publication, they usually contacted a commercial photographer or took it themselves.

Then, in 1936, 26-year-old Shulman, fresh from UC Berkeley and with a love of his adopted Los Angeles and fascinated by photography, pointed his newly acquired vest-pocket Kodak camera at a recently constructed house in the Hollywood foothills designed by Richard Neutra.

The resulting photographs were shown to the renowned architect, who liked them, bought them and asked Shulman to take more. Other assignments followed from other architects making their mark in Los Angeles, and Shulman's hobby soon became his career.

What Shulman did in the subsequent years on assignment for a roster of leading architects and interior designers, and for just about every design journal and numerous magazines, was no less than to create an art form.

If anything distinguishes Shulman's photographs, it is their composition and how they are illuminated. He uses light to express the essence of man-made structures in much the same way and with the same genius the late Ansel Adams did with nature.

While he has traveled the world on assignments, Shulman has maintained a special focus on Los Angeles, which has been his home since 1920, when his family moved here from eastern Connecticut. For the last 36 years, he has lived in and personally and elaborately landscaped a Hollywood Hills house designed by Raphael Soriano.

Of all the periods of architecture that Los Angeles has experienced and that Shulman has documented on film, he says the most exciting was the '50s. "It was a glorious period in Los Angeles' history, in terms of the care and detailing that went into design," Shulman said in a recent interview.

Shulman noted that in the '50s, in addition to Neutra and Soriano, those practicing architecture in Los Angeles included such pioneers of the modern style as Rudolph Schindler, Gregory Ain and Harwell Harris. He avoid, with a smile, mentioning any favorites.

"They had divergent styles and artistic egos then, just like architects do now," Shulman said. But he added what made them different from some of the architectural stars of today was their prime concern to please their clients, "not an AIA (American Institute of Architects) jury or an ephemeral publication." He dismissed some of today's more publicized structures as "facade architecture."

It was a remark of a professional who does not have to worry about his next assignment. With a wall decorated with dozens of awards and commendations, including a coveted medal for photography from the AIA, and as the author of the definitive "The Photography of Architecture and Design" (Whitney Library of Design, $27.50), Shulman continues to be in demand.

"Of course, my fees have changed a bit," he observed, noting he received $2 apiece for the photographs he took in 1936 of the Neutra-designed house, compared to $2,500, plus liberal expenses, from a corporation for a photograph of its headquarters for a cover of an annual report.

But Shulman was quick to add that his fee schedule varies, depending on the age and accomplishments of the architects involved. He has been known to donate his time and talent to photograph student projects that have captured his fancy, and to allow such non-profit organizations as the conservancy to reprint his photographs at no cost.

Also in demand by book and magazine editors and curators and historians is Shulman's photo collection, the size of which even he cannot estimate. "Just give me the name of any architect, any year within the last 50, and I should have a photograph," he said with pride.

Shulman holds on to images, mementoes and memories with a sure and affectionate hand. Rummaging through his studio he produced, among other things, a photograph of the 6th Avenue bridge over the Los Angeles River, which won him his first award 50 years ago, and a letter from Frank Lloyd Wright, complimenting him on his work.

The letter prompted Shulman to talk about the art of architectural photography. "You have to consider the building's siting. That is most important; then what distinguishes it; what is it to do?" he mused. "But first that feeling for the siting, how you are going to point the camera, must come from the heart."

Shulman added that almost always when he has taken on an assignment, the architect or owner comments that the building is hard to photograph. "I tell them 'don't tell me a building is hard to photograph. You're talking to Uncle Julius.' "

—Sept. 11, 1985

Lautner Still Ahead of His Time

A SELECT JURY OF THE AMERICAN INSTITUTE OF ARCHITECTS WILL BE MEETing shortly to review nominations for the organization's highest and most coveted award, the Gold Medal.

Among those nominated last year from California and eventually losing out to Canadian Arthur Erickson was John Lautner, the maverick designer of a variety of lyrical, singular structures in Los Angeles and elsewhere.

The hope here is that Lautner once again will be nominated and somehow the power, originality and genius of his imaginative designs will overcome the prejudices and parochialism of the profession's establishment, and that at long last he will receive the recognition he so richly deserves.

For nearly 50 years, Lautner has been leading an almost monastic existence in Los Angeles, bucking tradition, styles, fashions and fads to produce woefully few structures. It is a price the architect has paid for trying to incorporate the latest building technology into original designs to serve both the environment and the user.

BUT THE RELATIVELY FEW DESIGNS BY LAUTNER THAT HAVE BEEN REALIZED ARE landmarks that promise him a place in architecture history, with or without an AIA Gold Medal. Though some were built decades ago, they are still ahead of their time, and I suspect 50 years from now, they still will be ahead of their time. Such has been his vision.

In Los Angeles, his buildings include the Chemosphere house, an octagon-shaped structure that sits like a flying saucer on a single concrete column in the Hollywood Hills, overlooking the San Fernando Valley. But the house is more than just an entertaining, odd-shaped object.

Here Lautner, in 1960, created a unique living space on what was an unbuildable, steep site without resorting to the usual bulldozing to create pads and havoc with the sensitive hillsides. The solution was lyrical and logical, and unexpected.

Also unique is the expressive Carling house above Mulholland Drive, which features a living room wall with a built-in softa that swings out on a hinge onto a terrace to provide exterior seating. Built in 1950, the indoor-outdoor wall still works, a tribute to Lautner's training as an engineer.

Lautner's design, in 1963, for the Silvertop house in Silver Lake is another example of his marriage of engineering and architecture to create a futuristic form that not only engages the eye and mind, but works well as a space for living.

Beyond Los Angeles, there are singular structures in Palm Springs (for Bob Hope), Aspen, Colo., Anchorage, Alaska, Hawaii and Mexico. And, of course, there also were some select commercial buildings in the 1940s and 1950s, including a variety of eye-catching coffee shops that gave rise to the so-called Googie style. The style, which at first was heckled for its flamboyance, recently has been heralded in various architectural histories for its expressionism.

"His designs have been unique; every structure a one of a kind," declares renowned architectural photographer Julius Shulman, who has observed Lautner's work since the designer came West after studying at Taliesin to supervise, in 1939, the construction of Frank Lloyd Wright's Sturgis house in Brentwood.

At 75, Lautner is still young and looking to the future, though his practice is limited.

"I guess one of my problems is that I have cared more about creating a sympathetic space that enriches the client's life and work—spaces that provide a service—than about being trendy," said Lautner recently while philosophizing in his cluttered Hollywood office.

"I'm afraid I am just not into the superficial facadism with all its phony rationales that seem to preoccupy architecture these days," he added.

LAUTNER ALSO TOOK STRONG EXCEPTION TO THE CURRENT FAD AMONG SOME architects to pervert materials for effect, or in straining to be witty by use of a grab bag of historical references.

"It is amazing what architects are getting away with in the name of art, thanks to an undiscerning media," declared Lautner. "You people have let them get away with it; you and those sheep-like clients, who want to be trendy, even if it means getting a building that doesn't wear well or work.

"But I don't want to criticize. It is too easy. I want to create."

HE THEN DESCRIBED A HOUSE HE DESIGNED THAT IS IN THE LAST THROES OF construction in Malibu. Its soaring concrete form hints of being another striking Lautner structure.

This is not an architect who looks over his shoulder to see what might have worked in the past, or to mimic others, or who grovels for peer approval. Like his designs, Lautner is an original. There are not too many unselfconscious, honest ones left in architecture today.

If Lautner receives the medal, it will be he who honors it, rather than it honoring him. But one cannot be sanguine about his chances. Too often the award has gone to businessmen and politicians posing as architects rather than to the profession's dwindling true theoreticians and innovators.

THAT IS NOT TO BE TAKEN AS AN INSULT TO GOLD MEDALIST ERICKSON, WHO, in addition to having offices in Vancouver and Toronto, maintains one in Los Angeles as he supervises the completion of his design of California Plaza.

Out of respect for Erickson, I assume last year's award went to him primarily for his individualistic designs in and around Vancouver rather than the competent but not particularly inspired commercial effort on the lobotomized Bunker Hill

Having experienced Erickson's stunning Museum of Anthropology at the University of British Columbia and the powerful campus of Simon Fraser University, and having welcomed his presence here, I am still hopeful that he will have other opportunities to apply his broader talent to the wanting Los Angeles cityscape.

Hopefully, Lautner also will have the opportunity, embodying, as he does, so much of the city's faith in the future.

—Sept. 14, 1986

Lautner was not honored.

194

When Lefcoe Missed the Ham, He Quit

ARGUMENTS CONCERNING LIFE, LIBERTY AND THE PURSUIT OF ZONING changes continue at the Los Angeles County Regional Planning Commission, just as they did before George Lefcoe retired last month as a commissioner, but they are not the same.

During his eight-year tenure, Lefcoe not only brought rare insight to the commission's hearings, helping explain the often obtuse planning process to a confused public and press, he did it with an equally rare humor.

As if Los Angeles County was not so fragmented and far-flung, and its government not so dense and convoluted so as to confuse those who question its shaping and misshaping, now we must struggle without the aid of Lefcoe.

"I have no doubt that you and others will be able to find the answers to our multitude of planning problems," Lefcoe said in a recent interview. "But whether those answers will be appropriate, or right, is another matter," he added with his characteristic laugh.

ACTUALLY, LEFCOE, WHO IS THE DISTINGUISHED HENRY BRUCE PROFESSOR OF Equity at the USC Law Center, admitted to having had increasing difficulty over the years finding answers.

"A problem has been the rigid state planning and environmental statutes," he explained. "While minimizing arbitrary planning abuses, they also have minimized our ability to come up with creative solutions. At times, I have felt more like a traffic cop at a 'stop' sign than someone who should be deciding whether there should be a road there at all."

Following the theme of traffic in another direction, Lefcoe commented on how, in planning discussions, much more time seems to be spent on reviewing minor parking problems than larger and ultimately more important matters of design.

"Listening to our Planning Commission, you could easily believe that we were actually an off-street parking authority, mandated by law to rescue for every stray vehicle a free and available resting place at every corner," Lefcoe said.

BACK TO THE BROADER ISSUE OF PLANNING, LEFCOE DECLARED HE FELT THAT too much time also was spent on developing detailed general plans— again to satisfy state statutes—and too little time fine-tuning specific plans. "We should be looking less at the sweep of the county from a perspective of 10,000 feet up in the air and more at the bits and pieces of neighborhoods and landscapes, from the level of the street."

But that perspective also has its problems, Lefcoe added. He recalled a hearing where a woman from the San Gabriel Valley began crying because someone wanted to build a house on a corner lot that her young daughter and friends used as a playground.

"That the person who owned the lot wanted to build exactly the same type of house the woman lived in made no difference," Lefcoe said. "She and her neighbors were opposed to it. They also were opposed to chipping in and buying the lot for a playground, or even just maintaining it. It was something we call in law a 'freegood' and they wanted it kept that way."

Lefcoe added that such parochialism tended to wear him down. "The environmental rhetoric of homeowners was fine, and I agreed with much of it, but the reality was that most just wanted to stop something down the block, not do anything positive. A few developers, at least, recognized that good design and good planning was good for marketing."

WHEN APPOINTED TO THE COMMISSION BY SUPERVISOR EDMUND EDELMAN, Lefcoe said his hope was to act as a sort of mediator on planning matters while somehow improving the environment, "protecting views and hillscapes and promoting bike paths and nature preserves."

Among projects that pleased him was one in Valencia, where the required flood control channel was turned into a linear pedestrian park. "The developer's plan really did not look inspired on paper, but it turned out just fine," said Lefcoe. "In contrast, I remember some development for Agoura looked great on a paper, but in execution was a real disappointment."

Often frustrated by the protracted and parochial planning process, Lefcoe would turn to humor to try to put the project that was being reviewed into perspective. One of his memorable efforts involved Playa Vista, an ambitious and controversial mixed-use project proposed between Westchester and Marina del Rey and encompassing the sensitive wetlands there.

Wearied of the heated push and pull of the developer and the surrounding community, he suggested jokingly that a disputed water channel be divered east into landlocked Culver City, creating waterfront property there.

"SINCE THEY WOULD BE GETTING A MARINA AND WETLANDS OUT OF THE development, something of real value, residents there would be much more willing to work toward a solution," Lefcoe commented.

Asked to discuss some mistakes he might have made as a commissioner, Lefcoe replied that "like Lot's wife, we try not to look back. If we do, we'll cry salty tears."

He did say that a mistake might have been made that he retired before, and not after, Christmas. "I really missed the cards from engineers I never met, the wine and cheese from development companies I never heard of and, especially, the Honeybaked ham from, of all places, Forest Lawn, even though the company was never an applicant before the commission when I was there," Lefcoe said.

"But because I miss them is why I think it was a good idea I resigned," he added. "I do not think it is wise to stay in public office for too long a time."

Lefcoe used the ham from Forest Lawn as an illustration.

"My first Christmas as a commissioner—when I received the ham—I tried to return it at once, though for the record, I did not because no one at Forest Lawn seemed authorized to accept hams, apparently not even for burial. My guess is that no one of the many public servants who received the hams ever had tried to return it," said Lefcoe.

"When I received another ham the next Christmas, I gave it to a worthy charity," Lefcoe recalled. "The next year, some worthy friends were having a party, so I gave it to them. The next year I had a party and we enjoyed the ham."

"In the fifth year, about the 10th of December," said Lefcoe, "I began wondering, where is my ham? Why is it late?"

Lefcoe sighed and laughed. "So much for the seduction of public officials. It was then I thought it was time to retire, though it took me two more hams and three years to finally do it."

—Jan. 25, 1987

Cliff May's Quintessential Houses

THE LOS ANGELES MULTIPLE LISTING SERVICE, IN ITS TYPICALLY TERSE style, described well the four-bedroom, four-bath house being offered through Coldwell, Banker real estate office in Brentwood:

"Exciting custom Cliff May ranch on a cul-de-sac, up a private drive in Sullivan Canyon. House has a wonderful feeling of seclusion and privacy, nestled among the trees, high beamed ceilings, skylights, and great flow to patios thru sliding glass doors. Room for horses and small pool. . . ."

Calling it a Cliff May ranch and not simply a California ranch was quite fitting and noteworthy. More than any other designer, architect or developer, it was Cliff May who perfected the graceful, informal, low-slung, single-story style marked by the mingling of interior and exterior spaces.

Though the style and its thousands of variations dot the city and in particularly, suburbanscapes across the country, some outstanding examples of the better appointed and sited Cliff May ranches can be seen in Sullivan Canyon north of Sunset Boulevard.

THERE ALONG OLD OAK AND RIVIERA RANCH ROADS, SET BACK ON WELL-landscaped large lots behind splitrail fences, adobe walls and horse corrals, are some of the pricier Cliff May ranches. There are no sidewalks, and many of the numbers can't be seen. The owners like it that way. But almost all of the houses along these streets are Cliff May ranches. (The one offered through Coldwell, Banker is listed at $895,000.)

At the end of Old Ranch Road, and very difficult to see beyond an imposing gate protecting a 50-or-so-acre expanse, is May's masterpiece, a sprawling, skylight structure he christened *Mandalay* when he began building it in 1953.

May lived there for more than 30 years, expanding and improving the structure to accommodate his family, entertain his friends and clients, and to test out new design concepts. May now lives elsewhere, and the ranch is currently listed for sale for $22.5 million.

Sitting in his modest office at the foot of Riviera Ranch Road about a mile from his beloved Mandalay, May frowns at the mention of the prices being asked for his creations, including the amount for his own home.

"WHEN I BEGAN DESIGNING AND BUILDING MY RANCHES BACK IN 1931, MY aim was to keep them affordable. After all, it was the Depression," May says. Though nearing 80, he is still in practice and as sharp as ever.

"But I also wanted the houses to be attractive, and somehow express and serve the California life style of informality, outdoor living and, of course, the sunshine," May adds. May did not attend architecture school, nor is he a registered architect; he simply describes himself as a designer.

What May did was to combine the informal layout of the California adobe courtyard house with the practical construction of a board-and-batten bungalow. In effect, it was a marriage of the Hispanic style and Yankee ingenuity that was party of May's heritage.

His first ranch-style house with its living room oriented not to the front and the street but to a rear patio sold quickly in San Diego for $9,500. After building and selling easily about 50 more ranches, May moved to Los Angeles to expand his business and improve upon his design.

Among his innovations was moving the garage from the backyard to the front yard and attaching it to the house, or simply putting the car in a breezeway under a shed roof: ergo, the carport.

"The only reason people had put their cars in the backyard was because they had replaced horses and that is where the barns were. The barns simply had become the garages," May says. "Moving cars and their garages to the front saved all that driveway space and cut down on some terrible accidents people had backing up. Now the backyard could really be used for the children and entertaining."

As for the house itself, May did away with the boxy room arrangements—favored in the East and mimicked in the Midwest—for informal, free-flowing combinations of living and dining areas. Spaces also were defined by their use, such as the family room and the entertainment area, and were marked by their openness, flexibility and orientation through sliding glass doors to rear terraces and landscaping.

WHAT EVOLVED WAS THE QUINTESSENTIAL SUBURBAN RANCH. LAUNCHED IN Southern California with May at the helm, the style gained steadily in popularity in the late 1940s and 1950s, paced by an expanding suburbia. By the 1960s the ranch and its ubiquitous backyard barbecue had become a symbol of suburbia.

While over the decades designing about 1,000 custom homes, May also sold plans for an estimated 18,000 other houses and numerous subdivisions. On his office wall is large map of America covered with pins: red pins for locations of his custom-designed houses, green for subdivisions of fewer than 25 of his houses and gold for subdivisions of 25 or more of his houses. There also are blue pins for houses and projects for which he has won awards and yellow pins for houses that have been featured in magazines.

In addition, over the years May's plans and concepts have been freely adopted and adapted with some license by architects and builders around the world. "I guess you can say that it is a compliment, of sorts," May says.

But wherever the ranches might be constructed, it is in Southern California that the style was shaped, and in Sullivan Canyon that it flowered, cultivated with a rare talent by May.

—Feb. 7, 1987

Charles Lee's Glory days

IMPRESARIO H. L. GUMBINER WANTED SOMETHING BETTER, MORE SUMPtuous than his Tower Theatre downtown, recalls architect S. Charles Lee, who had designed the Baroque-styled extravagance at Broadway and 89th Street for him in 1927 with an interior modeled after the Paris Opera House.

So the Beaux Arts-trained Lee dipped further back into history and, on a 35-foot-wide lot a block and a half away at 615 S. Broadway, designed the Los Angeles Theatre as if Louis XVI were his client.

After all, Gumbiner had made a fortune with the Tower Theatre, which was the first built in Southern California for the talkies—"The Jazz Singer" premiered there—and the first to be air-conditioned.

WHEN THE LOS ANGELES THEATRE OPENED IN 1931 FOR THE WORLD PREMIER of Charlie Chaplin's "City Lights," the $1.5-million design by the then 32-year-old architect defined the phrase "movie palace."

It also turned out to be the last such palace built on Broadway, then beginning to feel the effects of the Depression and the competition of Hollywood Boulevard for the title of the "Great White Way of the West."

Gumbiner eventually would go bankrupt, while Lee went on to design other theaters and buildings of note before giving up architecture in the 1950s to become a successful developer. Of the many projects with which he has been involved, Lee considers the Los Angeles Theatre one of his favorites, and on a recent tour there, talked about the design.

Behind the theater's exterior marked by a bright terrazzo sidewalk and an ornate facade of Corinthian columns was a luxurious lobby that Lee says was fashioned after the Hall of Mirrors at Versailles, extended to a two-story height and focused on a fountain on the mezzanine level featuring strands of crystal simulating falling water.

"We thought for 35 cents a person should be able to get their art as well as their entertainment," Lee said. "The idea of combining art and entertainment we copied from the church, just as we copied some of the decorations from the French."

LEE WAS PARTICULARLY PROUD OF THE LUXURIOUS DESIGN OF THE BASEMENT, which, when the theater opened, included a ballroom where people waiting for seats or the next show could dance, eat in an adjacent restaurant or even view the film on a small screen that by a prism device reflected the big screen in the auditorium above.

There was also a spacious smoking room and marble-encrusted men's and women's rooms, the latter including 16 private toilet stalls, each faced with a different color marble.

Downstairs was a room decorated as the inside of a circus tent where children could be left in the care of attendants provided by the theater. Upstairs behind the balcony was a soundproof room, where parents could see and hear the film while comforting their crying children.

Other features included a board in the lobby wired to each seat in the theater that showed ushers where there were vacancies. And, of course, there was the auditorium itself, replete with crystal chandeliers, plush and easily accessible seating and ornate decorations.

The theater is still very much in operation, though worse for wear. Gone are the special rooms and furnishings; the carpet designed by Lee is threadbare and patched; the snack bar and arcade games clutter up the lobby; and the men's and women's rooms have lost their glitter and attendants.

But the scale and details of the theater are impressive and evocative, and if not in all its past glory, certainly in part glory.

—Feb. 21, 1987

Designing Women

For Mother's Day on Sunday, Barbara Coffman plans to take her 3-month-old daughter Caelainn and husband Arlan on a tour of construction sites of projects she has designed.

"An architect also can be a mother," Coffman said.

"But it is tough," Rebecca Binder added, referring to both professions as her 16-month-old son, Max, exercised his expanding vocabulary in the background.

Also apparent is that it is not easy simply being an architect and a woman, let alone a mother.

According to the Los Angeles-based Assn. for Women in Architecture, women composed an estimated 30% of the nation's architecture student body, but only 4% of the nation's 60,000 registered architects, and fewer still of any prominence in the large, established firms.

This harsh reality has in recent years prompted more and more women to establish their own firms—by themselves, with other women, or in full partnership with a man. As a result sprouting up across the local landscape has been an increasing number of buildings designed by women.

Coffman's projects have ranged from residential remodels and new houses to a shopping mall and an award-winning temporary pavilion at the Los Angeles County fair. In Santa Monica Coffman has a brawny single-family house nearing completion at 452 22nd St. and the start of a more interesting apartment complex at 2454 4th St.

Among Binder's designs are a playful Eats restaurants at 411½ Main St. in El Segundo, an idiosyncratic addition to a house at 15119

Valley Vista Blvd. in Sherman Oaks and a distinctive High Tech-styled condominium at 116 Pacific St. in Santa Monica, the latter in partnership with Jim Stafford. All have won major awards from the American Institute of Architects.

Binder's latest design is her own house, at 7741 81st St. in Playa del Ray, a well-chorused melange of materials expressing a very functional and personal arrangement of space that takes advantage of the structure's site and light.

Brenda Levin also has done her own house, but as the principal of her own firm she is best known as an accomplished restoration architect. The impressive list of her projects includes the Oviatt and Fine Arts buildings, at 617 S. Olive St. and 811 West 7th St., downtown, and the Wiltern Theatre and Pellissier Building, at the southeast corner of Wilshire Boulevard and Western Avenue. All are landmarks that have been recycled with a respect for the original structure and a concern for details.

In addition, Levin designed the renovation of the Downtown Women's Center, at 333 S. Los Angeles St., and is directing the continuing refurbishing of the Grand Central Market, at 315 S. Broadway, and the architectural orientation of Eliot Levin Abel, her 6-year-old son.

While she was with the firm of Welton Beckett & Associates, Norma Sklarek served as project director for the design of the bright, breezy Terminal One at LAX, bringing the $50-million project in on time and on budget.

Soon after its completion in 1984, Sklarek joined with Margot Siegel, who had designed the co-generation plant and cooling tower at LAX, and Kate Diamond, to form the firm of Sigel Sklarek Diamond. Among Diamond's designs is a small-striking office building at 870 Vine for Otto Nemenz International.

The firm has since garnered some impressive commissions, attracted other women architects into the fold—most recently Alicia Rosenthal from Benton/ Park/ Candreva— and has grown to 20 employees, three of whom at present are pregnant.

Also involved in the design of the ambitious Terminal One project was Margot Hebald-Heymann, a mother of two and for the last 10 years the principal of her own firm. Among her many projects are the interiors of the Oxnard and Simi Valley childrens' dental clinics, and with the Luckman Partnership the plan for the Universal City metro rail station. And, of course, she also has designed her office, at 1320 on the Santa Monica Mall.

Seraphima Lamb's most recent project is what she calls a very practical, well-detailed house at 3318 The Strand, in Hermosa Beach. Other projects include being sub-architect to Kajima International on the design of a major warehouse and office for Kenwood Stereo at 2201 Dominguez St., in Carson.

Lamb explains that she formed her own office when she realized that after 12 years in male-dominated firms she felt she had risen as high as she would. "In architecture like in so many other things there is very much an old boys' network," she adds. "But it is changing."

And, as a result, also changing is the design of the cityscape.

—May 9, 1987

Remembrance for UCLA's Harvey

THE RENAMING, A FEW WEEKS AGO, WITH SOME FANFARE, OF A BUILDING AT UCLA in Westwood for Harvey S. Perloff prompted some thoughts of the first and late dean of the university's Graduate School of Architecture and Urban Planning.

No doubt, naming what previously had been labeled the Architecture Building for a planner would have pleased Harvey, who, for 15 years, presided over the uneasy peace there between the ego-involved architecture and planning faculties.

To most persons who knew him, it was Harvey, not Mr. Perloff, or Prof. Perloff, or Dr. Perloff, or The Dean. Unlike so many pretentious persons in the tenure-obsessed academic community, Harvey did not hide behind titles, the authorship of numerous studies and books or laurels, of which he had many to his credit.

Simply calling him Harvey, as he preferred, was more informal and made him more accessible. That and a ready smile were part of his charm, and a reason he was relatively successful in bridging the gap of the rhetoric of the school and university, and the reality of the city and nation.

HARVEY WAS IN A CLASS BY HIMSELF IN HIS ABILITY TO "CO-OP" SELF-absorbed academics, autocratic administrators, vain donors, fatuous politicians and merciless journalists, and gain research grants or donations, participate in a prestigious planning effort or a major seminar, or flog a report or the school itself, and garner yet another award.

University buildings certainly have been named for persons who have done less.

But there was much more to Harvey than just being a genial power broker. For me, what distinguished Harvey was that he cared deeply about the human condition and cities, believed with the fervor of a zealot that planning and design could make a difference, and that the university should play a critical role in the effort.

And despite the reality of the politics of universities and cities, and the egos of master architects and planners, which battered him over the years, and his caring causes, Harvey somehow remained an optimist. For this you had to admire him.

From when I first met him in 1969 to the last time I saw him shortly before his death in 1983, Harvey had an agenda of good works for which he was trying to raise support.

IN 1969, IT WAS A "NEW TOWN INTOWN" CONCEPT, AND IN 1983, A VISION of a better Los Angeles through better planning. His optimism was infectious, and whenever I left him I felt a surge of enthusiasm and a hope that perhaps the city could be saved from itself.

When Harvey died I did not write an obituary or an remembrance or attend the numerous memorials that were held for him. I just did not want to think of Harvey being dead and his optimism no longer around from which to draw upon.

I fantasized with envy that Harvey had gotten one of the marvelous travel and study grants, and that he and his loving wife, Mimi, had gone off for a well-earned sabbatical abroad, would return enthused as ever, and call me. Politics as ever, he would begin the conversation with a statement that he liked a particular column, adding "but had you thought of. . ." or better yet "I shouldn't be telling you this, but. . . ."

The call never came.

IN ADDITION TO MEMORIES, HARVEY DID LEAVE AN IMPRESSIVE VOLUME OF work, including 17 books and numerous reports and articles. His last was an article reflecting on his 15 years at UCLA and what the next 15 years might bring.

His thoughts in the article about the future I found particularly revealing and provacative, especially as they specifically relate to UCLA, and generally other schools of architecture and planning, and to the design and planning professions at large.

"I am convinced that the pressures of rapidly changing technology and international competition will once again—and very soon—put education and research at the forefront of national concerns," he wrote, adding if so "a great deal will be expected of us in the professions dealing with the environment, with building and with social progress."

With this in mind, Harvey declared that the school's architecture and urban design program "has to go some distance further in learning how to combine technology with good design and how to better combine both technology and design with human needs and aspirations."

As for the planning program, he wrote that it had to strengthen its built and natural environment concentrations, and planning research, the latter "not only in the realm of theory, but also in action research and community-oriented research."

CONTINUING THIS THEME OF APPLIED EDUCATION, HARVEY DECLARED THAT the school was strong enough "to lead the way in actually *creating* a better architecture and a better urban planning.

"Southern California provides us with just the right context to demonstrate that architecture and urban planning should be and *can* be much better than they are now, for the area is still growing, not only in numbers but in internationalization and in sophistication."

He concluded:

"In the next few years, I would like to see the School undertake some truly courageous and even surprising plans for the future of the Los Angeles area (in design, building, planning and human relations) as a prototype for other cities—at the same time that we advance the theoretical and methodological bases of our profession.

"It would be an appropriate goal for the School to be known not only as a leading school of architecture and urban planning but also an important contributor to the actual creation of a better tomorrow."

To the end, Harvey was optimist, dreaming grand thoughts for his profession, his school and his city. May they be kept alive.

—May 24, 1987

An Architect With the Wright Stuff

TWENTY-EIGHT YEARS AFTER HIS DEATH, FRANK LLOYD WRIGHT IS STILL the greatest, most recognizable, name in American architecture. In a long career that spanned 70 years, including some very productive ones in Los Angeles, the flamboyant Wright was almost constantly in the public eye promoting and producing new design concepts.

So bright was his star, so strong his personality and public image, that Wright left much of the profession in the shadows, including the architecture careers of his own talented sons, John and Frank Jr.

To establish his independence as an architect based in Los Angeles, Frank Jr. altered his name to simply Lloyd Wright. John in his California practice was less identified with his father, a situation helped by his invention of the Lincoln Logs building set for children.

And though Lloyd Wright designed some singular structures here, including the Wayfarers Chapel in Palos Verde and the Samuels-Navarro House in Hollywood, he remained in the shadow of his father's reputation, acording to his son, Eric Lloyd Wright, an architect himself.

"THERE IS NO QUESTION ABOUT IT THAT GRANDFATHER WAS A FORCE, AND though an inspiration to father, dominated his practice long after he died in 1959 and until father died in 1978," commented Wright recently while discussing his heritage and his own career as a third generation architect.

Wright made his remarks sitting comfortably in the shade of a tree on an expanse of land he owns above Malibu. On the land is a mobile home which serves as his architecture office, and nearby the foundations of a distinctive home and studio he has designed for him and his family and practice, and which he is handcrafting with the help of his sons and friends.

Having worked and studied under his grandfather for eight years and then his father for 22 years, the 57-year-old Wright said that it took him some time to come to terms with his heritage. "I feel now nearly 10 years on my own, keeping my practice small and in control, and more and more confident in my creativity, I can talk with some objectivity," declared Wright.

Wright said in some ways his family heritage has made it more difficult for him as the chief designer in his three-person office. He explained that some potential clients expect him to produce drawings and designs like his grandfather. "Among the things I learned from him, and my father, was not to be an imitator," he said.

However, Wright said he does embrace his grandfather's concept of organic architecture, which he explained was an architecture that grows out of the site, the needs of the client, the nature of the materials, and a hope that it improves the surrounding area, and, generally, society.

"I guess you could say I'm an idealist. But I think architects should be idealists, for what they create affects so many more persons than just themselves, and in all probability will be around for a good many years," added Wright.

"Grandfather did not try to create unique buildings just to be different, but rather to solve the problems presented by the sites and the users," said Wright. "Today it seems a lot of architects just want to be different."

Because of what Wright termed the pandering and politics of the architecture profession, he said he does not enter competitions, vie for awards or belong to the American Institute of Architects. "I guess being a renegade is a family tradition," he explained, adding that he felt, as did his grandfather and father, that such activities are not really motivated by the creative and social aspects of architecture, but simply self promotion.

"It is a tough business, and when growing up I was not drawn to it," said Wright. "At mealtime all I always heard was about the problems of architecture, the battles grandfather and father were having with contractors and clients. It also was their lives, and came before their families, and I guess I resented that also. What I wanted to be was a farmer."

When Wright was 15 years old he went to work during the summer in his grandfather's studio at Taliesin in Spring Green, Wis., and fell in love with the design process. "The talk in the drafting room about buildings, the passion with which grandfather reviewed plans, the models—everything—was just so exciting."

In time Wright went on to study architecture as an apprentice at Taliesin West, in Scottsdale, Ariz. "And while grandfather there was still grandfather, he also was Mr. Wright. It was there I began to realize the responsibility that came with my name," said Wright. "There was the family, and there was the architecture, and the architecture came first."

And while that was the way it was with his grandfather and father, it is apparent that that priority is somewhat different with Eric Lloyd Wright. He has been quite select in his commissions, which include being a consultant in the restoration of various Frank Lloyd Wright landmarks across the country, and the designer of a few residences here, a small office building in Glendale, an animal shelter in Ojai and a church in Philadelphia.

This has left him time to be with his wife, Mary, and two sons, Devon, a landscape contractor, and Cory, a music student, and work on the house and studio he designed. "My goal is creating a life, of which architecture is a part," he said.

—Oct. 25, 1987

205

Ain's Contributions Remembered

I NEVER MET GREGORY AIN, WHO DIED A FEW WEEKS AGO AT THE AGE OF 79 after a lingering illness, but through his architectural designs and writings I knew him, and respected him.

From the 1930s to the early 1960s, Ain practiced and preached in Los Angeles a rare, humanistic architecture in which he considered design a tool to improve the lives of people and communities.

It is a design philosophy as appropriate today as it was then, and prompts a new appreciation of Ain's struggle to produce user-friendly, affordable housing and well-planned neighborhoods. Certainly, he deserves to be listed among the architectural heroes of Los Angeles.

Despite lean years in the profession during the 1930s and '40s, Ain produced an impressive body of work in the spirit of his selfless social consciousness. This included dozens of innovative single-family and tract houses, a few office buildings and some distinctive apartment complexes.

Among those still to be seen and admired is a two-story, four-unit project at 1281 S. Dunsmuir Ave., just west of the Crenshaw District. Despite a narrow, sloping site, Ain, in a 1937 design, manipulated the cubist-styled units to create an open, informal plan focused on a row of private gardens.

The result, under severe constraints, was a modernistic update of the tried and true bungalow court, inexpensive housing sensitively rendered.

Though not a stylistic ideologue, Ain championed a modern design vocabulary that he embraced and hadlearned as an apprentice at separate times to both R. M. Schindler and Richard Neutra, two lions of the modernist movement. In his later writings and comments, Ain indicated that Schindler tended to be more sensitive to function and Neutra to style.

"Ain idolized Schindler," recalls architect John Blanton, who for a time also worked for Neutra. "But Ain was more user-oriented; he wanted his designs to work for the client, and therefore might compromise style. Because of this, clients loved him."

Blanton also remembered Ain as an engaging and sympathetic teacher, an impression shared by others. Ain taught for a number of years at USC and in the mid-1960s, was dean of the school of architecture at Penn State. He returned to Los Angeles in 1967, but because of varying illnesses, sadly, never fully resumed practice or teaching.

In his prime, Ain continually tried to extend the modernist idiom to build affordable housing. It was a dream for which he won in 1940, at the age of 32, a coveted Guggenheim Fellowship to study low-income housing. Among his sponsors were the renowned Walter Gropius and Mies van der Rohe.

During this time, Ain also designed about 20 small, well-planned houses for middle-income families, who otherwise, because of no alternatives, would have most likely ended up in ticky-tacky tract models, according to architectural historian Esther McCoy in a definitive study of Ain included in her book "The Second Generation." (The book is out of print but available through Hennessey & Ingalls, Santa Monica.)

McCoy notes that Ain "performed this service deep in the shadow of Neutra and Schindler, bringing to it a complexity greater than Neutra's and a simplicity greater than Schindler's." She adds that "Ain was part of that small select group of the '30s—Harwell Hamilton Harris, J. R. Davidson, Thornton Abell, John Lautner—that gave substance, variety and surprise to the Los Angeles scene."

In the 1940s, Ain continued to champion the need for well-designed, affordable housing in well-planned subdivision, particularly to serve the flood of families expected in the postwar years. As a member of a jury judging a competition in 1945, sponsored by a national construction materials corporation, Ain warned that if architects did not meet this neeed, builders would, with poor designs.

Declared a report of the jury said to have been written in large part by the social-minded Ain, "too many architects in their zeal to promulgate new and frequently valid ideas withdraw from the common architectural problems of the common people."

Definitely not withdrawing from the fray was Ain. With Simon Eisner as planner and Garrett Eckbo as landscape architect, Ain in the postwar years pursued the development of a 280-unit cooperative in Reseda. It was to be a model community, sensitively planned with parks and playgrounds and a variety of modern-styled housing for a mix of families. But because the mix included minorities, the project could not get the needed backing of the Federal Housing Administration, and failed.

MORE SUCCESSFUL WAS A TRACT DEVELOPMENT IN MAR VISTA, WHERE AS A principal in the firm of Ain, Johnson & Day, and in association again with Eckbo, Ain in 1947 planned about 100 houses on a 60-acre tract. But even there the FHA haunted him, reducing the number of units it would finance and requesting that in the interest of "good business practices," ranch and salt box designs be mixed with his modernist schemes.

A persevering Ain eventually produced 52 compromised, partially prefabricated, 1,050-square-foot houses there that sold in the late 1940s for about $11,000 apiece, which was then a bit pricey for the area. Though the Mar Vista houses have been substantially altered over the last 40 years, they are still touted as an Ain design (and sell for about 20 times the original price.)

But in my opinion, it really is not the designs that distinguished Ain's career, conscientiously rendered and accomplished as they were. What marked his work, and for which I am confident he will be remembered, was its motivation: The belief that design could, and should, be socially and environmentally responsible; indeed, that in its use there is an obligation to better serve mankind.

Such beliefs elevate architecture, and remind us of its marvelous and exciting potential. For that we thank, and remember, Gregory Ain.

—Jan. 24, 1988

Quincy Jones' Architectural Legacy

"THERE IS NO UNIMPORTANT ARCHITECTURE," THE LATE ARCHITECT Quincy Jones once said, adding that everything in the built environment affects people and, in turn, the world, whether it is good or not so good.

It was with this attitude in mind that the Los Angeles-based Jones shaped a variety of distinguished projects in a prolific career as an architect and educator that spanned 34 years, ending in 1979.

Indeed, Jones designed almost every type of structure: inexpensive to luxurious single-family houses, garden apartments and apartment towers, small branch libraries and large university research libraries, school buildings, office complexes and factories, churches, performing arts centers, an embassy, a funeral parlor, a tennis club and an entire college campus.

For nearly 20 years, he was associated with the USC schools of architecture and fine arts and for a time served as the dean of the two schools.

THE VAST BODY OF WORK GENERATED BY JONES BY HIMSELF AND WITH VARIOUS associates over the years garnered about 70 awards. These included a 1950 honor award from the American Institute of Architects for the design of a house, and, in partnership with Frederick Emmons, the institute's firm award in 1969; It remains the only Los Angeles firm to win the award.

Jones also designed a succession of houses for himself, the last being the 1965 conversion of a large, wood-clad photography studio at 10300 Little Santa Monica Blvd. near Century City into a stunning, singular home and office. Because the shape and materials resemble a New England barn, a mood Jones enhanced by planting clusters of trees on the street edging the site, the structure became known as the "barn."

Despite its urban setting, adjacent to a busy boulevard and in the shadow of some cold commercial office structures, the barn as maintained by the architect's widow, Elaine Sewell Jones, is a warm anomaly, a softly styled informal oasis in an increasingly frenetic setting.

The sense of space, the subtle natural and artificial lighting, the concern for detail, such as in the use of the re-sawed redwood and the wooden window grills, the selective furnishings and extensive plants are combined in the barn into a distinctly Modernistic Craftsman style. Whatever it might be called, the barn exudes a welcomed gentility.

Among the more prominent projects Jones and his associates designed in Southern California are the University research Library at UCLA, the Annenberg School of Communications at USC, the chemistry building and carillon tower at UC Riverside, the Brentwood and Palos Verde branch libraries, the Warner Bros. Record building in Burbank, and the master plan for Cal State Doninguez Hills.

Jones also was involved in two noteworthy efforts in Los Angeles' rich legacy of residential architecutre, the Crestwood Hills project in Kenter Canyon in Brentwood, and the case Study House program.

In Crestwood, he joined with architect Whitney Smith and engineer Edgardo Contini to design a number of attractive, modest, functional houses as part of a cooeprative housing effort. And while the cooperative faltered, the housing in time flourished, to set an example of sensitive land-use planning and design.

As for the Case Study House program, Jones was one of a number of architects selected to design individual houses to showcase how the latest construction materials and methods might be adapted to produce attractive, affordable structures.

Though his custom projects generally were in a Modernist mode popular in the 1950s and '60s, Jones was not a stylistic ideologist. "His designs grew out of the problems, and within the constraints of materials, space, the site and the budget," explained his widow, who is cataloguing the architect's writings and voluminous drawings.

"And always on his mind," she said, "was the need of the user, the people who would use the building, whether a place to live, or work, play or worship. That's what his architecture was all about."

—March 26, 1988

A Missionary Among Architects

HONORED LAST WEEKEND AT CAL POLY POMONA'S SCHOOL OF ENVIRONmental Design was architect Ralphael Soriano, who practiced in Los Angeles with distinction in the 1930s through the '50s.

Now 83 and living in Claremont, Soriano, is best remembered for his pioneering use of steel framing for housing and office buildings and his disciplined designs in the severe, smooth international Modernist style.

The style, distinguished by flat roofs and ribbon windows accenting a light, horizontal look, was introduced to Southern California in the 1920s by Austrian emigres R. M. Schindler and Richard Neutra, both of whom Soriano had worked for at various times.

Schindler and Neutra, along with other disciples of the style, in time pursued a more relaxed Modernism, using wood and raising roofs. But Soriano held true to his vision of a strict, reasoned marriage between architect and engineering, prompting architectural historian Esther McCoy to describe him as "a romantic technologist" who had become a "true missionary."

As a result of his approach, Soriano did not have a particularly active practice, and many of the projects he designed that did get built unfortunately were demolished or extensively remodeled.

Just recently bulldozed, despite the protests of the Los Angeles Conservancy and other preservationists, was the Colby apartment complex on Beverly Green Drive in the Palms District. This design by Soriano in 1950 had won a national American Institute of Architects honor award, one of several he garnered over the years.

Surviving as originally designed by Soriano and in excellent condition is a steel-and-glass house and studio, tucked high in the Hollywood Hills on a lushly and lovingly landscaped site at the end of a curving driveway at 7875 Woodrow Wilson Drive. It was designed by Soriano in 1949 for the eminent architectural photographer Julius Shulman, and last year was declared by the city a Historical-Cultural Monument, as well as being honored by the local chapter of the American Institute of Architects.

"Though Soriano was very rigid in the selection of the materials," Shulman recalled recently, "he also was very sensitive to the needs of the client and felt that the ultimate test of architecture was not in the construction but the use."

Shulman added that "after living here 40 years, there is not one change I would make." But he did say that his wife, Olga, had moved the furniture around to take better advantage of the views of the gardens through the extensive glass walls. He noted that she could do that because Soriano had designed the house as an open plan consistent with the Modernist style.

Soriano also experimented with all-aluminum houses, designing one at 11468 Dona Cecilia Drive, Studio City, for friend Albert Grossman, an architectural product representative, who still lives there. Though since expanded, the house at the time of construction in the 1960s was distinguished by being completely prefinished at the factory, including its 28 glass sliding doors.

One of Soriano's larger projects still standing and an excellent example of his design philosophy is the Adolph's office building, at 1800 Magnolia Blvd., Burbank. It was constructed in the 1950s using a modular system of steel columns and aluminum framing, which allowed considerable flexibility in locating offices and work spaces enclosing a pleasant courtyard and swimming pool. Hints of the ambitious structure are expressed in the facade and can be seen from the street, exuding the spirit of the 1950s and the concern then for form and function.

—May 14, 1988

ON A SAD NOTE, RAPHAEL SORIANO, ONE OF THE ARCHITECTS WHO PARticipated in the original Case Study House program, passed away a few weeks ago. He was 83 years old.

—July 31, 1988

IX

PERSONAL PREJUDICES

THE INCIDENT WAS NOT EXACTLY OF THE MAGNITUDE OF THE BERNHARD Goetz affair, but it does say something about the current state of urban civility and design, and the rights of pedestrians and responsibilities of automobile drivers.

It happened on a gray Saturday afternoon a few weeks ago in Santa Monica on a pleasant neighborhood commercial street along which my wife and I like to stroll, shop, eat ice cream and take in the sights.

While the walk for me is diverting, a nice break from my weekend gardening, for my wife it is an essential exercise now that she is in the last few weeks of her pregnancy.

The incident occurred at a gasoline station and mini-market similar in siting and design to the type I recently criticized in these columns for its lack of concern for streetscapes and its potential danger to pedestrians.

The column was prescient, for as we were walking past the station where three cars were lined up at the street-side pumps, the third car, a Porsche, lurched out of line, off the station's asphalt driveway and onto the concrete public sidewalk. Apparently the driver wanted to get ahead of the other cars to an empty forward pump, a common maneuver at self-serve stations.

Whatever the reason, we were forced to step with some trepidation into the street to give the car a wide berth as it edged along the sidewalk, only stepping back onto the sidewalk after it passed us. So much for pedestrians having the right-of-way, even on sidewalks.

However, after we had taken a few steps on the sidewalk, the Porsche began backing up. Startled, I stepped in front of my wife and tapped the left rear fender of the car to alert the driver and yelled "stop." The car stopped.

As we cautiously side-stepped left past the car, which was still hogging the sidewalk, I commented to the driver that "sidewalks are for pedestrians." The response was a sharp obscenity.

Perhaps out of naivete, I was expecting an apology, a simple "excuse me," or "I'm sorry," the type of courtesy one hopes for but unfortunately seldom gets on a city street these days.

Annoyed, I called the driver's attention to the condition of my wife, who was then eight months pregnant. Cursing us, the driver got out of the car to see if I had caused any damage by my tapping.

Provoked, I slapped the car, denting with my right palm the left rear fender. It was amazing to me how soft the fender felt as it folded in. And how nice.

My gesture prompted a scene, drawing some enthusiastic spectators and a call for the police. Within minutes, three police cars converged on the gas station, sirens blaring and lights flashing. The Santa Monica police obviously take pride in their response time.

Though I admitted slapping the fender and the police said the driver admitted driving on the sidewalk, no citations were issued. Patrolman Joseph Gardner, the officer in charge at the scene, said in effect that we were both in the wrong and urged us to go our separate ways.

Legal and emotional issues aside, the entire incident could have been avoided if the station had been designed to be more sensitive to the streetscape, limiting its curb cuts and putting up some sort of barrier between its service area and the sidewalk.

As it now exists, cars using the station have preempted the sidewalk, leaving the pedestrian out in the street and in the cold. In effect, the station has expanded to the curb at the public's expense. And as we learned, it is hard to argue with a car, even if you do have the right-of-way.

According to police and planners, the conflict between pedestrians and vehicles at curb cuts and cross walks, as well as at gasoline stations and mini-markets, has become an increasing source of incidents.

The problem has been noted by the Santa Monica Planning Department and Planning Commission, with the department studying specific zoning and building requirements for gasoline stations, now that the city's land use element has been approved.

City Manager John Jalili and Planning Director Paul Silvern say they would like to see some requirement for existing as well as proposed service stations and markets along busy shopping streets to better define their boundaries and take into consideration the safety of passing pedestrians. "It is an obvious problem," Jalili said.

MEANWHILE, THE CONTINUING WAR BETWEEN PEOPLE AND CARS IN THE LOS Angeles area continues, with pedestrians having to be very much on the defensive.

Aggravating this small war is what seems to be an increasing, corresponding lack of civility. Common courtesy or simply politeness apparently are seen these days as a mark of weakness when being tough, if not coarse, is in vogue. On the street and behind the wheel one is taught to be on guard, a posture that does not generate amiability.

Good fences may or may not make good neighbors, but by separating pedestrians and vehicles along sidewalks bordering gasoline stations and markets they could prevent people from becoming enemies.

—Feb. 17, 1985

A Public Park As A Private Preserve

THE GATHERING WAS TO BE A CELEBRATION OF CHARLIE STONE'S THIRD birthday and the nation's 209th, in short, a Fourth of July weekend family picnic.

But the gathering last Saturday also turned out to be a celebration of another sort—the right of the public to use a public park—and raised some disturbing questions about the management of the Hollywood Bowl by the Los Angeles Philharmonic Assn., and the responsibility of Los Angeles County for its park lands.

A week earlier, a decision had been made to hold the celebration picnic in a public park. With three infants, a smattering of toddlers, parents, grandparents, a great-grandmother and friends, totaling 18 persons, it was felt that no one's home should be subject to such a crowd.

Because it was near a grandmother's house, central to all and easy to find, a sylvan spot on the western slop of historic Whitley Heights was selected. And because of the recent heat wave, the picnic also was scheduled for 4 p.m., a little later than usual in the hope that it would be cooler.

The spot is in Milner Park, which had been the site of 23 houses when the land was condemned enarly 30 years ago for a movie industry museum. Ironically, among the homes eventually demolished were those of former movie stars, including one which a studio had built for Bette Davis, replete with a thatched roof and spider-web windows.

As various plans for a new museum were bandied about, the site on the east side of Highland Avenue was declared a park by the county. In time, the county turned most of the land into a large, raw parking lot for the nearby Hollywood Bowl, while the remaining hilly section adjacent to Whitley Heights was graded for picnic areas— a gesture to the neighborhood that was never happy with the condemnation.

However, when we arrived at 4 p.m., the parking lot adjacent to the picnic area in the southeast edge of the park, the farthest one from the Bowl and a steep mile away, it was blocked by security guards. They said the lost was needed for patrons of the concert scheduled for 8 that evening.

Shrugging our collective shoulders, we drove off to deposit our cars in the Heights, and innocently descended on the park on foot through another entrance, the food and drink in arm and the infants and toddlers in tow.

No sooner had we settled down at two of the 14 tables in the picnic area and begun giving out party hats to the children, than four guards arrived to inform us brusquely that the area was reserved for Bowl patrons and that we had to leave. There is nothing like the hint of authority backed by identification badges to bring out the worst in fledgling bureaucrats, even if only parking attendants for an evening.

Incredulous, we protested, making Milner hill our Bunker Hill, and asked that the guards or their superiors produce permits or leases to support the claim that the public area was for the private use of the Los Angeles Philharmonic Assn., its friends and patrons.

"This area has been reserved by the Bowl for eight years," snapped a guard who identified himself as Bill Carr, as if the lapse of time made it legal and qave him and the other guards the right to threaten to bodily remove us.

It appears not everybody has to sit besides the paths leading up to the Bowl or in their seats to enjoy a supper *alfresco* before a concert, in keeping with a Los Angeles tradition. (As I learned later, all you have to know is to phone the Hollywood Bowl at 850-2060 to reserve a table; at least that was the policy before this article was written.)

As for the permits we requested to see, none of the guards or their superiors could produce anything—one wouldn't even show his identification badge.

However, subsequent inquiries have disclosed that the county has leased the land at no cost to the association for its use on days concerts are scheduled. Presumably, this was for the parking, but in time has included the picnic areas, as well as by default, the operation of the park for the entire year. It seems that Milncr Park, in effect, has become the private domain of the Philharmonic Assn. Give an institution an inch and it will take a mile, especially when a compliant public agency strapped for park maintenance funds is involved.

The lease and subsequent withdrawal from the park's management by the county seems oddly magnanimous, considering that the land was acquired with public funds through a public process for a public purpose, in this case as a museum.

It was bad enough that the park was an afterthought to rationalize a particularly harsh condemnation, but worse than that, most of the park really is just a parking lot, with a little green strip left over only because it was too hilly to grade for more parking spaces to serve the Bowl. And now it seems even the strip is being gobbled up or, as a Whitley Heights resident commented, "bowled over."

As for the party, it went on as scheduled with a few Bowl employees looking on. Six other people did sit for a time at two of the 12 other tables, but left when friends told them they were having dinner elsewhere in the park. A few other persons also came and left.

When we finally policed the area and packed up to leave at about 7 o'clock, a total of nine persons in addition to our party had used the area, nowhere near the 50 for which the area had been reserved, according to the guards.

We also noticed as we left, that the sprawling parking lot nearest the picnic area was vacant, except for an ugly large blue steel container. The container is said by heights residents to store equipment used by the Police Department for motorcycle practice it holds most Sunday mornings in the parking lot, waking up nearby residents in the process. This the Bowl management allows.

The use of Milner Park is very much an urban-design issue. Public parks are vital to the well-being of any city and its residents; a place where people should be able to relax, play and be reminded that before the city, there was a wilderness, if only just open space in which to stretch out and feel free.

They should not be used as storage areas for vehicles or as private preserves. For the county to allow such uses under whatever arrangement it might have with the Philharmonic Assn. is an abdication of a public trust.

—July 14, 1985

Fighting Traffic Terrorism Abroad

THE ONLY TERRORIST I OBSERVED IN EUROPE DURING A TWO-MONTH SO-journ there were drivers; the only acts of terrorism—traffic.

And the traffic, brought on by increasing car ownership, threatens to hold hostage the architecture and ambiance of Europe's historic communities and city centers.

The sorry situation exists despite most cities having accessible and, generally, efficient mass transit systems, serving in particular city city areas. It seems the car culture there is as pervasive as it is here. Such is human nature, spurred on by multinational values.

Unlike here, however, many European communities have not surrendered to the car. After years of mimicking America's perverted planning practices and bulldozing, urban renewal efforts that threatened to lobotomize their cities, they are standing up to the terrorists.

TO BE SURE, THEY HAVE BUILT FREEWAYS, RING ROADS AND UGLY PARKING garages, as we have. But with increasing conviction, and in increasing numbers, they are balking at the continued shredding of established neighborhoods and historic districts in the name of progress to accommodate traffic.

Under different names and different programs, and to varying degrees in various countries, the planning and design emphasis these post-urban renewal days in Western Europe is on human-scale, people-oriented, pedestrian-encouraging development.

Instead of cutting down trees and widening streets, the usual bureaucratic knee-jerk solution in Los Angeles, European cities are planting flower beds and widening sidewalks, installing benches, approving sidewalk cafes, encouraging vendors and generally trying to expand pedestrian zones and creating humane environments.

At the same time, particular care is being paid to preserve historic sites and buildings from the ravages of the automobile and tourist buses. The practice appears not just to be a case of preservation being good for tourism, and therefore business, but of genuine pride.

IN SELECT NEIGHBORHOODS, STREETS AND ALLEYS ARE BEING MADE INTO landscaped cul de sacs, odd shaped lots into playgrounds and sitting areas, parking patterns are being changed to widen sidewalks, and everywhere landscaping is being encouraged. Making a difference is the concern for details, on a human scale, on a block-by-block basis.

Remarked a planner-politician in Barcelona, Spain: "We have had enough of grand plans, along with the thick reports and long speeches. It is time to go to work and look at each block, each district, and see what can be done simply to make life for residents there better."

As for the harsh realities of the increase in driving, planners have come to understand a basic traffic engineering principle that contends that traffic abhors a vacuum; that the easier you make driving through a particular area (as opposed to around it), the more cars it will attract.

Therefore, for example, even if an extra lane or two for cars could be created easily along, say, the *Champs Elysees* in Paris, traffic there would not necessarily be eased. And, of course, in the process, the magnificent scale and special ambiance of the grand boulevard would be irreparably harmed—just as sections of Wilshire Boulevard or San Vicente Boulevard would be if their center malls would be whittled away. (The latter from time to time has been proposed—in the name of progress, of course.)

THE CONCLUSION OF THE YEARS OF DEBATE IN EUROPEAN PLANNING AND political circles on how to resolve the war between cars and people in neighborhoods and city centers is that, given human nature and love of the automobile, a truce is impossible; that in areas of conflict, the pedestrian environment must have priority and vehicles the responsibilities.

The shift in policy favoring pedestrians has resulted in traffic jams on the edges of these districts approaching gridlock, with honking horns, fender benders, fights for parking spaces and chaos. For pedestrians, it is a wonderful comic opera; for drivers, frustration.

The reaction of officials, and residents, has been to generally shrug their shoulders, smile and, in effect, to say, "Too bad, if you don't like it, don't drive, or change your driving habits. But we are not going to knock down any more buildings, cut down any more trees, narrow any more sidewalks so you can drive a few miles faster."

Western European cities appear to be taking a tougher line in their fight against traffic terrorism, while not incidentally, better preserving what they have and creating much more inviting and livable communities. It is a dramatic and welcomed shift from what I had observed five years ago, when freeways, large urban renewal efforts in cities and antiseptically designed new communities in the suburbs—ideas that had been in vogue in the 1960s—were still being pursued.

VERY SHORTLY, A SIMILAR DECISION IS GOING TO HAVE TO BE MADE IN THE LOS Angeles Area; whether we will continue to be held hostage and have the various critical decisions shaping the region dictated by traffic terrorists, or whether we can break free to begin to protect and improve our work and residential communities.

The decision cannot be put off simply because of the hope of Metro Rail. Even if a feasible system moves forward, it has been long obvious that Metro Rail or an expanded light rail will not solve the region's growing traffic problems. At best, if redesigned to serve the region's demographics, instead of its politics, they will offer a transportation alternative to a limited population.

Prompting the decision, as well is the obvious—the inability of city, county and state bureaucrats to make the existing transportation system of buses and network of roadways function to their capacity, and the reasonable reluctance of local communities to yield more land and ambiance to accommodate alien traffic.

July 20, 1986

View of Santa Monica and Beyond

To CATCH UP WITH WHAT HAS HAPPENED IN ARCHITECTURE AND DESIGN IN the Los Angeles area while away for two months, I began by taking a walk in my Santa Monica neighborhood.

With sadness, I noticed one of my favorite buildings, a Spanish Colonial Revival delight of an automobile showroom at the southwest corner of 17th Street and Wilshire Boulevard, had been demolished. A fire in May apparently had damaged the structure beyond repair.

The red-tiled, two-story structure, featuring an interior decorated as a Moorish castle replete with ornate chandeliers, was designed by Edwell James Baume in 1928, when the city's design community was in the throes of an exotic revivalism flavored by the movies.

Simonson Mercedes Benz Co., which owns the prime site and building, has said it will try to reconstruct the showroom in the same engaging style. I tend not to like new old buildings, for in their modern construction they usually lose both authenticity and charm, and end up as some sort of ersatz confectionary, like a Beethoven piano sonata being played by Liberace.

In this case, I hope I am wrong, and that with a respect for quality that has distinguished the Simonson dealership for decades, somehow the charm of a lost and lamented style can be captured in the new showroom. Wilshire Boulevard, from Westwood to the ocean, certainly needs all the help it can get.

With the march of out-of-scale high-rises competing for attention, the lack of sign control and, generally, the crass commercialism of developers and retailers, and the insensitivity to design of Santa Monica and Los Angeles officials, the boulevard is turning into yet another L.A. *schlock* strip.

ELSEWHERE IN SANTA MONICA, A SUBDUED HISTORICISM MARKS THE SOUTH-east corner of 15th Street and Montana Boulevard.

There, housing the popular Montana Mercantile cookingware company is a recent high-tech rendition of the Streamline Moderne style. It was designed by Kanner Associates with round corners, glass brick, white steel railings and a horizontal emphasis, details that had distinguished the popular style of the late 1930s.

Though I found the effect a bit too institutional, and the signs—particularly the lettering of "Hemisphere,"—incompatible with the style, the building is well scaled and welcome.

A nice touch also are the benches set in the 15th Street facade.

However, they would have been better placed on Montana to view the passing parade there of shoppers. The street, which has been labeled "Croissant Canyon," is becoming quite gentrified; its increase in trendy shops and attractive eateries, and decrease in neighborhood services being spurred on by the spending of yuppies receiving what, in effect, are substantial monthly cash subsidies under the city's perverted rent control system.

As for the rental housing stock, a walk up and down the nearby alleys indicated that it continues to deteriorate. Apartment complexes are in need of paint, window sashes are rotted and stucco above the rear parking bays was falling on the shiny new cars of tenants.

It is depressingly apparent to someone like myself, a former renter, now a landlord, that the system as it has evolved in Santa Monica is not working, at least not for housing and those who need it.

However, it seems to be doing fine, perpetuating a fat bureaucracy, and as a political tool with which to bribe renters who vote.

The alleys that apartments back up to were not in a much better condition, with broken pavement, garbage strewn about by the collectors and, during rush hours, cars racing up and down, taking short cuts to avoid the traffic and lights on Montana and Wilshire. And this in a reasonably sized community with a local government that talks a lot about quality of life.

North of Montana, expensive private houses continue to expand and rise, like giant souffles too big for their dishes and the oven. The eclectic Tudoresque style, with a garish gazpacho of materials popular a few years ago among builder/developers, seems to have been replaced by an encrusted, nouveau-French chateauesque style. Simi Valley has come to Santa Monica.

But for real ugly, there is a new strip of stores at the northwest corner of Euclid Street and Montana that is attributed to Pacific Southwest Development Inc., at least according to the approved architectural drawings.

With its prison-like gray grill against a cheap stucco facade rising to a false, peaked third story, a fake front column offset on its base, and a particularly bad color selection, the concoction gives Postmodernism a bad name.

And, as if Postmodernism, with its tricky, often obtuse use of architectural allegories, did not have enough of a problem with the public at present without would-be designers embracing it as a gimmick.

—Aug. 10, 1986

A correction concerning that failed piece of facadism at the corner of Euclid Street and Montana Avenue in Santa Monica.

Pacific Southwest Development Co. informs me it was the general contractor of the building, not its designer, as I had noted in a column earlier this month. The architect was Kurt Beckmeyer and the designer was Lynn Paxton.

If only the design of the building could be corrected as easily.

—Aug. 21, 1986

Viewing Downtown in Wheelchair

AS IF THERE WAS NOTHING MORE HEINOUS DEMANDING ATTENTION ON Skid Row, a policeman there recently issued a jaywalking ticket to Chris Morland.

But Morland was not jaywalking in mid-Main Street between 5th and 6th streets, as cited. What Morland was doing there was operating an electric wheelchair to which he has been confined for the last 12 years.

It was not that Morland, a talented photographer who works for the city's Community Redevelopment Agency, did not want to ford Main Street at the corner in the designated pedestrian crosswalk. He could not. There were no access ramps there to allow him to negotiate the high curbs.

The only way for him to cross the street without asking a passer-by to help him maneuver the wheelchair off the curb was to drive to the mid-block where the sidewalk dips into an alleyway on the same level with the street, and then to cross the street to the opposite alleyway and up to the sidewalk.

MORLAND SAID HE DOES NOT LIKE TO ASK ANYONE TO HELP HIM OFF CURBS AT corners, especially in generally hostile Skid Row. "Once a man there offered to help me, and when he got my chair down in the street, he robbed my camera," the photographer explained.

Morland also said he does not like to get to the other side of streets by traveling along in the traffic lanes from crosswalk to crosswalk, as many persons in electric wheelchairs do. "I've been sideswiped and hurt doing that," he said. "No, I prefer sidewalks."

The problem is getting onto and off the sidewalks. According to Morland, other similarly handicapped persons and various associations of disabled persons, there is a serious lack of access ramps in downtown Los Angeles, as well as elsewhere across the city.

"But it is particularly bad downtown, where a lot of disabled persons work and an increasing number live," said Morland, who lives in an apartment on Spring Street.

THIS IS THE POINT MORLAND WAS GOING TO MAKE IN TRAFFIC COURT REcently in contesting the $10 jaywalking ticket. But when he appeared on a not guilty plea, the judge did not take any testimony.

Instead, he simply dismissed the ticket with the comment that Morland in a motorized wheelchair was operating a vehicle and obviously had been improperly charged.

Morland said later that it was apparent that the judge did not want to confront the problem; that because of the lack of access ramps, disabled persons who want to use and enjoy the city's sidewalks, often must break the law by riding in streets to seek out alternative curb cuts.

"The judge was acting just like the city does when disabled people try to tell them that the lack of access ramps, among many other things, is denying us our rights and freedom: They don't want to solve the problem, they just want to avoid it," Morland added.

ALSO AT THE COURTHOUSE TO TESTIFY ON BEHALF OF MORLAND AND THE rights of the disabled were Lou and Yvonne Nau, both of whom are confined to wheelchairs, have been fierce local proponents of the rights of the disabled.

"California has some very good laws," said Yvonne Nau, who is past president of the Mayor's Advisory Committee on the Disabled. "The problem has been enforcement. There has been a lot of lip service about the needs and rights of the disabled, but everyone, from the governor and mayor on down, seem to want to get away with doing as little as possible for the least amount of money."

"Particularly bad have been builders and architects," added Lou Nau. He said that complying with the accessibility codes usually is an afterthought in the building and design process.

As a result, Yvonne Nau commented that access for the handicapped in many public places, such as a restaurant, is through the rear. "It is amazing that they just have not simply put up a sign that states, delivery, garbage and the handicapped to the rear."

"ON THE WAY TO DINNERS, WE'VE PASSED THROUGH AND SEEN MORE RESTAUrant kitchens than kitchen inspectors," added Lou Nau.

According to the Naus and Morland, among other problems handicapped persons must contend with are the attitudes of RTD bus drivers.

They charged that many drivers, even those of buses with wheelchair lift ramps, pass by handicapped persons waiting at stops. Yvonne Nau said drivers just do not want to be bothered and take the time to operate the lifts.

Private transportation, in general, also is a problem for the handicapped. Specially equipped automobiles are expensive, as is insurance, which for some handicapped persons is quite difficult to obtain.

AND YVONNE NAU ADDED THAT FOR THOSE WITH CARS, A CONSTANT ANnoyance is the failure of the city to enforce parking spaces for the disabled. She explained the Police Department had turned the responsibility for enforcement over to the city's Transportation Department, which, at best, responds to complaints only during weekday work hours. "No one seems to want to be bothered," she said.

When Morland and others agitate for a more accessible environment, they contend they are treated like pariahs. "Like the judge, you could tell that he just wanted me and my problem to go away."

But the problem of providing an accessible environment for the handicapped to lead full and productive lives will not go away. Indeed, the problem is expected to increase, along with the projected dramatic increase over the next few decades of the nation's elderly population.

And as persons live longer the probability of becoming hand-icapped, temporarily or permanently, sharply increases. Already an estimated 32 million to 35 million Americans—about one out of eight persons—suffer some form of sensory or mobility impairment.

Yet, as anyone who has been temporarily or permanently disabled can testify, our buildings and streets are a maze of hurdles. As the advocates of a barrier-free environment declare, despite the enlightened laws calling for accessibility, there is still much to overcome.

AT PRESENT, WE DESIGN AND MANAGE OUR CITIES AND OUR BUILDINGS AS IF everyone is a robust 25-year-old in perfect health, and will remain that way the rest of his or her life. Little thought seems to be given to the problems of the handicapped or elderly, as well as to children, and persons not in the best of condition.

"Society wants us not to be a burden, to work and lead full lives, and so do we," Morland said. "But if you can't drive, or a bus won't stop for you, or you can't get up on a sidewalk, or easily enter a building, it's tough."

May most of us never know how tough.

—March 1, 1987

A Design That's Worth the Wait

I HATE WAITING, BE IT FOR DENTISTS, DOCTORS, MOVIES, RESTAURANT TABLES, meetings, births, arriving planes and departing planes; indeed, almost anything.

Some people, while waiting, apparently can read, knit, do their nails, doze, meditate or simply vegetate with seems a contented purpose. I can't

For me, waiting is a non-activity, a void of time that I tend to fill with random thoughts and emotions, depending on what I am waiting for—a late plane with a loved one aboard, or, say, root canal surgery. One productive process I often engage in, however, is to examine the design and style of the surroundings; the mood, view and scale of the space; the flow of people through it; the function of the furnishings and fixtures, and the color schemes and lighting.

Much of what I see is bad or banal. There are medical waiting rooms that try to be modern and relaxed but look like motel lobbies; corporate reception areas draped in leather, chrome and wall hangings that take on the shallow aesthetic of furniture showrooms, and government offices that are as friendly and fragrant as a meat packing plant, but usually not as functional.

These thoughts came to mind recently while I waited to meet relatives arriving at LAX at various times at three different terminals. Thanks to an efficient roadway system and luck finding parking spaces, I was early each time. The planes were late, giving me a lot of time to experience the terminals.

Two of the terminals were anonymous, noisy expanses, with regimented seating and limited views, a place at best for processing people. As such, they were typical, unfriendly airline waiting areas. The third was the recently completed first stage of a remodeled and expanded Delta Air Lines terminal, and it was a delight.

Here at last is a terminal at LAX that through its designs announces to all that they are in Los Angeles. Palm and citrus trees, exotic plantings, Art Deco detailing, subtle "hot" and "cool" lighting, and varying terraces and seating areas were evocative, welcoming and comfortable.

What the design firm of Gensler & Associates Architects has created under the roof of a terminal is the beginning of a palm-shaded Southern California pedestrian streetscape, lined with clusters of shops and restaurants, sidewalk cafes, parks, and an array of seating and planting areas.

"We want to make people feel they are out of doors, walking along a street, or sitting in a par," project designer Andy Cohen explained. He said the lighting was designed to create the feeling of being under a sky and the various seating areas shaped and sited to allow people to view the passing parade of passengers, or look at the planes, or find a quite spot to read or think.

THE CLUSTERS OF PASSIVE AND ACTIVE AREAS WERE QUITE CALCULATED. "We wanted to create a sequence of events lining the street to lead passengers along, and shorten the experience of going from ticketing to the plane," project manager Ron Steinert said. "And we didn't want people waiting for a plane to feel they were in a room and confined."

According to Edward Friedrichs of Gensler, the design grew out of a concern of the architects and the client, originally Western Airlines before it was absorbed into Delta, that the waiting experience not be a static one.

"They recognized that LAX was a hub terminal where a lot of passengers would be waiting for planes, and that a waiting passenger tends to be a disgruntled passenger." Friedrichs said. "Waiting is a big complaint, so a decision was made to concentrate on how waiting can be made more pleasant."

I still hate waiting, and try to avoid it however I can. But in what Gensler and Delta have so far created at LAX there is the promise; of at least a tolerable purgatory for those waiting, and an affable architectural welcome for those arriving.

—Jan. 23, 1988

Rumbles on the Livable City Turf

GROWING LIKE A FRAIL PLANT OUT OF THE VARIED SLOW-GROWTH, PRESERvation and community movements in Los Angeles and other metropolitan areas across the country is the concept of the livable city.

The concept generally envisions a city of distinct neighborhoods with a sense of pride, place and history, bolstered by safe streets, good housing, shopping and schools, friendly playgrounds, revered landmarks and a host of cultural attractions.

In sum, it is a city that encourages walking, bicycling, saying hello to neighbors, smiling at passers-by, planting flowers in the front yard or in a window box, strolling along shopping streets, picnicking in parks, or not hesitating to go downtown.

There are fragments of this in most cities, even in auto-oriented Los Angeles; enough so to nurture the hope of more.

At the core of this hope is the thought that cities should be designed to serve and enrich the people who live there, not to fulfill some market-driven or textbook vision packaged by an architectural and planning elite doing the bidding of real estate interests.

The radical thought that cities should be first and foremost about people who live and work there, and not those who design, build and profit from them, has made "livability" a rallying cry here and elsewhere of residents and neighborhood groups doing battle against intrusive, destructive and insensitive development. It is a concept that to succeed must be of a neighborhood scale and sensitivity.

But in gaining increasing attention and acceptance, it was inevitable that those in the development community and their architectural and academic sycophants who ignored, disdained or distorted the neighborhood-based concept for decades, should now try to co-opt it.

An example is a conference scheduled this week in Pittsburgh, Pa., entitled "remaking cities." Sponsored by the American Institute of Architects and the Royal Institute of British Architects, it promises to be another self-serving and congratulating exercise that has come to mark such efforts.

THE PROBLEM IS NOT THE SUBJECT MATTER. ACCORDING TO A PACKAGE OF slickly designed materials I received to get me to write a glowing story to prompt "high-quality representatives from your readership" to attend, the conference will focus on how cities can become more livable to compete better for new businesses and people in the emerging post-industrial age.

Much of it sounded like one of my columns, right down to the statement that to achieve the "local pride and a sense of identity and uniqueness" that marks livability "new coalitions of public-private investment, especially in the neighborhoods, are top priority. Citizens must be enfranchised to determine policies that affect their local communities."

And making the conference even more appealing is that scheduled to speak there is Britain's Prince Charles, who, as I fondly wrote about recently, has become an outspoken advocate of more user-sympathetic and historically sensitive designs; in short, pro-livability.

It was Prince Charles a few months ago, who declared in a speech in London that for 40 years the planning, architectural and development establishment has been doing it their own while "we, poor mortals, are forced to live in the shadow of their achievement."

Everywhere he went the prince said, "it was one of the things people complain about most," adding that "if there is one message I would like to deliver. . . in no uncertain terms it is that large numbers of us in this country are fed up with being talked down to and dictated to by the existing planning, architectural and development establishments."

All this is quite enticing, except when you begin to note who, in addition to the prince, are the speakers, and read a background paper on the structure and anticipated results of the conference. It seems that our well-meaning, community-sensitive British friends have been had, and the rhetoric of livability appropriated by the American version of the establishment that the prince takes such strong exception to.

WITH A FEW EXCEPTIONS, THE CONFERENCE'S SPEAKER LIST IS DOMINATED BY those who, at best, in the past have ignored the gut neighborhood issues on which livability is based, to act as apologists for antiseptic designs that have segregated our cities.

At worse, a few have been the hatchet men who chopped up neighborhoods they will now discuss how to save. And nearly all are cut from the patronizing, paternalistic weave of the corporate, bureaucratic and academic cloth, colored by a pandering journalist or two.

According to the background paper, the primary goal of the conference is to produce a set of policy recommendations to be, among other things, presented to legislators, developed into a national educational television series, debated "in a Fred Friendly forum on public television," discussed in a book on the future of the cities, and, lastly, "packaged for presentation to local leaders and grass-roots participants in the community process as well as for use in colleges and universities."

Give us a break. Indeed, give a break also to all those activists who are not paid to attend the interminable hearings and meetings involved in the shaping of their neighborhoods, and then have to endure the putdowns by self-proclaimed professionals whose egos won't quit.

As if the conference organizers had not learned from the past fiascoes of urban renewal and similar ventures with which they were associated, such efforts as livability begins, and ends, at the neighborhood level. The days of master mega planning, mammoth multicolored reports, and intricate model making are as dead as the credibility of the big-bang conference.

To be sure, there will be some sound and fluff in Pittsburgh this week, but in all probability, the effort will produce nothing more than a pleasant few days for select civil serpents and others, a little play in the media, another line or two on the *vitae* of fawning academics, and an exchange of business cards.

Perhaps it would be too much to hope to expect that some of the conference funds be diverted to a grass-roots effort to improve the livability of one of Pittsburgh's struggling neighborhoods; that in addition to the hot air, something of substance and value comes out of the gathering. To that end, I offer my proxy to Prince Charles.

—Feb. 28, 1988

224

Aid for Creative, Not Con, Artists

EVERYBODY LOVES THE CREATIVE ARTS. THEY ENRICH OUR LIVES FIGUR-atively, while also enriching our cities literally by generating spending and jobs, and invigorating neighborhoods.

Happily, within the last decade there has been an awakening in Los Angeles to this potential, as evidenced by the construction and expansion here of major cultural institutions, the announced plans for more, arising design consciousness and the increased arts offerings in scattered galleries, schools, theaters and makeshift facilities across the city.

But much, much more needs to be done, especially if Los Angeles is to match its burgeoning economic power and become a center of culture and distinction, let alone emerge as a more engaging and livable city. So states a recently released report on the arts here, drafted by a blue-ribbon citizens' task force.

The report declares that "while the city is unique both in physical form and ethnic composition," what cultural boom there has been "has not really touched much of its population" because of a lack of adequate support for artists and outreach programs, among other things.

According to the report,"the arts in Los Angeles are woefully under-funded and poorly promoted by any regional or national standards." It notes that the city's per capita spending is less than one-fifth that of New York City, "although Los Angeles rivals New York as the country's most important cultural center."

With this in mind, the report recommends that Los Angeles enact a so-called Percent for Arts program under which a fee of 1% be levied on major private construction projects and on all city capital improvement projects. In addition, it calls for a hotel bed tax and increased city allocations. The report concludes that these steps could produce about $25 million annually, providing a healthy source of funds for the arts.

Such programs have been successfully initiated by a host of other cities. As task force chairman Robert Maguire declared in a letter to the development community, the Percent for Arts concept is "an effective, long-term strategy for supporting the arts without placing a disproportionate burden on any one part of our economy." The letter was sent to generate support for the concept, which will be a subject of City Hall hearings over the next few months.

There should be little debate over the Percent for Arts concept, and certainly little over the need for the funds it would produce. Many legitimate cultural groups not blessed with well-heeled and connected board members are struggling to survive, while other well-intentioned efforts are stillborn. There is, across Los Angeles, a fertile creative art scene waiting to be seeded.

HOWEVER, WHAT SHOULD BE QUESTIONED AND DEBATED IS THE TASK FORCE recommendations on how the seeding should proceed.

Disturbing is that the prime recommendation of the report is the creation of a private, nonprofit arts organization, to be called the Los Angeles endowment for the Arts, to develop a cultural master plan for the city and to administer the funding.

We understand too well that such an organization was in part conceived to circumvent some of the management problems that the City's Department of Cultural Affairs has suffered in the past and to avoid the political pressures that most likely will arise in the City Council over the allocation of the percent funds in the future.

The council does have a history of making messes of departmental honey pots, with few members displaying any sensitivity for cultural efforts. To them, an arts event is inviting a glad-handing movie star or two to a fund-raising dinner. No doubt, if the Department of Cultural Affairs was given the task of administering the funds, the council would get sticky fingers.

But not altogether successful and without incidents of skimming and scams have been the efforts of some "nonprofit" and "public-private partnership" experiments, including a few that have involved persons who played a role in drafting the task force recommendations.

The first and highest order of business of some who work for endowments or similar "nonprofit" entities tends to be to endow themselves, followed by controlling the use of the funds to fulfill an elitist view of the arts and build up a favor bank to feather possible nests in the future.

Though they may coat their actions with impressive rhetoric and disingenuous smiles, the actual aiding of needy artists, frail arts institutions and worthy cultural experiments more often than not is incidental. But if it happens, you can be sure the nonprofiteering elite will take credit, just as sure as they will be filling their glasses and plates at the wine-and-cheese buffet celebrating the event.

THE REPORT'S RECOMMENDED PRIME ASSIGNMENT OF THE ENDOWMENT TO draft a "long-term" cultural master plan also deserves to be questioned. The development of such plans tends to turn out to be costly, self-perpetuating labors, full of sound and fluff, signifying little and effecting less. It is the sort of undertaking that former cultural affairs General Manager Fred Croton would have loved.

What the city also does not need is another boondoggle, such as the Pershing Square revitalization effort where, under the guise of a public-private partnership, hundreds of thousands of dollars of public funds have been spent on salaries, consultant fees, cross-country trips, receptions, dinenrs and a trumped-up competition, leaving the cupboard, and park, bare.

it would be a tragedy beyond repair to the Los Angeles cultural community if the Percent for Art program was turned into a relief act for art and architecture dilettantes and their favorites and family.

Somehow, the program must be shaped and safe-guarded to serve creative artists, not con artists.

—Aug. 14, 1988

A modified program was eventually approved.

Public Art Can Make a Difference

THE COOKIE-CUTTER SHAPING AND SIMILAR MODERNIST AND POST-Modernist styling of most of the recent mini-mall, shopping center and office projects here and across the country have created, I feel, a deadening architectural banality.

In their predictable and cliche designs, the developments could be anywhere, and nowhere. Whether located along a suburban shopping strip or downtown, they seem to float on islands, usually in a sea of parking spaces, bearing no relationship in massing, scale or style to their neighbors, neighborhood or city, nor to the architectural traditions of the region.

The resulting scene "is a specter of 'placelessness," ' declared Ronald Lee Fleming and Renata von Tscharner in "Place Makers," published in 1981. The authors observe that most malls and plazas have become dead spaces, void of any meaning or connection to our roots and asipirations, and telling no tales, aggravate the present condition of angst and anomie that afflict our age.

With this in mind thcy make an impassioned plea for "place makers" and "place making," objects, be they sculptures, murals, landscaping, furnishing, fountains or fragments, that "help define, revel, enrich, reinforce, expand or otherwise make accessible place meaning."

In short, public art that tells you where you are, to paraphrase the book's subtitle.

Once only thought of as sculptures or statues commemorating great events or people, public art over the last decade has become much more imaginative and controversial.

In almost every major city there is now some sort of government-aided or encouraged effort to encourage public art, including Los Angeles, where the city's Community Redevelopment Agency has made it a requirement of its program.

Our public spaces need such art desperately, given the continued misshaping of our communities by developers and architects more interested in generating maximum exposure and maximum returns than creating buildings that might better serve the user, and the city.

HOWEVER, SOME OF THE PUBLIC ART HERE AND ELSEWHERE THAT HAS BEEN produced under various well-intentioned programs seems like afterthoughts, dropped on plazas just as arbitrarily as the buildings they front were dropped on the city.

Just as there are bad buildings, there is also bad art, self-indulgent or inappropriate exercise that instead of telling where you are, as Fleming and Von Tscharner suggest, tell you where you can go, or something to that effect.

The George Herms concoction, "Moon Dial," at the northwest corner of Santa Monica and Beverly boulevards in Beverly Hills. In most neighborhoods, the collection of rusted buoys would have been towed away by now for scrap.

227

Seeking to avoid such an embarrassment, and ever sensitive to the less-than-enlightened local interest groups, the Santa Monica Arts Commission (SMarts) is at present welcoming comments on five works of public art proposed for the Third Street Mall. After years of political posturing and back-room bartering, the city last month broke ground for a $10.5-million renovation of the mall and nearby parking structures.

The proposals are on view in the storefront window of 1345 3rd St. through Sept. 6, when a three-member jury will weigh the public comments and their own prejudices and make a decision. At stake is a healthy $450,000 for artist fees, construction, fabrication, transportation and installation, which will make the project one of nation's more exorbitant public art efforts to date.

Whatever the price, the mall certainly needs something to lend it an identity, if not some verve, for the plan by the San Francisco-based ROMA Design Group approved by the city is a mixed bag of weak architectural cliches. The proposed Disneyland-like lighting, signage, fountains, street furniture and clock tower entryways pay little respect to the city's unique bay-side setting and architectural history.

The feeling here is that the mall will succeed, not because of the design, but despite it. this is due in large part to an increasing general interest in the economic potential of downtown Santa Monica; an interest prompted by a latent recognition of its desirable location near the ocean, freeways and affluent residential neighborhoods, and the increased inaccessibility of other urban areas, such as Westwood and West Hollywood.

Looking at the future of downtown Santa Monica, its success most likely will not be dependent on opening the mall to traffic and more parking garages. More critical, I feel, will be the development of a range of housing within walking distance of the area. Only then will the mall fulfill the image of a promenade the city and vested real estate interests are anxiously promoting.

As for the five public art proposals that were winnowed down from 50 submissions, they include a conceptual scheme by Vito Acconici that looks like the mall after the earthquake; three overblown and overworked integrated steel forms by Guy Dill; a playful collection of giant topiary in the form of dinosaurs focused on a fountain by Claude and Francois LaLanne; a series of sculptures of acrobats performing stunts a la Muscle Beach by George Segal, and a large reverse flow fountain that can also serve as an amphitheater by Athena Tacha.

I found the Acconci scheme too heavy-handed; Dill's too static, and Segal's too cute, with Acconci and Segal's also begging for new ideas, and Dill's for attention. None of them displayed anything unique to the site, or new.

This, for me, left the LaLanne and Tacha schemes. I like both for the inviting water elements, but the LaLanne's more for the additional dimension of the fanciful dinosaur sculptures. Santa Monica being different, deserves something different.

So into the mail slot at 1345 3rd St., goes my vote for the proposal by the LaLannes, and for public art.

—Aug. 21, 1988

After the column appeared, there was a marked increase in the voting, with the result that the LaLanne proposal won.

Modest Proposal For a Better L.A.

HAPPILY, THE DODGERS WON THE WORLD SERIES IN FIVE GAMES. AS AN avid fan who has followed the team since learning to read by studying the sports pages of the Brooklyn Eagle in 1940, I do not know if I could have handled any more of the tension the games generated. They were exhilarating, and exhausting.

And even though I had tickets to the seventh game at Dodger Stadium, I am glad they closed down the A's in alien Oakland. You never know how fans will react after such an event, and Elysian Park, where the stadium is located, has suffered enough. Remember last year, when fireworks that the Dodger organization set off nearly burned down the park?

While the Dodgers, bless them, have done well since moving to Chavez Ravine in 1962, the park has not. Touring it reveals groves of dead trees, eroded hillsides, damaged picnic grounds, overflowing trash cans, broken fountains, generally poor maintenance and inappropriate uses, such as the city using some nooks and crannies there as dumping grounds.

And this, the last remaining public portion of the public land grant establishing the city in 1781; the city's first and oldest park, officially "forever dedicated" as such in 1886; the site of the first botanical gardens in Southern California; and a vital open space, particularly for the adjacent communities of Chinatown and Echo Park.

One would hope that in some way Elysian Park, which as the Dodgers' neighbor, accommodated the construction of the stadium and bears the brunt of traffic to and from the games, could benefit from the success of the Dodger organization.

Actually, as part of the original agreement that gave the Dodgers Chavez Ravine and allowed roads to be cut through the park, the organization was to set aside 40 acres for a recreational area in Elysian Park on which they would spend $500,000 for development.

In addition, according to a 1962 article written by former Mayor Norris Poulson who helped shape the agreement, the Dodgers were to spend $60,000 a year to help maintain the park. But the funds instead went into the city's general fund, ending, for reasons unknown, after 18 years.

Meanwhile, the irrigation lines that had been serving the park and were destroyed when the stadium went in, never were repaired. The result is the dead trees you can see from the even-numbered sections of the reserved and upper-deck sets in Dodger Stadium.

In addition, when new roads were cut and others widened over the years toe ase the crush of cars in and out of the Dodgers' raw parking lot, there was no compensation to the park, in either land or maintenance funds. and this, as the Dodgers became one of the more successful and profitable sports enterprises in history.

Certainly, if the Dodgers can afford millions of dollars in deferred payments to players no longer with the team, and at the urging of such fans as myself, dangle millions more for free agents, they could afford to aid ailing Elysian Park.

With this in mind, I proposed that the stadium parking fee be raised from $2 to $3, withh the additional dollar being channeled to underwrite specific projects in Elysian Park. Considering that parking at some other stadiums is considerably higher—it's $7 at Shea Stadium in Flushing Meadow, N.Y., $5, if you are lucky, at the Coliseum—I feel the amount is modest, as is the proposal.

The increase would generate an estimate $1.5 million a year, an amount equal to Kirk Gibson's salary, that could be used for the hiring of more park ranger, more park maintenance personnel (if only to pick up the beer cans and other garbage thrown from the cars departing the stadium after a game), repairing the irrigation system that the construction of the stadium damaged, or planting new bushes and trees.

With the funds a foundation on which to build a new pride in the park, perhaps it is time for the city's Department of Recreation and Parks, in cooperation with the ever-vigilant Citizens Committee to Save Elysian Park, to undertake a needed master plan for the entire area. Also included in the process should be the Department of Water and Power, whose Elysian Reservoir is surrounded by the park, and the Police Department, whose academy also is in the park. The park has suffered enough from patchwork planning.

As Tommy Lasorda will never let us forget, it was teamwork that powered the Dodgers to their unlikely ultimate triumph in 1988. Perhaps it also might work for Elysian Park, with a little help from the Dodger organization.

—Oct. 30, 1988

Welcome to a Sadder City

DEAR FORMER PRESIDENT REAGAN: WELCOME BACK TO LOS ANGELES, TO be sure from a design and development point of view, a very different Los Angeles than the one in which you and Nancy once lived.

In your waning days as president, one of your more popular lines was to ask people whether they were better off now than they were 8 years ago. No doubt a select portion of L.A.'s population is, judging from the over subscription of the pricey-per-plate testimonials honoring you; the sizes and costs of the custom designed houses rising here like souffles; and array of gilded autos being turned over to the parking attendants at the doors of overpriced eateries.

But as a returning resident, I think you should know about another Los Angeles existing beyond the privately guarded residential islands, such as Bel Air where you will be living, the scattered upscale retail enclaves and restaurants-of-the moment, and the glittering new museums, art galleries and performance centers.

From my perspective, this other Los Angeles which many of us see and experience is a much less livable city today than it was 8 years ago, due, frankly, in part to your tenure as President.

Take, for example, housing. In 1980, in Los Angeles, the need for affordable units was estimated at 50,000. In 1988, the estimate was 250,000, following repeated deep cuts in federal aid for low and moderate income housing, consistent with your policy of disinvestment in urban America. To feed a bloated defense budget, you starved domestic programs.

The private sector did not come to the rescue as you promised. Generally ignoring affordable housing, it instead indulged in questionable land deals and built speculative projects, such as mini malls, consuming tens of billions of dollars strewn about by a deregulated thrift industry. (And now we have to bail them out at no little damage to the federal budget.)

To be sure, not speculative was the purchase by an unidentified consortium of a multi-million dollar house in Bel Air, and its lease to you and Nancy, with an option to buy. I presume some sort of preferred subsidy is involved, probably of the form that was to aid low income families to buy their project apartments under one of the housing assistance programs scuttled by you.

The private sector did for a while undertake an encouraging wealth of historic rehabilitation projects that benefited the city. However, that trailed off considerably after you signed the Tax Reform Act of 1986, which eliminated many of the incentives for such efforts, as well as for housing development.

Meanwhile, there has been in Los Angeles a depressing increase in the number of people living in unsafe and unsanitary garages, raw sheds, and recreational vehicles. And what decent housing is available is costing more and more; one study estimated that 150,000 families here spend at least 50% of their income on rent.

Then there are those who cannot even find shelter, however makeshift, and are homeless. The latest estimate put their number in Los Angeles at 50,000, including at least 10,000 children. They are scattered in street scenes as depressing as any Third World City slum. And just saying "no" to the problem won't make it go away.

You probably will never visit these areas, if only because contending with our increasingly congested roadways to get there would be too difficult. At times, it also will be hard for you to get to your office in Century City, or your ranch above Santa Barbara. As an ex-president, you no longer can take a helicopter wherever you want to go, or have the roads in front of you cleared by a police escort.

This seems fair, for it was your administration that emasculated a variety of transit programs that could have helped relieve the mess. For the record, we note that your last budget called for a whopping $100 million cut in funds for our frail Metro Rail project. Instead, billions were squandered on plans for a railroad line in the desert to carry MX missiles nowhere. At least if located in L.A., it also could have carried people.

Not helping our freeways, and lungs, either was your easing of auto emissions standards, which, in effect, has encouraged the production of gas guzzlers, and our increased dependence on foreign oil.

And then there were your vetoes of the clean water acts, your smudging of the Clean Air Act, the super fund, the national forests, off-shore oil rights, and your appointment of such stewards of the environment as James Watt. Consequently, I don't think you and Nancy will find Santa Monica Bay, or the Santa Monica Mountains, as attractive as you might remember them.

I therefore expect you will be spending more and more time at home. When looking out at the Los Angeles skyline from your living room, bear in mind that many of the glittering high-rise towers you will be seeing are foreign owned. They have been snapped up by the Japanese and others at bargain prices as the unprecedented budget deficits incurred by you turned the United States in just 8 years from the world's largest creditor nation into the world's largest debtor nation.

This means that for the next 50 years, or however long it takes our children to mend the damage you did to our economy, it is going to be a little tougher in L.A. repairing infrastructure and improving city services, as well as buying a house and getting a mortgage.

As for design, during the last eight years, there seems to me to have been an emphasis on how things look, rather than how things work. Playing to this, I feel, was the penchant of Post Modernist styling for self-indulgent and self-promoting pastiches.

The result was an architecture viewed less as a social art aesthetically serving a human need—a traditional definition of the craft—and more as a photo opportunity. In this respect I feel it reflected the values of your administration.

Your city which you referred to in your farewell address a few weeks ago might be "shining," "more prosperous, more secure and happier than 8 years ago," especially if seen through the smoked glass windows of a stretch limo in which you and Nancy probably will travel.

But the city of most of the residents here at present when compared to 8 years ago is more inequitable, more threatening, uglier and sadder.

Jan. 22, 1989

Acknowledgments

The articles and commentaries included here were culled from ten years of writing for "The Los Angeles Times," and to the editors there who if not encouraged me in my attempts to raise the public's design consciousness then at least humored me, I give my thanks. At the risk of offending a few who I do not mention, I want in particular to thank Jean Sharley Taylor and Dick Turpin, who countless times stood by me when readers and special interests took exception to my articles; Kurt Liepman, who collaborated with me on many of the headlines; also Lou Desser, Dave Kinchen, Dave Meyers, Ruth Ryon, Evie De Wolfe, and Carole Powers, who at times edited and proofed my copy; Marilyn Kelker and Irene Vasquez, for finding clippings I had lost and generally keeping my in-and-out basket relatively uncluttered; and Dave Laventhol, Tom Johnson, Bill Thomas, and Shelby Coffey III for tolerating my prejudices.

Deserving special thanks beyond the confines of "The Times" are Tish O'Connor and Dana Levy, who with their professional expertise and personal warmth encouraged and organized this folly; Aaron Silverman, for his aid and advice; Chuck Rosin, for his enthusiasm; Doug and Regula Campbell, for their perspective and passion; Bruce Corwin and S. Charles Lee, for providing The Los Angeles Theater as a backdrop for the cover photograph; and the countless community activists, dedicated professionals, preservationists, students and others concerned with the drift of planning and design in Los Angeles. Their efforts prompted many of the columns.

Finally, my thanks and love, to my mother, Sadie, for always being so supportive, and to my wife, Peggy, who often accompanied me as I traveled across the region to look at a building, or a streetscape, or scene, and then back home had to suffer through me writing of these columns and more; being asked to read many of them before they were submitted; having to correct some of the grammar; and, when taking exception to a few of them, debating them, under deadline, of course, while dinner and the children waited.

Index

Abel, Eliot Levin, 201
Abel, Thorton, 207
AB 283, 19
Adolf office building, 210
Aerospace Museum,
    L.A., 96
Ain, Gregory, 88, 191,
    206–207
Alex Theater, 138
Alexander, Christopher,
    82, 135
Alexander, Diane, 43
Alleys, 121–123
Ambassador Hotel,
    141, 152
American Institute of
    Architects (AIA), 78,
    84, 88, 106–107, 192,
    223–224
American Legion Hall, 174
American Planning
    Assoc., 46, 50
Andalusia, housing
    court, 186
Angel's Flight, 32
Appleton, Mechur &
    Assoc., 34, 126, 127
Architectural Collective,
    133–135
Architecture Forum, 85
Architecture Plus, 85
Art of Building Cities
    (Sitte), 24, 61
    City According to Artis-
    tic Principles)
Arts + Architecture, 76,
    77, 89

Baldwin, Grayce, 173
Baldwin Hills, 74, 182
Barker Development Co.,
    60–61
Barnay, Don, 87
Barnsdall Park, 66, 179
Baum, Edwell James, 217

beaches, Los Angeles, 171,
    189–190
Becket, Welton, 152, 201
Beckmeyer, Kurt, 219
Bel Air, 230
Belmont Heights, 168
Belmont Shore, 168
Benton/Park/Candreva,
    201
Berheimer, Adolf and
    Eugene, 174
Berkus, Barry, 36–38
Berlant, Tony, 167
Beverly Center, 114
Beverly Fairfax, 47
Beverly Hills, 34, 69, 107,
    125, 139, 182, 187
Beverly Theater, 139–140
Beverlywood Homes
    Assn., 112
Biberton, Edward, 167
Big Sleep, The (Chandler),
    181–182
Binder, Rebecca, 200–201
Blacker House, 146–147
Blake, Eddie, 170
Blake, Dennis, 170
Blanton, John,
    177–178, 206
Bluff Park, 168
Board of Education, L.A.
    (Unified School
    District), 55, 73–76
Board of Education,
    N.Y., 75
Board of Supervisors, L.A.
    County, 97
Boehm, Gottfried, 108, 110
Bogaard, Claire, 143
Bowen Court, 185
Boyle Heights, 47, 106, 142
Bradbury Building, 143
Bradbury, Ray, 89
Bradley, Tom, Mayor, 18,
    46–47, 51, 53, 63, 115,
    118, 129

Braude, Marvin, 44, 49, 53
Breaker's Hotel, 168
Breall, Bob, 67
Breed St. synagogue, 142
Brentwood, 18, 66
Brentwood Gardens, 13
Brockman Building, 141
Brockway, Leon, 186
Brown, Edmund G. Jr., 124
Brown Derby,
    restaurant, 170
Brown, Lance, 108
Bruce, Henry, 195
Buchanan, Charles, 186
Bungalow Heaven, 148
Bunker Hill, 31, 61, 95, 110,
    115, 183
Burbank, 13, 41
Buttrick, White &
    Burtis, 162

Cabrillo Maritime
    Museum, 103
California Office of His-
    toric Preservation, 179
California Plaza, 32, 115,
    117, 128
Cal Poly Pomona, 188, 209
Cal State Dominquez
    Hill, 208
Caltrans, 113, 123
Campbell, Alexander, 171
Campbell & Campbell,
    128, 155, 171
Camrose Bungalows,
    144–146
Canfield-Moreno
    Estate, 141
Cannon, Sheila, 45
Caplan, Barbara, 130–131
Carling House, 193
Carr, Bill, 214
Carthay Circle, 13, 42,
    129–131
Cascades Park, 176
Case Study Houses,
    76–78, 80–81, 89,
    209, 210
Center City West, (Crown
    Hill), 30, 32, 127
Century City, 18, 49, 69,
    112, 114, 232
Central City Assn., 23, 127
Central Library, 31, 95, 138
Chavez Ravine, 229
Chandler, Raymond,
    179–183, 185
Chatterton's, 153
Chemosphere House,
    170, 193

Chernow House, 106–107
Children's Museum, 159
Choy, Barton, 177
Citicorp Building, 25
Citizens Committee,
    Elysian Park
City Administrator's
    Office, 60
City Council, L.A., 16, 18,
    26, 31, 42, 46–47,
    59–60, 115, 144–146
City Hall, L.A., 98, 189
Civic Center, L.A., 97–98
Claremont, 209
Coalition of Concerned
    Communities, 43
Coast Savings, 25, 94
Coffman, Barbara, 200
Cohen, Andy, 222
Colby Apartments, 209
Coldwell Banker, 197
Coliseum Commis-
    sion, 230
Columbia Savings and
    Loan, 139–140
Colorado Place, 90
Community Corp. of
    Santa Monica, 34,
    70–71
Communtiy planning
    boards, 52–54
Community Redevelop-
    ment Agency (CRA),
    23–27, 31, 34, 56, 58,
    78–79, 82, 88, 106, 116,
    119–121, 128–129
Concerned Citizens for
    South Central L.A., 45
Connolly-Berens,
    Janet, 163
Constructivism, 104
Contini, Edgardo, 209
Corcoran, Mike, 163
County Museum of Art,
    77, 130
courtyard housing,
    185–186
Craftsman style, 34, 43,
    143, 149, 150–151
Cresticon (Litton Indus-
    tries), 15, 16
Crestwood Hills, 208
Critical Edge, The
    (Marder), 85–86
Cultural Affairs Commis-
    sion, L.A., 23
Cultural Affairs Dept.,
    L.A., 226
Culver City, 66, 174,
    175, 196

Davidson, J. R., 206
Davis, Bette, 213
Davis, Pierpoint, 186
Davis, Walter Swindell,
    164, 186
DeBretteville and Poly-
    zoides, 143
Deconstructivism,
    103–105
Delta Air Lines, 222
Detroit St., 72
Deukmejian, George,
    Governor, 124
Devereaux, Peter, 169
Diamond, Kate, 201
Disney Concert Hall, 107,
    109–110
Disneyland, 154, 161
Dobbyn, Irma, 44
Dodgers, L.A., 229–230
Downing, Andrews
    Jackson, 184

Eats Restaurant, 200
Echo Park, 15, 16, 47.
Eckbo, Garret, 207
Eckstut, Stanton, 32
Edelman, Ed, 140, 146,
    152, 196
Ehrenkrantz Group, 32
El Pueblo de los Angeles,
    189
Elysian Park, 229–230
Emmons, Frederick, 208
Encino, 47
English, Barton, 146–147
Ennis-Brown House, 138,
    155–159
Erickson, Arthur, 88, 89,
    193, 194
Europe, 215–216
Exposition Park, 96, 150
Ezra, Edmond, 115

Fairfax district, 33, 58, 140
Fairway Building, 14
Farewell, My Lovely
    (Chandler), 181
Farrell, Robert, 145
Fed. of Hillside and
    Canyon Assoc., 45
Fed. of Organizations for
    Conserving Urban
    Space, 45
Ferraro, John, 31
Fickett, Edward, 177
Filler, Martin, 85–86
Fine Arts Building, 201
Fine, Mark, 35

Finn, Howard, 145
First Interstate World Center, (Library Tower), 13
First Methodist Church of Hollywood, 174
Fleming, Ronald Lee, 227
Flower St., 115–116, 119–121
Flores, Joan Milke, 120, 145
Ford Foundation, 158
Forest Lawn, 196
Fort-Brescia, Bernardo, 91
Fox Plaza, 95–96
Fredenburgh, Harold, 94
Freeman House, 157
Friedrichs, Edward, 222
Friends of Hollyhock House, 67
Friends of the Schindler House, 179
Friends of Westwood, 126, 127

Gamble House, 151, 164–166
Garbutt-Hathaway Mansion, 16
Garcia, Dan, 41, 44, 47, 49, 53
Gargosian Art Gallery, 167
Gartz Court, 143
Gaylord, Richard, 168
Gehry, Frank, 32, 58, 88, 96, 100–105, 108, 110–111, 167
Gehry House, 102, 104
Gensler Assoc. 59, 60, 91, 222
Getty Art Center, 66
Getty Trust, 155–159
Gibson, Kirk, 230
Gill, Irving, 88, 168, 186
Goetz, Bernhard, affair, 221
Golding, Arthur, 91
Goldrich & Kest, 140
Goldstone, Bud, 188,
Goldwyn Library, 103
Goodhue, Bertram, 95
Graves, Michael, 93, 99, 104
Greene and Greene, Charles and Henry, 88, 146, 151, 164–166
Gross, Sylvia, 42
Grossman, Albert, 210
Gruen & Assoc., 68
Gumbiner, H. L., 199
Gurin, David, 133

Hall, Mark, 44, 67
Halprin, Lawrence, 95, 128
Hamilton, Calvin, 17–18, 46–47, 50, 56, 118
Hancock Park, 113
Hardy Holzman Pfeiffer, 95
Harris, Harwell, 191, 206
Hathaway Hill, 15–17
Havenhurst Dr., 161
Hebald-Heymann, Margo, 201
Heilman, John, 126
Heineman, Arthur, 185
Helfeld, Edward, 50, 88
Hendrickson, Donald, 164
Hermosa Beach, 201
Highland Park, 13, 43, 66
Hightower Elevator Assn., 173
High Window, The (Chandler), 180, 183
Hines, Tom, 91–92
Hodgetts, Craig, 78, 80, 167
Holden, Nat, 31
Hollein, Hans, 89
Hollis, Doug, 184
Hollyhock House, 67, 179
Hollywood, 79, 80, 82, 144–146
Hollywood Heights, 172–174, 180
Hollywood Heritage, 79
Hollywood redevelopment, 31, 79
homeless, 105–107, 233
Homestead Group, 72
Hope, Bob, 193
Hope St., 13, 127–129
Horatio West Court, 186
housing, affordable, 34–35, 81–83, 105–107, 142, 233
housing, in-fill, 33
Howery, Donald, 118, 119–120
Hoye, Dan, 160
Hunt, Myron, 147, 164
Huntington Sheraton, 141, 147–148

Ince/Triangle Studios, 175
Irmas Housing, 107
Irvine, 37–38
Irving Thalberg Building, 175
Isozaki, Arata, 100

Jack's restaurant, 163
Jahn, Helmut, 96, 99
Jalili, John, 212
Jan Development Co., 144–145
Janss Corp., 60
Japanese American Cultural and Community Center, 56
Japanese Village, 31
JCA architects, 33
Jencks, Charles, 93, 104
Jerde, Jon, 32, 143
Jewett, Ken, 127
Johnson, Phillip, 93, 103–105
Johnson, Scott, 95
Jones, Eliane Sewell, 209
Jones, Quincy, 88, 208–209
Julio, Rolando, 164

Kamnitzer & Cotton, 35, 91
Kanner Assoc., 217
Kaplan, Josef, 161–162, 171, 184
Kappe, Ray, 78, 88, 178
Kay, Carl, 173
Kazor, Virginia, 112, 114
Keikyu USA Inc., 147–14
Kenter Canyon, 208
Kinney, Abbott, 167
Kohn Pedersen Fox, 94
Koning Eizenberg, 34, 71
Kornwasser & Friedman, 140
Koshalek, Richard, 78

LaBrea district, 140
LaCienga Blvd., 86
Lagreco, Charles, 133–13
Lake, Laura, 43, 44, 126
LaLanne, Claude and Francois, 228–229
Lamb, Seraphima, 201
Lambert, Henry, 94
Langdon Wilson Mumper, 94
Lasorda, Tommy, 230
Lautner, John, 88, 193–194, 207
Lee, Charles, 199–200
Lefcoe, George, 195–196
Lehrer, Ruthann, 143
Lemesh, Dana, 163
Le Parc communities, 36, 38
Lepis, Alice, 113
Levin, Brenda, 201

Library Square, Tower, 26, 31, 94, 119, 128

Lincoln Heights, 72

Lindsay, Gilbert, 57, 60, 119

Little Sister, The (Chandler), 182–183

Little Tokyo, 15, 31, 56–60, 65

Long Beach, 32, 72, 168–169

Long Goodbye, The (Chandler), 179–180

Lorimar-Telepictures Studios, 175

LA Law, 93

Los Angeles Beautiful, 124–125

Los Angeles Coliseum Commission, 150

Los Angeles Conservancy, 66, 120, 121, 138–139, 143, 160

Los Angeles Family Housing Corp., 106–107

Los Angeles International Airport, 49, 201

Los Angeles Prize, 89

Los Angeles Theatre, Cover, 199

Los Angeles Times garage, 98

Los Angeles 200 Committee, 38–40, 63

Los Feliz, 13, 153

Los Feliz Theater, 153

Lowy, Allan, 53

Lowe, David Ming-Li, 166

Luckman Partnership, 201

Lynch, Kevin, 176

MacArthur Park Community Center, 184

MacArthur Park, 183–185

Magic Castle, 174

Maguire, Robert, 61, 225

Maguire/Thomas, 94

Makinson, Randell, 151, 165–166

Malaga Cover Plaza, 163–164

Malibu, 182, 194

Man, Alexander, 45, 125–126

Mandarin Jade (Chandler), 182

Mangurian, Robert, 167

Manhattan Beach, 154, 162, 177–178

Manhattan Beach Pier, 154

Marina del Rey, 196

Marlowe, Philip, 179–182

Martin A.C., 86

Mar Vista, 13, 33, 72, 207

May, Cliff, 171, 197–198

McCartney, Patrick, 43

McCormick, Ken, 151

McCoy, Esther, 90, 206, 209

McKinley mansion, 141

Mendoza, Peter, 42

Meier, Richard, 89, 155, 158

Melrose Avenue, 22, 46, 86, 117, 119, 131–132, 162

Melrose Hill, 13, 152–153

MGM Studios, 175

Mies van der Rohe, 92, 206

Milden, Marty, 112

Mills, Mark, 108

Milner Park, 213

mini-malls, 20–22, 30, 35, 136

Miracle Mile Residential Assn., 42

Mission Viejo, 18

Mitchell, Kathy and Terry, 121–122

Milland, Ray, 163

Modernism, 19, 92, 227

Molina, Gloria, 31

Monrovia, 143, 176

Montana Avenue, 13, 136–137, 161, 211–212, 217–218

Montana Mercantile Cookware Co., 217

Monterey Park, 176, 177

Montevideo Country Club, 28

Moore, Brian, 45

Moore, Charles, 32, 93, 104

Moore's Market, 164

Moore Ruble Yudell, 155, 172

Morland, Chris, 219–221

Morphosis, 167

Moss, Eric Owen, 78, 80

Mt. Washington, 47

Mulholland Drive, 193

Museum of Contemporary Art, L.A., 76–81, 100–102, 129

Museum of Modern Art, N.Y., 103–105

Nadel Partnership, 87

Nau, Lou and Yvonne, 220

Nemenz, Otto, 201

Neutra, Richard, 177, 191, 206, 209

Newport Harbor Art Museum, 84

New Theory of Urban Design, A (Alexander), 82, 135

New York City, 19, 26, 32

Nicholas, Frederick, 110

Nodal, Al, 184–185

Nota, Dean, 178

Not Yet New York, 43, 48, 49

North Hollywood, 33, 47, 58, 66, 107

North Palos Verdes Drive, 163

North Westwood, 67

Ocean Front Walk, 119, 166

Ocean Hills, Leisure Village, 36

Ocean Park, 34, 70–71, 106

Oldesnburg, Claes, 101

Old Pasadena, 141

Olmsted and Cheney, 163–164

Olympics, 1984, 15, 45, 143

Olympic Blvd., 107, 113

Open Space Task Force, 128

Otis/Parsons, 13, 184

Oviatt Building, 201

Oxford Properties, 25

Pacific Coast Builders Conf., 36

Pacific Design Center, 13

Pacific Palisades Residents Assn., 126

Pacific Southwest Development, 218

Palisades Park, 187, 189

Palms District, 209

Palos Verde Estates, 163–164

Park Plaza Hotel, 183

Pan Pacific Auditorium, 140, 142, 151–152

Parkhill Partners, 99

Pasadena, 72, 82–83, 91, 144, 147–148, 151, 182, 185

Pasadena Civic Center, 13

Pasadena Heritage,
143, 146
Paxton, Lynn, 219
Peck/Jones Partnership,
59, 60
Pei, I.M., 94
Pellissier Building, 201
Perloff, Harvey, 88, 202
Perloff, Mimi, 202
Pershing Square,
22–24, 226
Philharmonic Assn., 214
Photography of Architecture and Design
(Shulman), 192
Pico Union, 34, 106
Pike, the, Long Beach,
13, 32
Pisano, Giovanni, 87
Pisano., Mark, 114
Pittas, Michael John, 109
Planning Commission,
L.A., 41, 47, 51, 53, 75
Planning Dept., L.A.,
16–18, 46, 47, 49, 55, 61,
75, 115, 118, 127, 129
Playa del Rey, 176, 201
Playa Vista, 43, 196
Post Modernism, 91–93,
99, 233, 227
Poulson, Norris, 209
Pratt House, 151, 155
PRIDE, of Pasadena, 14
Prince Charles, HRH, 223
Programmatic, "pop,"
architecture, 169–170
Progressive Architecture,
91–93, 133
Proposition U, 41–42,
48–53, 55, 72
Proposition 13, 52, 63
Project Restore, 157
Pryor, Luann, 168–169
public-Private partnerships, 29–30
Public Works Dept. L.A.,
115–116

Raffi Cohen Industries
(RCI), 97
RAND corp., 39
Randy's Donuts, 170
Rashoff, Marty, 116
*Raymond Chandler
Mystery Map of
Los Angeles*, 180, 182
Raymond House, 168
Ratkovich, Wayne, 32, 143
Reagan, Ronald, 55,
230–233

Rebecca's Restaurant, 167
Recreation and Parks
Dept. (L.A.), 24
Redondo Beach, 41
Reed, Chris, 137
Regional Planning
Commission (county)
28–29, 195–196
Reinway Court, 186
Reliance Development
Corp., 25, 94
rent control, Santa
Monica, 70–71, 141, 218
Richardson Nagy Martin,
36–38
Richman, Neal, 71
Ridgewood-Wilton Neighborhood Assn., 112
Riviera Ranch Road, 197
Rivington Place
housing, 141
Roberti, David, 75
Robinson Gardens, 187
Rodia, Simon, 188
ROMA Design Group, 227
Rosenthal, Alicia, 201
Rosin, Charles, 42, 58,
129–130
Rosin, Lindsey, 129
Rounds, Jay, 139
Ruskin, John, 86, 105
Russell, Pat, 131, 145

Saltzman, Laura, 88
Samson Tyre & Rubber
Co., 170
Samuels-Navarro
House, 204
San Diego, 198
San Fernando Valley, 38,
49, 193
San Francisco, 19
San Gabriel Valley, 195
San Pedro, 42
Santa Monica, 66, 70–71,
90, 121–122, 136–137,
181–183, 186, 211–212,
217–218
Santa Monica Blvd.,
125–127
Santa Monica Pier,
154–155
Santos, Adele Naude, 78,
80, 82
Savitch, Fran, 120
Schindler House, 178
Schindler, R.M., 178, 191,
206, 209

Second Generation
(McCoy), 207
Seventh Street Market
Place, 31
Sedway Cooke Assoc., 72
Selznick, David O., 175
Sewell, Tom, 166
Shapiro, Dan, 53
Sherman Oaks, 18, 33, 66
Ship's, 66
Showa Village, 15, 31,
59–61
Shulman, Julius, 191–192,
210
Sidewalk Cafe, 164
Siegel, Margot, 201
signage, 25–26
Signal Hill, 168
Silver Lake, 15–17, 47
Silvertop House, 193
Simi Valley, 38, 201
Simonian, Judith, 184
Simonson Mercedes, 217
SITE, 24
Sitte, Camillo, 24, 61
Skidmore Owings &
Merrill, 19, 94
skid row, 27–28
Sklarek, Norma, 201
Smith, Alexis, 185
Smith, Elizabeth, 78
Smith, Kathryn, 179
Smith, Tim, 177
Smith Whitney, 209
Snelling, George, 131
Snyder, Art, 145
Snyder, Jerry, 56
Solomon, Dan, 82
Soriano, Raphael, 191,
209–210
Southern California
Association of Governments (SCAG), 114
Southern California
suburbs, 35–39
South Park, 95, 129
South Pasadena, 66
Stafford, Jim, 201
Stalk, Arnold, 106–107
Steinert, Ron, 222
Stern, Robert A.M., 93
Stevenson, Peggy, 79, 144
Stirling, James, 108,
110–111
Stone, Charlie, 213
Storer House, 162
Street Scene festival,
117–118
Studio City, 14, 33, 41, 47
Sullivan Canyon, 197

unland-Tujunga Area
    Residents Assn., 42
unset Blvd., 133–135, 197
weeny, Robert, 178

Tail 'o Pup, 169–170
aliesin, 193, 205
arzana, 176
arzana Property Owners
    Assn., 44
emporary Contemporary
    Museum, 57, 58
eraswa, Toshikazu, 56
ognetti, Gina, 137
opanga Canyon,
    28–29, 66
opping, Kenneth, 53, 56
orrance, 106, 162
ower Theater, 199
ransportation Dept.,
    L.A., 113–114, 118,
    120–121, 130, 132
rump's, 143
scharner, Renata
    von, 227
urner, Richard, 184
wentieth Century Fox
    Studios, 174

JCLA, 31, 32, 68–69,
    127, 202–203
Jnified School District,
    see Board of Educa-
    tion, L.A.
Jnion Church, 157
Jniversal City, 201
Jrban Innovations
    Group, 31
Jrban Land Institute, 27,
    29–30, 35
JSC School of Architec-
    ture, 92, 151

Valdez, Patssi, 185
Van de Kamp's Bakery, 170
Vanderlip, Frank, 163
Van Nuys Blvd., 13, 21
Van Tilburg, Johannes, 38,
    59, 60
Venice, 47, 66, 166–167
Vidal, Olivier, 90
Villa d' Este, 186
Villa Primavera, 186
Villa Riviera
    Apartments, 168

Wanamaker, Marc, 175
Warner Center, 49
Watt Industries, 15
Watts Towers, 187–188
Wayfarers Chapel, 204
Webber, Staunton &
    Spaulding, 164
Weil, Martin Eli, 67
Weinstein, Richard, 32
Welton Beckett &
    Assoc., 90
West Adams, 13, 72,
    149–150
Westchester, 41, 196
West Hollywood, 106,
    109, 124, 133–135, 143,
    161, 186
West Coast Gateway
    competition, 108
West Los Angeles, 18, 33,
    49, 155
Westmoreland Pl., 164
Westpark, 36
Westside Pavilion, 49
Westwood, 33, 41, 43, 47,
    48, 67–69
Whitley Heights, 213
Wigley, Mark, 104
Will Rogers Park, 187

Williams, Gary, 18
Wilmington HomeOwners
    Assn.
Wilshire Blvd., 69,
    115–116, 127
Wilshire district, 31, 33
Wilshire Stakeholders, 31
Wilson, Theo, 173
Wiltern Theater, 138, 201
Wilton Place, 114
Winogrond, Mark, 109,
    134–135
Wojciechowski,
    Christopher, 28
Wolfe, Bonnie, 173
Woo, Michael, 75, 79, 82,
    120, 121, 144–146
Wright, Frank Lloyd,
    66, 142, 162, 179, 192,
    204–205
Wright, Lloyd, 204–205
Wright, Eric, 204–205
Wu, Ted, 123–124

Yalch, Bill, 164
Yale School of
    Architecture, 93
Yamashiro Restaurant, 174
Yaroslavsky, Zev, 44,
    49, 130
York-Ames, Donna, 163

Z lots, 37
Zimmerman, Bernard, 170
Zwebell, Arthur and Nina,
    161, 186

Sam Hall Kaplan is an award-winning journalist with a love for cities. At present the Design Critic for the *Los Angeles Times*, Kaplan also has been an urban affairs reporter for the *New York Times*, has held various public planning and development posts, taught and lectured extensively, and written for various popular and professional journals, and radio and television. Books include *L.A. Lost & Found: An Architectural History of Los Angeles*, *The Dream Deferred: People, Politics and Planning in Suburbia*, and *The New York City Handbook*. He has received grants from the National Endowment for the Arts, the Graham and Ford foundations, and awards from numerous professional and community associations. He is the father of four children and lives in Santa Monica, California.